Routledge Revivals

Party and Professionals

Originally published in 1981, this study fits into a wider context of works analysing the impact of the social revolution on the structure of Chinese society since 1949. *Party and Professionals* focuses on the teaching profession in relation to social ranking. As a part of the intelligentsia, the socialist government has an ambiguous relationship with teachers of all levels and this work aims to highlight the government's political interactions with teaching professionals. This title will be of interest to students of Asian studies, Politics, International Relations and History.

Party and Professionals

The Political Role of Teachers in Contemporary China

Gordon White

Routledge
Taylor & Francis Group

First published in 1981
by M.E. Sharpe Inc.

This edition first published in 2016 by Routledge
2 Park Square, Milton Park, Abingdon, Oxon, OX14 4RN
and by Routledge
711 Third Avenue, New York, NY 10017

Routledge is an imprint of the Taylor & Francis Group, an informa business

© 1981 M.E. Sharpe, Inc.

Publisher's Note
The publisher has gone to great lengths to ensure the quality of this reprint but points out that some imperfections in the original copies may be apparent.

Disclaimer
The publisher has made every effort to trace copyright holders and welcomes correspondence from those they have been unable to contact.

A Library of Congress record exists under LC control number: 81005256

ISBN 13: 978-1-138-65347-4 (hbk)
ISBN 13: 978-1-138-65349-8 (pbk)

Gordon White

Party and Professionals

THE POLITICAL ROLE OF TEACHERS IN CONTEMPORARY CHINA

M. E. Sharpe, Inc.
ARMONK, NEW YORK

Portions of the Appendix first appeared in *Chinese Education* XII:4
(Winter 1979-80), and are there so identified.

Library of Congress Cataloging in Publication Data

White, Gordon, 1942-
    Party and professionals.

    Includes bibliographical references.
    1. Teachers—China—Political activity. 2. Teachers' socioeconomic
status—China. 3. Communism and education. I. Title.
LB2844.1.P6W48   371.1'04   81-5256
ISBN 0-87332-188-X   AACR2

Printed in the United States of America

To my mother Vera and sister Judith,
both members of the teaching profession.

Contents

Contents

Acknowledgments

My first thanks go to the Department of Political Science (SGS), Australian National University, and the Institute of Development Studies, University of Sussex, for their financial and institutional support for the project of which this book is a part. Penny Lockwood of the Australian National University contributed greatly through her meticulous and enthusiastic assistance in locating and cataloging relevant materials.

A special debt is owed to Ai Ping for doing such an excellent job in translating those materials in the Appendix that originally appeared in <u>Chinese Education</u> XII:4 (Winter 1979-80); the balance, and majority, of the Appendix translations were drawn from such standard U.S. and Chinese government sources as SCMP, JPRS, NCNA, etc. Doug Merwin, my editor at M. E. Sharpe, Inc., helped me a great deal through his initial encouragement, his ability to keep me up to schedule and his invaluable advice on the structure and content of the book.

Several people read the text in various drafts, and the final manuscript has benefited greatly from their comments. I owe particular gratitude to Ron Dore, Joel Glassman, Ann Kent and Jon Unger. Thanks also to Vincent Oates who was very helpful in providing me with copies of relevant articles from the magazine <u>People's Education</u> from his personal collection.

Many people have been involved in typing successive drafts — my particular thanks go to Judy Rix of Australian National

University, and June Hutfield and Penny Barraclough of the Institute of Development Studies.

Finally, my very special gratitude goes to Christine White who has helped me through some difficult times with her love and encouragement and without whom I would never have completed this work.

Gordon White
Brighton
August 1980

The Ideological and Policy Context

1

This case study is part of a wider effort to assess the impact of socialist revolution on the structure of Chinese society since Liberation in 1949 and the role of the socialist state in the process of postrevolutionary transformation. In the tradition of successful Marxist-Leninist revolutionaries, the leaders of the Chinese Communist Party (CCP) have sought to use the ideological, political, administrative, and coercive powers of the state to restructure Chinese society along socialist lines. The political authorities have attempted to regulate levels of social prestige, confer or withhold power or influence, and determine the differential allocation of material income. To the extent that they have been successful, the specific social positions of individuals, groups, strata and classes, and the stratification system in general, are determined by a process of conscious distribution.[1] The three basic variables of stratification analysis — power, prestige, and material welfare — can thus be seen as distributive social goods to which different sectors of society have differential access.

In their efforts to change Chinese society, Party leaders have not faced a tabula rasa. They have had to confront patterns of differentiation and inequality inherent in the social division of labor of the old society they sought to replace and the new society they seek to build. In the realm of society, the position of individuals and collectivities depends on their market position, their possession of skills, knowledge, or other attributes which command differential exchange values on the market. These attributes are the material basis of their differential

1

political claims to prestige, power, and material privilege.

The social position of an individual or group in China — and
in other socialist societies — is thus determined by the imperatives of state and society, political distribution and market allocation, what the Polish sociologist Bauman calls the realms
of "officialdom and class."[2] Each of these realms embodies a
distinct structure of power: on the one side, political power
resting on the normative and structural resources of the state;
on the other side, social power resting on position in the social
division of labor. The actual social position of an individual or
group depends on the mutual interaction and interpenetration
between these two systems of power. This interaction takes
the form of politics, distributive politics; stratification and inequality are the structural outcomes of this political process.
On the one hand, those who possess market power try to "cash
in" or "realize" their exchange values to acquire favorable
symbolic prestige, access to political power and material benefits; on the other hand, the socialist state, impelled by its di-
rectional nucleus, the Party, attempts to impose a system of
social differentiation which, to a greater or lesser degree,
clashes with the imperatives of the market. This is a structural contradiction in socialist society and expresses itself be-
haviorally in terms of distributive politics. This latter process
of pressure, persuasion, exchange, and bargaining is the subject of our investigation. Thus in our attempt to elucidate new
dimensions of stratification in postrevolutionary Chinese society, we are less concerned with the traditional sociological
question "Who ranks where?" than with the traditional political
science question "Who gets what?"

We shall pursue this inquiry by focusing on one occupational
group, professional teachers. This group is important as one
section of the intelligentsia (zhishifenzi) who possess the specialized skills and knowledge so crucial to the strategic aims
of socialist development.* Evidence from the socialist coun-

---

*For the purposes of this study, the "intelligentsia" are defined in terms
of formal educational qualifications, i.e. senior high school and above.

tries of Eastern Europe suggests that the intelligentsia have proven a politically problematic group, and their relationship with the ruling parties has been fraught with tension and ambiguity. The Chinese case is comparable. By virtue of the favorable market position embodied in their scarce skills and knowledge, the Chinese intelligentsia possess, to varying degrees, independent resources of social power which they have used to set the terms of cooperation with the socialist state, protect their autonomy from untoward political incursion, and improve their material and symbolic standing in society.

The Party's relationship to teachers has been particularly ambiguous. Since teachers are "cultural intellectuals" not engaged in directly productive activity, the Party has regarded them as less sacrosanct than their technico-scientific counterparts, exerting greater political pressure with less fear of immediate damage to economic objectives. At the same time, teachers have attracted political pressure because of their multifaceted importance for socialist development: i.e. leaving aside their economic and technological role in training personnel for the modernization effort, they are ideologically crucial for transmitting "correct" attitudes to rising generations and politically crucial as a key component of the system of mobilization, control, and compliance which links the state with the nation's youth.[3]

We intend to describe and analyze the process of political interaction between the Party and the teaching profession over the question of distribution. This process has several aspects: the ways in which the political authorities have sought to reshape the social identity and regulate the social, political and economic position of teachers, and their degree of success in this endeavor; the methods by which teachers themselves have sought to ameliorate or defend their access to scarce social goods and the nature of the political resources they have mobilized in their contest with the Party. The results of our inquiry should throw some light on the general question of the relationship between state and society in socialist contexts, particularly on the capacity of the revolutionary party to restructure society along socialist lines.

We shall deal with the teaching profession as a whole, at primary, secondary, and tertiary levels. There are important differences between teachers at these three levels which will become apparent as the analysis proceeds. We shall only deal with teachers in "regular" state-run schools for reasons of data availability and analytical convenience. Teachers in other types of schools, notably private, part-time or "people-run" (min ban) schools, have faced special problems which are not discussed here.

CCP policies toward professional teachers have been highly ambiguous since 1949, fluctuating in time with the major swings in the general political and ideological environment. Official policies toward the teaching profession have varied along with changing Party policies toward the intelligentsia as a whole, a subject dealt with extensively by other scholars.[4] The teaching profession has experienced periods of greater and lesser political pressure, and different kinds of political pressure.[5] This ambiguity derives from competition between alternative policy strategies which reflect different historical stages of "socialist transition," the ideological positions of different groups within the CCP leadership, and different constellations of interest and attitude in Chinese society generally.

Specific issues in educational policy have been discussed in detail elsewhere.[6] In this first section I shall provide a brief description of competing ideological positions and trace their implications for policies toward teachers. There are three major sets of perceptions and priorities which I shall call the "first revolution," the "modernization motive," and the "continuous revolution." Let us discuss each in turn.

a) The "first revolution"* refers to the structural and insti-

---

*This description of the "first revolution," as of the following two ideological positions and policy packages, is very much a model, or "ideal type," simplifying for the sake of analytical clarity and explanatory power. Any detailed examination would reveal conflicts and ambiguities within each model: between central, local, and basic levels of the state; between different segments of the state (for example, more conciliatory educational organs vs. more militant political agencies); or between individuals and groups within the Party.

tutional transformation of the "old society" engineered by the
CCP between 1949 and 1956: the change in the systems of own-
ership in industry and agriculture and the consequent redistri-
bution of power and productive assets, and the rapid expansion
of the state apparatus, notably the Party, which gradually pene-
trated all sectors of society and acted as a kind of central ner-
vous system for political mobilization, communication, regula-
tion, and control. In structural terms, this initial period of
"socialist transformation" brought major changes in class relations; in attitudinal terms it meant a major propaganda effort
to educate the Chinese population in the unfamiliar values of
socialist revolution; in institutional terms, it established new
organizations or remodeled old ones to embody the new values
and act as instruments of CCP policy.

The educational system was perceived as an important tool
for changing class relations and social attitudes. For schools
to be effective agents of social change, however, their personnel had to be politically reliable. For this reason, the new revolutionary government viewed the existing body of teachers with
some concern. They saw teachers as politically problematic
on three grounds. First, in terms of class background, most
teachers — in middle schools and colleges — were scions of the
"exploiting classes" (notably "landlord" or "rich peasant") or
other undesirable strata in prerevolutionary society. This was
a natural result of the class bias in access to educational opportunities before 1949. Over the long term, the Party planned
gradually to replace the existing corps with a new generation
of "working class intellectuals" drawn from more "reliable"
classes. Prerevolutionary class antecedents aside, however,
the social position of teachers in postrevolutionary society was
politically ambiguous. The general definition of the social
"status" (chengfen) of "teaching personnel" (jiaoyuan) was laid
down in the official decisions on the nationwide differentiation
of chengfen in August 1950. According to these decisions, since
their work in prerevolutionary society had not been exploitative
and thus qualified as a form of "labor," teachers could be
counted as part of the diffuse category of "brain-power laborers"

(naolide laodongzhe), along with editors, reporters, doctors, artists, authors, and white-collar office employees. More specifically, teachers were defined as subgroups within two narrower strata — "free professionals" (ziyou zhiyezhe) and "employees" (zhiyuan) — depending on the organizational context of their job before 1949.[7] Thus they were cleared of exploitative connotations and assigned a social status which was neither honorific nor invidious. From the outset, however, as members of the "intelligentsia," a segment of the "petty bourgeoisie," they were subject to the ambiguity inherent in the Party's view of intellectuals in the early years, i.e. as valuable but unreliable, a "vacillating" group which needed close supervision. As we have suggested, moreover, as part of the cultural wing of the intelligentsia operating in the "superstructure" (along with writers, artists, reporters, etc.), teachers have been the object of more intense political concern than technical intellectuals such as engineers, technicians, scientists, and doctors.[8]

Second, teachers were suspect in terms of their personal political "histories" (lishi) or dubious "social connections" (shehui guanxi) because many of them had either joined or supported the Guomindang (Kuomintang) during the Civil War period. One official source in early 1952, for example, claimed that only a minority of teachers had actively supported the revolutionary movement before 1949, another minority had taken an active counterrevolutionary stand, and the great majority had been passive, timorous, and demoralized.[9] In the Party's view, the overriding political task in the early years was to establish an effective network of supervision and control in basic-level educational units which could identify and neutralize such dubious elements. Over the longer term, a new generation of politically reliable teachers would emerge, a good proportion of them being Party or Young Communist League members.

Third, teachers were perceived as ideologically problematic, both as pertinacious carriers of "feudal" social ideas (notably the traditional concept of the scholar gentry) and as susceptible to noxious "bourgeois" (i.e. liberal) educational ideas and practices imported from the United States and Western Europe dur-

ing the first half of the twentieth century (for example, John
Dewey's pragmatist theories of education). In the early 1950s,
Britain and the United States were defined as morally degenerate and scientifically inferior to the Soviet Union, which
served as the major source of "advanced experience" in the
sphere of education.[10] On the other hand, the importance of
maintaining educational practices developed in the "old liberated areas" during the Chinese revolutionary war was also emphasized. The Party's main aim here was to bring about the
"ideological reform" (sixiang gaizao) of teachers, to fashion
them into reliable transmission belts for the theoretical and
practical imperatives of the new order.

These priorities were embodied in the educational policies
of the period of "socialist transformation" between 1949 and
1956. They exerted a dominant influence over policy in the initial phase of reconstruction and reform from 1950 to 1953,
notably in the successive political campaigns during this period. They were intended to be transitional policies, laying the
foundations for a new socialist educational system which could
fuel the fires of economic growth in the next major stage, that
of "socialist construction." It is clear, however, that the
Party's ambitious transformational aims could not be wholly
achieved in the short period of seven years. In consequence,
although the goals of the "first revolution" were increasingly
to be shouldered aside after the modernization drive began in
1953, they remained on the policy agenda at alternately subdued
and resurgent levels during the next two decades.

In terms of the relationship between the Party-state and the
professionals, the political logic of the "first revolution" was
separatist, tending toward a system of virtual apartheid between
"red" administrators or Party officials and "expert" teaching
personnel. The official terms describing the Party's relationship to intellectuals in general and teachers in particular were
"utilization and transformation" — both concepts implied that
teachers were to be the object of state action, necessary irri-
tants to be tolerated and used rather than coequals in the socialist endeavor. Understandably, this created patterns of an-

tagonism and distrust which continued into the 1960s and found
expression in successive political movements, notably the
Hundred Flowers movement, the Anti-Rightist campaign, the
Socialist Education movement, and the Cultural Revolution.
This continuity of issues and alignments was thrown into sharp
relief during the Cultural Revolution, notably in its earliest stage,
when Party cadres and sections of the student body castigated
teachers with "bad" class backgrounds or political histories
and accused them of displaying their "reactionary class stand"
by discriminating against worker-peasant students, opposing
Party leadership, and corrupting the youth ideologically. The
same themes were resurrected in the campaign to "clean class
ranks" (qingli jieji duiwu) among teachers which was launched
in late 1967.[11]

Thus the key issues, alignments, and attitudes of the "first
revolution" lived on in schools and colleges beyond their theoretically allotted time-span: the question of teachers' "complicated" (fuza) class backgrounds, the tension between politically
"impure" intelligentsia and "pure" Party cadres and students;
the notion that teachers are crypto-apostles of "feudal," "bourgeois" and foreign ideas, or covert supporters of alien political
forces, notably the Guomindang or United States imperialism.
The importance of these issues during the Cultural Revolution
demonstrated vividly their persistent presence in the interstices
of the new generation of issues which arose between 1956 and
1966. It is to the latter that we now turn.

b) The Modernization Motive. The new set of dominant priorities which emerged in the mid-1950s focused on the long-
term goal of socialist modernization (xiandaihua). Although the
Party had been proclaiming the ultimate goal of comprehensive
modernization from the outset, this did not become the overriding determinant of policy until the inauguration of the First
Five-Year Plan in 1953.[12] From the perspective of the time,
the main task of the revolution was being reoriented from sociopolitical transformation to economic development. The new
strategy was incorporated in a new "general line" embodying
the key priorities of rapid economic growth (particularly indus-

trialization) and technological progress measured in terms of
"advanced world levels." The main ideological themes were
speed, efficiency, economy, expertise, and modernity.

This shift of priorities brought major changes in policies toward the intelligentsia. There was a fundamental reevaluation
of their position in the new socialist society, notably their relationship to the Party. They were to be legitimized ideologically
and admitted as partners in the socialist project. The separatist policies of the "first revolution" were superseded by a
strategy of accommodation, co-optation, and cooperation. Political pressures on intellectuals were to be reduced. First,
the political significance of their "complicated" class backgrounds was downplayed as historically obsolete, because, it
was argued, intellectuals educated before 1949 had changed
their "class standpoint" and many of the new intellectuals
trained after 1949 came from working-class families.[13] Party
leaders emphasized the progress made by intellectuals in remolding themselves ideologically. For example, Zhou Enlai
claimed in 1956 that 40 percent of the intelligentsia were now
"progressive," 40 percent "intermediate," 10 percent "backward," and only 10 percent "counterrevolutionaries or other
bad elements."[14] Second, the Party leadership attempted to
abolish the invidious "petty-bourgeois" connotations of the term
"intelligentsia" by recategorizing them as members of the
"working class" (gongren jieji) and thus on a sociopolitical par
with manual workers. As we shall see later, this conceptual
shift was accompanied by a wide range of changes in specific
policies toward intellectuals.

This general policy reorientation had important implications
for members of the teaching profession who were a numerically
dominant section of the new intelligentsia, as Table 1 demon-
strates.

The overwhelming majority of teachers were working at the
primary level, as Table 2 shows.

According to the categories of the mid-1950s, teachers at
different levels belonged to different strata within the intelligentsia. University professors, almost all of them older aca-

Table 1

Number of Technical Personnel, by Professional Fields,
for Selected Years, 1949-1964
(the figures are year-end and are in thousands)

Professional field	1949	1952	1955	1956	1957	1958	1959	1961	1964
Engineers and technicians	126	212	626	730	800	901	1,000	(n.a.)	(n.a.)
Agricultural specialists	16	68	165	250	389	786	872	(n.a.)	(n.a.)
Teachers	834 (70%)	1,441 (70%)	1,632 (56%)	1,830 (55%)	2,116 (55%)	2,489 (52%)	2,670 (52%)	2,851 (48%)	3,004 (41%)
Scientific research personnel	3	8	11	20	28	32	36	(n.a.)	(n.a.)
Medical and public health specialists	180	244	370	411	452	466	480	(n.a.)	(n.a.)
Cultural affairs specialists	35	70	88	91	94	99	99	(n.a.)	(n.a.)
Total technical personnel	1,194	2,043	2,892	3,332	3,879	4,773	5,157	5,943	7,237

Source: J. P. Emerson, Administrative and Technical Manpower in the PRC,
Washington, D.C., U.S. Department of Commerce, International Population Reports
Series P-95, No. 72, p. 37.

demics teaching before 1949, were counted as "higher intellectuals" (gaoji zhishifenzi). The much larger number of college
lecturers (jiangshi) and assistants (zhushou) were viewed as a
"reserve force" of higher intellectuals.* Beneath these two
groups were the majority of "ordinary intellectuals," among
whom middle-school teachers occupied a higher standing. Primary school teachers just about qualify as "intellectuals," since
many of them have completed senior middle-school education, but
they have often been described informally as "petty intellectuals."

---

*According to Emerson (op. cit., pp. 12-13), in 1956 "higher intellectuals"
included university teachers of lecturer rank and above, doctors of visiting
physician rank (zhuzhi yishi) and above, scientific researchers of the rank of
research assistant (zhuli yanjiuyuan) and above, and all engineers.

Table 2

Number of Teachers by Level of School: Selected Years, 1949-1964
(in thousands as of start of school year [c. September 1])

Level of school	1949	1950	1954	1955	1956	1957	1961	1964
Higher schools	16 (1.7%)	20 (2%)	37 (2.1%)	42 (2.3%)	58 (2.8%)	70 (3%)	135 (4.2%)	145 (4.3%)
Secondary schools	82 (8.8%)	87 (8.6%)	179 (10.1%)	187 (10.3%)	237 (11.6%)	284 (12%)	550 (17.3%)	611 (18.2%)
Primary schools	834 (89.5%)	901 (89.4%)	1,555 (87.8%)	1,594 (87.4%)	1,749 (85.6%)	2,010 (85%)	2,500 (78.5%)	2,600 (77.5%)
Total	932	1,008	1,771	1,823	2,044	2,364	3,185	3,356

Source: Emerson, op. cit., p. 93.

In the context of the drive for modernization, the role of the educational system was to select the brightest members of the new generation and develop their talents in ways conducive to economic development. The pedagogic process was to be knowledge-centered and academic in spirit and content. The role of teachers was seen as crucial, particularly in the more strategic sectors of education-specialized middle schools and colleges — which produced skilled personnel for the five-year plan. The new deal for the intelligentsia in 1956 was also a new deal for teachers: their class origins were redefined as politically unimportant and their progress in ideological reform was praised.[15] In his cardinal report in early 1956, for example, Zhou Enlai cited statistics from four colleges in the cities of Beijing, Tianjin, and Qingdao which showed an increase of 18 percent to 41 percent in the proportion of "progressives" and a decrease of "backward elements" from 28 percent to 15 percent over the previous few years.[16]

Given the importance of integrating the teaching profession into the modernization drive and establishing a new relationship between them and the state, Party leaders identified four main priorities. First, there has been a perennial need to guarantee

a constant supply of talented and capable teachers to meet the
manpower requirements of educational expansion and the technical requirements of the general occupational structure at any
given time. In distributive terms, this means that the Party
must guarantee teachers (particularly at secondary and tertiary
levels) a level of material and symbolic benefits sufficient to
make teaching an attractive career prospect for talented youth.
Second, the Party aimed to improve the "productivity" of existing teachers by strengthening their job commitment and allowing scope for their professional ambitions. To this end, the
Party has not only offered distributive benefits, but also has
encouraged teachers to think of their job as a "specialization"
(<u>zhuanye</u>) or "profession" (<u>zhiye</u>), a distinct realm of intellectual expertise and an object of pride. Party spokesmen also
emphasized the distinction between young and old teachers,
urging the former to emulate and learn from the latter's superior knowledge and experience. Third, the Party leadership
wanted to construct an effective working relationship between
teachers and political-administrative cadres in schools and
colleges. This has required a precise demarcation of the powers and responsibilities of the two groups, and a reduction of
political pressure on teachers to minimal levels compatible
with the routine requirements of control and supervision.
Fourth, Party leaders sought to integrate teachers fully into the
nation's political life through various types of political recruitment, notably into the Party itself. This process of political
co-optation, it was felt, would prevent polarization within school
and college staffs and enhance both the professional and administrative quality of the educational system.
    CCP leaders apparently agreed on this new relationship be-
tween Party and professionals in 1956. Over the next decade,
however, disagreement emerged within their ranks. One section of the leadership — particularly associated with Liu Shaoqi
and Deng Xiaoping — sought to retain the priorities of 1956.
They continued to identify rapid economic and technological
modernization as the pivotal goal of development policy and emphasized the need for conciliation and cooperation in relations

with the intelligentsia. In this study, I refer to this group as
the "socialist modernizers" or "developmentalists" and locate
them on the center-right and right of the Chinese political
spectrum.* Their political influence has been dominant in several periods: 1956-57, 1959-1963, and 1977 onward after the
death of Mao Zedong, the removal of the "Gang of Four," the
return of Deng Xiaoping, and the inauguration of the "Four
Modernizations" program.[17] It is surprising to note the re-
morseless predictability with which the concepts and policies
of the "socialist modernizing" tendency have resurfaced in each
successive period.

c) The Continuous Revolution. In the period between the
Great Leap Forward and the Cultural Revolution, a competing
definition of the central priorities of socialist development
emerged. This approach was closely associated with Mao Zedong and particularly with his theories of "continuous revolution" and "the continuation of class struggle in socialist society." Mao and his adherents wished to bring about simultaneously both the modernization and the continued revoloniza-
tion of Chinese society during the period of socialist construction. Advocates of the theory of continuous revolution, whom I
am calling "Maoists" or "radicals," argued the need to transform both forces and relations of production, both base and
superstructure, simultaneously. In practice, however, they have
tended to give relative prominence to social, political, and ideological priorities over those of rapid economic and technological development. They have advocated a more active role for
the Party and its political allies in transforming society in general and the intelligentsia in particular. This implies a more
antagonistic relationship between Party and professional which,
in many aspects, is a return to the separatist, transformative
tradition of the "first revolution."

The theoretical terms of debate and the concrete policy dif-

*Other Western commentators have dubbed them "Liuists," "managerial
modernizers," "pragmatists" or "moderates," and their domestic opponents
labeled them as "revisionists."

ferences between these competing groups have been described
in extenso by Western scholars. I shall focus here on the "radical" approach to education and its effect on the teaching profession. Educational policy has been one of the major areas of
ideological and political contention over the period from 1958
to 1976.[18] The radicals, notably Mao himself, identified the
educational system as a key determinant of the values and
structure of the new socialist society. In their view, the postrevolutionary educational system was still dominated by "bourgeois" intellectuals and "bourgeois" values and, in consequence,
was not fulfilling its progressive historical role. "Revisionist"
policies toward the educational intelligentsia were not only
failing to keep them on the straight and narrow, but were actually protecting and reinforcing their noxious influence in the
schools. Worse still, the Party itself was being subverted and
its policies perverted by these very intellectuals. With the
"bourgeois academic authorities" given their head, schools had
become centers of elitism and depoliticization.

Thus radical reforms were needed, and as Mao pointed out
in 1964, the teachers were the key to educational reform.[19] As
a result, the radicals have imposed quite severe political demands on teachers. The social role of teachers has been redefined: they are not primarily conveyors of knowledge but war-
riors in an ideological class struggle which rages fiercely in
the schools. "To Be a Teacher," read the title of an article in
a Shanghai newspaper in 1965, "Is to Make Revolution."[20]
Teachers must devote their primary efforts to the ideological
transformation of their students and, if they wish to be effective, must achieve their own ideological transformation in the
process. The slogan of "education must serve proletarian politics" is thus counterposed to the allegedly "revisionist" or
"bourgeois" notions of "intellectual knowledge in the first
place" and "professionalism in command." Accordingly, teachers must reorient their curricula away from academic book-
learning to living practical education linked to the concrete realities of the outside world. Students must be dissuaded from
"reading dead books in a mechanical way"; teachers who can

"only plant grain on the blackboard" or "operate a machine on
paper" must take steps to integrate theory with practice. This
involves the breaking down of the wall between school and society through the principles of "open door schooling" (kaimen
banxue) and "education must be combined with productive labor." This requires teachers to spend more time outside their
schools planning practical curricula, doing manual labor together with their students, and receiving "reeducation" from
both students and the working masses. In these ways, it was
hoped that intellectuals could be "laborized" and the gap between mental and manual labor could be reduced. Maoist analyses admit that this reorientation is a painful process for most
teachers since, as a group, they are "basically bourgeois" and
are thus naturally attracted to the "revisionist" themes of the
"socialist modernizing" educational strategy: after all, the
latter safeguards their professional autonomy, locates their
primary responsibility as transmitting academic knowledge
within the schools, and guarantees them special social status
as an "expert" group. The Maoist challenge rejected all these
professional perquisites.

Thus, although radical ideology has allowed in theory for the
existence of "revolutionary teachers," in practice the required
characteristics of this group have been defined so narrowly as
to confine them to a minority of younger teachers with "good"
class backgrounds and innate "class feelings" which make them
naturally incline toward Maoist ideas. Many teachers, notably
"old" teachers with allegedly "bad" class backgrounds or problematic "histories," have been automatically judged beyond the
political pale.[21] Prerevolutionary class backgrounds and political affiliations were thus judged to be politically significant
even in the new stage of socialist construction. Radical spokesmen have also tended to define teachers as a whole as a suspect
group, as potential "agents of counterrevolutionary restoration," and thus "the objects of revolution in the period of socialist revolution." According to the radical Shanghai group
and their associates in the 1970s, the politically problematic
nature of teachers had historical roots. In a speech in May

1976, for example, radicals Chi Chun and Xie Jingyi delivered
the following analysis:

(Teachers) are left over from the Guomindang period. We did not have our
own teachers and professions. After 1949, we relied on them to cultivate new
ones gradually, but the cultivation was done in a manner that followed their
old ideological systems.... Except that there was no hailing of Generalissimo
Chiang Kai-shek, the rest was about the same.[22]

Teachers are on the "wrong" side of several dichotomies:
mental vs. manual labor, people in authority (in the classroom)
vs. those without authority (their students), and experts vs.
"red" cadres or masses. In most cases, the practical logic of
radical appeals has demanded the supervision and "reeducation" of teachers through practical experience (notably manual
labor) and by other more "reliable" and "progressive" social
forces, notably political, administrative or military cadres or
the "masses," including both their own students and outsiders
such as local workers and peasants, or PLA (People's Liberation Army) soldiers.

To summarize, each of these three paradigms of the nature
of the socialist transition contains a distinctive image of the
social position of teachers and their relationship to the Party-
state: the transformational separatism of the "first revolution,"
the "socialist modernizing" offer of rapprochement and cooperation, and the "radical" return to "revolution" in a new form of
mobilization and confrontation. During the 1960s and early
1970s, the policy context was ambiguous as the issues and antagonisms from the period of the "first revolution" were resuscitated during the Socialist Education movement and the
Cultural Revolution and intermingled with the clash between
developmentalist and radical conceptions of socialist construction. Each of these sets of policies left its imprint on the political sociology of basic-level educational units, affecting relationships among teachers, and between teachers and their pupils, educational cadres, and various mass groups. This created a complex pattern of interests and attitudes, many of which
have found political expression in the alliances and antagonisms

visible in successive political movements.

Each paradigm has carried its own set of <u>distributive impli-
cations</u> for teachers in general and for different strata and
groups within their ranks. The political logic of the "first revolution" was hard on the teaching profession, as was the radical
strategy at a later date. "Socialist modernizing" policies, on
the other hand, have been aimed at ameliorating the distributive
position of teachers. Over time, this complex mix of policies
has created significant fluctuations in the symbolic status, political influence and material comfort of teachers in general
and different groups of teachers — old and young, Party and
non-Party, "progressive" and "backward," skilled and unskilled,
proletarian and bourgeois. The impact of these policies has
given rise to distributive politics in various forms.

The rest of this study is devoted to a detailed examination
of this political process.

The Social Prestige of Teachers

2

From the outset, CCP leaders assumed they had both the responsibility and the capacity to manipulate the relative prestige of specific social groups and strata. By a variety of means the CCP has in fact influenced — directly and indirectly, deliberately and unintentionally, positively and negatively — the symbolic standing of teachers as a distinct occupational group. On their side, teachers — like other members of the cultural intelligentsia — seem to have been particularly sensitive to the question of prestige and have exerted their best efforts to gain symbolic recognition from the political authorities and to blunt the impact of Party policies which threatened to undermine their social standing.

I am dividing my discussion of this question into two parts: first, the prestige of teachers among the general population and, second, the specific question of the relationship between teachers and students in the schools.

1. The General Prestige of the Teaching Profession

In this section we are concerned with the social honor or respect (zunjing) accorded to teachers by society at large. In Chinese parlance, this is referred to as "social status" (shehui diwei). The competing policy paradigms discussed earlier have meant that the Party's attitudes toward, and impact on, the social status of teachers since 1949 has been ambiguous and vari-

able. In the context of the political imperatives of the "first
revolution" in the early 1950s, the Party regarded it as essential — for both ideological and practical reasons — to weaken
the strong link between high prestige and mental labor which
had been a key dimension of the prerevolutionary social system.
The traditional notion of "all occupations are lowly, only the
study of books is supreme (wan ban jie xiapin, wei you dushu
gao) was thought to be incompatible with the proletarian ethic
of the new socialist order. Much of the traditionally honorific
aura of the literati, moreover, had derived from the close relationship between formal education and bureaucratic power in
the imperial state apparatus.[23] This relationship was reflected
in popular sayings such as "study books to become an official"
(du shu dang guan). In the early years after Liberation, therefore, the prestige deriving from the formal education of the prerevolutionary intelligentsia, particularly its higher strata, represented a potential threat to the authority claimed by the new
communist elite. Keenly aware of these links between knowledge, power and prestige, the Party thus felt it necessary to
restrain any "arrogance" or "cockiness" on the part of higher
intellectuals and to puncture any mythologizing about their
"glorious" and "elevated" past.

In the early postrevolutionary period, many older and senior
teachers did in fact tend to romanticize the past, pointing to the
great respect accorded to learning and the transmitters of
learning in traditional China. They wanted the new communist
government to maintain this tradition. Such nostalgia was mis-
leading (and often Machiavellian) since the heritage was ambiguous. The traditional prestige of learning had not been conferred automatically on teachers. In fact, they were often seen
as social failures, people who had aspired to government office
through success in the examinations, but whose failure —
through lack of talent, money, or connections — had forced them
into teaching.[24] The decline and fall of the Qing empire, moreover, had led to an increasing separation of the fields of power
and intellect as new elites grew up from different roots, notably
business and the armed forces.[25] During the latter part of the

Republican era, the social position of teachers at all levels
had been eroded by hyperinflation and a general decline in educational standards. As a result of these trends, the prestige
accorded to learning in general and teachers in particular appears to have decreased during the half-century before the
CCP's accession to power. Unfortunately, we do not yet have
enough systematic evidence to document the nature and extent
of this decline. Clearly it was only partial, for many of the
traditional si shu school teachers in the villages still retained
considerable prestige in the eyes of rural communities.[26]
Moreover, the prestige of the upper intellectual strata — notably college lecturers and senior-middle-school teachers in
the cities who had received Western-style education at home
or abroad — still remained substantial. The CCP viewed
this recently forged link between domestic prestige and
Western influence, particularly important in educational circles, with alarm and took steps to break it in the early
1950s.
    On the other hand, there were clear differences between the
social status of different strata of teachers, and CCP policies
in the early years reflected this fact. In the Republican period
(and before), the social status of the lower layer of teachers —
myriads of petty intellectuals eking out an existence as private
tutors, or employees in small private schools, or coaching colleges — had never measured up to the romanticized view of the
"tradition." The social standing of urban primary school
teachers had been particularly low during the Republican period; they constituted a kind of "underclass" within the teaching
profession. Thus the CCP's proclaimed intention to redistrib-
ute social goods and opportunities in favor of the previous un-
derdog classes and strata also involved a commitment to raise
the social position of primary school teachers. In the case of
college teachers, on the other hand, the problem was reversed.
Their command of specialized skills and Western knowledge
brought them high levels of prestige which often allowed them
to overawe the working-class cadres assigned to "lead" them.
Thus the Party's attempt to redefine the prestige of the teach-

ing profession involved both a leveling-up and a leveling-down.

In general, however, any systematic attempt to deflate the social image of intellectuals was precluded for several practical reasons. First, as the CCP strove to consolidate and extend its authority throughout China in the early years, it needed to win political support or minimize opposition from influential urban groups, including teachers. This caused constant tension between the moderating influence of the central political and governmental leadership and the "leftist" tendencies of basic-level cadres who wanted to "take the intellectuals down a peg." Second, teachers were too crucial to the CCP's new programs to be the victims of ideologically motivated attacks on their status. Great importance was attached to the reconstruction of the educational system after 1949 and to its expansion and adaptation to meet the manifold developmental needs of the First Five-Year Plan. Trained and experienced teachers were scarce; their skills and commitment had to be fully mobilized in the service of the Plan. Third, it was no easy task to motivate young people to go in for a teaching career. Some were deterred by the ambiguous official status of the teaching profession, some by the "troublesome" nature of the job (particularly at the middle school level), others by the existence of attractive job alternatives, particularly in the early post-Liberation years.[27] Because of the Party's own emphasis on "advanced" techniques and "specialist" occupations during the early years of the Plan and the consequent focus of public attention on higher levels of the educational system, there was a widespread feeling that the lower strata of the teaching profession, notably (but not exclusively) those in "regular" junior-middle and primary, part-time, or "people-run" schools, were functionally unimportant for national development. At a time when young people were constantly being encouraged to rise above mere material motivations and seek to make a "contribution" (gongxian) to the socialist motherland through their work, these jobs were seen as too "simple" (i.e. not a "specialty") and mundane. Young people felt that it would be very difficult to "make one's mark" in such occupations. Government officials charged with the task of mobilizing applicants for teacher-training institutions — "normal" schools, colleges, and universities — complained constantly that many prospective students felt that "teaching takes a lot of trouble and achievements in this field are not easily detectable; in other fields of work, on the other hand, success is as clear as the shadow of a pole."[28] This low evaluation of primary- and lower-secondary-level teaching was shared by many teachers in service, especially recent appointees. Since controls over the labor market in the early and mid-1950s were relatively loose, there was a tendency for young lower-level teachers to leave their jobs if an attractive alternative presented itself. This raised the specter of a large-scale "brain-drain" out of the teaching profession and a consequent decline in professional standards.

A debate in the magazine Xiaoxue jiaoshi [Primary School Teacher] in late 1953 illustrated some of these motivational problems. Primary school teachers wrote to the editor complaining that teaching was inferior to other professions, that they were inferior to their counterparts in middle schools, and the latter to academics in colleges and universities. One teacher complained that he had wanted to "participate in national construction directly" (i.e. by getting a job in the state sector of the economy) but had been contemptuously prevented from sitting the examinations for an engineering institute. Another correspondent reported that, in a survey of the career ambitions of 146 children in his school, only one wanted to become a teacher. This teacher expressed his worries as follows:

As far as future development is concerned, our country is taking the path of industrialization and our Five-Year Plan is concentrating on economic construction. This means that economic construction is most important and industrial workers are the people with the most prospects and prestige. If we use a theoretical metaphor, economic construction is playing the lead role and cultural construction is in the supporting cast. What's wrong if we primary teachers want to do jobs which are in the lead role? Moreover, I believe we could definitely do them better than those (industrial) workers whose cultural level is low. Everybody would like to do important things and contribute more effort to the nation. Isn't this all right? Why is it that some teachers have encountered criticism when they request a change of occupation? Possibly

some people say: "The work of primary school teachers is also important."
But I'd like to ask them this: "So why do a lot of people look down on primary school teachers?"[29]

The official response to these pressures was ambiguous, reflecting a clash between long-term egalitarian goals and short-
term developmental and political objectives. On the one hand,
the Party sought, over the long run, to redefine the very meaning of symbolic status and cancel the relationship between occupation and differential social prestige. Official spokesmen argued optimistically that "whether a person is honored by society today depends on his contribution to the nation and the
people, not on whether he is an engineer, teacher, or nurse."
On the other hand, it was recognized that popular motivations
change only glacially and that it was necessary in the short
term to pander to "incorrect," hierarchical conceptions of social status based on occupation, not selfless contribution to
society.

Thus, as the modernization program gathered pace in the
mid-1950s, Party leaders took specific steps to maintain or increase the prestige of middle and primary school teachers,
particularly the latter. This was particularly necessary as a
distributive substitute for significant improvements in teachers'
material position which were precluded by the diversion of
funds into the industrialization program. Party leaders ap-
proached the task from two directions: first, they sought to in-
flate through invidious comparison, seeking to encourage the
belief that teachers' status in the new society already far exceeded that in the bad old prerevolutionary days; second, they
attempted by a variety of concrete means to improve the image
of teaching prevalent among teachers themselves and among the
general population.[30]

Official propaganda in the early and mid-1950s thus highlighted the negative aspects of teachers' lives in the imperial
period and documented the deterioration of their prestige during
the Republican period. Party spokesmen tried to demonstrate
that the time-hallowed theory of the "lofty" (qinggao) status of
teachers had never accorded with reality and cited proverbs to

document their previously contemptible status. Take one example from old Beijing:

> There were two sayings which described the homes of the well-to-do: "an
> awning, a fish-pond, a pomegranate tree; a master, a sleek lapdog and a fat
> slave-girl." The status of teachers in old China could be compared with that
> of sleek lapdogs and bond maids. In the countryside, their status certainly
> wasn't high either. People thought this of them: "When young, they carry
> firewood and grain baskets; when they grow up they become a king among chil-
> dren; when they're old they sell flatcakes and sesame candy."[31]

   This point was particularly emphasized in the case of primary school teachers.

> In the old society, was there a teacher who didn't feel deeply the sufferings of
> social discrimination, when primary school teachers were called "book-
> teacher" (jiaoshujiang) [the suffix jiang is usually attached to manual trades
> such as bricklayers and carpenters and has a demeaning connotation] or "king
> of the kids"? The proverb says: "If your house has two measures of grain,
> don't become a king of the kids."[32]

During the Nationalist period, proclaimed the official media,
most teachers, particularly those in primary schools but also
more generally, had led a "chalk and eraser life" (fenca sheng-
ya), pushed around by politicians, bureaucrats, policemen and
soldiers, and ground down by inflation.[33] Not only had they
been despised by the general population, Party spokesmen argued, but they had also despised themselves. They cited Ye
Shengdao's celebrated novel of the 1920s, Schoolmaster Ni
Huan-chih, to illustrate the miserable position of teachers in
previous decades, particularly at the primary level.[34] In the
new socialist society, they maintained, such a situation was in-
admissible: it was the Party and government's responsibility
to raise the social standing of teachers among the general population.
   In a more positive vein, the propaganda system in the early
and mid-1950s carried many eulogistic accounts of the teaching
profession aimed at middle and primary school teachers themselves and at the general public. Professional teachers in the

"regular" school system were on the state payroll and thus
could lay claim to the prestige surrounding the role of "state
cadre" (guojia ganbu). They were also granted the honorific
titles of "people's teachers" (renmin jiaoshi) and "engineers
of the human soul" (renlei linghun gongchengshi). The latter
term was borrowed from the Soviet leader Kalinin and reflected
the high prestige accorded to the (real) engineer in the social
system of the early and mid-1950s.[35] The use of a technological analogy, "soul engineer," clearly reflected an attempt to
draw talented senior-middle graduates away from the more
prestigious careers in industry opened up by the First Five-
Year Plan and into normal colleges to meet the pressing shortage of middle school teachers.[36] For example, consider the
following extract from an article aimed at senior-middle school
graduates in 1956:

> I want to introduce to you those institutions which train a special kind of engi-
> neer for our country, a type with the honorific title of "soul engineer" — higher
> level normal schools for training people's middle school teachers. If we com-
> pare ordinary education to "industry," then higher normal schools can be com-
> pared to the "iron and steel industry." Our country's task of socialist con-
> struction needs all types of engineers, including those engineers of the human
> soul, people's teachers. Today's industrial revolution and cultural revolution
> are intimately connected. The two different types of engineers are both needed
> by the nation, and though their responsibilities are different, they are both
> contributing to the construction of the motherland. This requires that a large
> number of young people in the graduating classes of senior-middle schools
> should take the exams for higher normal schools.[37]

The analogy with the economic system was taken further. Not
only were teachers singled out for special praise as "models"
but were also incorporated into the "advanced producers" campaign in the mid-1950s designed to raise the technological
level of industry.[38]

Mass movements were also launched in the early and mid-
1950s to "foster the social habit of respecting teachers," particularly primary school teachers.[39] The Government Affairs
Council included in its "Directive on the Rectification and Improvement of Primary School Education," issued in December

1953, a specific call to the "popular masses" to "recognize primary school teachers as trainers of our new generation, shouldering a glorious and difficult task," to respect them and to "correct all derogatory and discriminatory treatment."[40]

The official media also encouraged a professionalist ethic ("specialist thought," zhuanye sixiang) among primary and middle school teachers, thus allowing them to include themselves within the prestigious ranks of "specialists" (zhuanjia).[41] This was designed to counteract the notions, widespread among middle school students, that they "could learn nothing and had no chance to become an expert in teacher-training institutions" and that "only those with poor results in their study go to normal schools."

The social position of teachers in the Soviet Union was widely popularized as a model in the early and mid-1950s. Soviet policies which conferred special privileges or honors on teachers were singled out for special attention (for example, study sabbaticals, long service medals, or "teachers' homes"). The allegedly prestigious social role of Soviet teachers received wide publicity through Soviet films, such as "A Teacher's Life" and "A Rural Female Teacher." Complimentary statements by Lenin and Kalinin about the teaching profession were frequently cited in the press, notably Lenin's remark that the Bolsheviks should "raise the status of our country's teachers to a level utterly unattainable by teachers in capitalist societies."[42] Delegations of Chinese teachers back from the Soviet Union reported that teaching was one of the most respected professions in socialist countries.[43] But the political impact of such reports was ambiguous. Many young Chinese who went to visit or study in the Soviet Union during this period expressed dissatisfaction when they returned home because the prestige of primary and middle school teachers in Soviet society was higher than in China.

In implementing these policies, the CCP leadership ran into a good deal of resistance from basic-level cadres, particularly in the countryside where cadres were overwhelmingly former poor peasants who distrusted intellectuals in general and teach-

ers in particular. Primary school teachers were one of their
most frequent (and most vulnerable) victims. Teachers in
rural primary schools complained that the Party's proclaimed
policies were laudable, but they just weren't being implemented:

These policies may be fine, but when they get to our county they totally change
their form and some even change their substance. In our area, many county
cadres use such pretty phrases as "glorious people's teachers" and "engineers
of the human soul" when they refer to teachers. But when they handle practical matters, it's not like that at all — they treat primary school teachers like
toilet paper.[44]

While the media praised the social importance of teachers, they
argued, educational cadres did not take them seriously (qing-
shi): one primary school teacher, for example, complained
that a colleague in his school had been transferred to commer-
cial work simply because he was a good worker and thus "too
valuable for teaching." While the official media maundered on
about how "glorious" their job was, teachers complained, local
cadres acted quite contrarily:

Once a member of our district committee came to Wang Zhuang Village on a
job and found that several teachers had gone home. He didn't look into the reasons thoroughly but criticized us in front of the masses: "The teachers here
spend more time at home than they do at work." This made us all very angry.
When some of our cadres here mention primary school teachers in conversation, they say: "Pah! If you tell them to go east, they don't dare go west.
Tell them to catch a dog, they don't dare say boo to a goose." Is this our so-
called "glorious workpost"?[45]

Complaints about such "deviations" by local and basic-level
cadres were a frequent theme in the specialized educational
media in the early and mid-1950s. Teachers charged that
cadres were damaging their "prestige" (weixin) in their local
communities and among their students; that cadres "looked
down on" (kanbuqi) teachers and regarded them as "one cut below" (di ren yi deng) themselves in the social pecking order.
Cadres were accused of perpetuating the "traditional historical
notion" that primary school teachers were a profession "with-

out prestige or profit."[46] One teacher from Shandong Province,
for example, wrote to a magazine to complain that he had been
barred from a film show by a gray-uniformed cadre who told
him: "Today the film's being shown for the entertainment of
cadres. Primary school teachers don't make the grade!" The
teacher felt deeply shamed by the incident: "My face turned
red right down to my throat and I left straight away in case I
should meet an acquaintance."[47] Another primary school
teacher from Anhui Province reported a case of discrimination
over food:

A meeting was held once at the district (qu) headquarters for administrative
cadres and teachers. When it came to mealtime, food was prepared only for
the cadres and not for the teachers. A teacher named Ma stupidly rushed over
to eat with the cadres but was ejected by a district cadre. We could only appease our hunger by going out to buy food.

A teacher from Hunan Province made a similar complaint
about clothing:

A district cadre said: "For winter this year, there are regulations for clothing. Cadres are to wear uniforms with four pockets, teachers are to wear
black uniforms with three pockets. You mustn't be lax about your clothes. If
you are, then there's no way to tell who is a cadre and who is a teacher."

Yet another case, from Shandong Province, showed the un-
pleasant personal repercussions of such differences:

In our district there's a teacher who fell in love last year with a female
teacher. Relations between the two were very good and they often spent time
together talking or helping each other study. But in the spring of this year,
the head of our district wanted to introduce the (female) teacher to a district
cadre. (The male) teacher replied as follows: "I'm already going steady with
(her)." But the district head said: "What prospects has a primary school
teacher got?"

Cadres in Liaoning Province were censured for calling primary
school teachers the "three petties": "petty teachers," "petty
intelligentsia," and "petty bourgeois." The following case was
cited as typical of such attitudes in the province:

In Lingyuan County, a cadre once visited a primary school. When some
teachers spoke to him politely, they were accused of "fawning." When some
teachers didn't talk to him at all, they were accused of "arrogance." The
teachers were thus between the devil and the deep blue sea.[48]

Similar complaints included cases of cadres treating primary
school teachers as secretaries, cooks or general skivvies, arbitrarily requisitioning their school buildings or educational
equipment, or making them deliver mail, sink wells, collect
fertilizer, or sell produce. There were also many cases of
petty discrimination by cadres in the distribution of medical
facilities, mailing privileges, the right to use telephones, and
so on, actions which teachers resented both in themselves and
as slights to their self-esteem.[49]

This pervasive clash between the modernization-oriented
policies of the central leadership and anti-intellectual "deviations" among basic-level cadres highlights the difficulties of
the transition from peasant-based revolution to urban-based
modernization. As we suggested earlier, cadres in both urban
and rural schools and education bureaus retained many of the
hostilities and prejudices of the "first revolution" in conflict
with the increasingly "developmentalist" emphases of the CCP
elite. In consequence, the impact of the political system on the
general social status of the teaching profession over the period
of "socialist transformation" from 1950 to 1956 was decidedly
ambiguous. The proletarian fervor of the immediate post-
Liberation years which undermined the prestige of the intelligentsia became interwoven with modernizing policies which attempted to bolster their social prestige as one means of gaining
their cooperation. Teachers, like other members of the intelligentsia, shared a sense of uncertainty which found expression
in criticisms voiced during the Hundred Flowers movement:
"At different times, intellectuals may be thrown into the fire
or pushed into the water, sent down to hell or lifted up to
heaven."[50] But the Hundred Flowers movement provoked a re-
version to the anti-intellectual themes of the "first revolution"
during the Anti-Rightist campaign. Teachers were one of the
prime targets of this backlash, and their public standing was

damaged by a barrage of propaganda about their "bourgeois" tendencies and a welter of humiliation and encroachments at the hands of school cadres.

The fluctuations of this early period continued into the 1960s and 1970s, this time in response to the struggle between left and right within the Party leadership. During periods when radical ideology and policy were dominant, official propaganda impugned the social value of professional teachers and, implicitly or explicitly, undermined their status in the eyes of the general population. During periods of "socialist modernizing" predominance, however, official propaganda changed course, waxing lyrical about the respected social position and crucial developmental role of teachers.

The first appearance of the Maoist critique of the professional integrity of teachers was during the "educational revolution" of 1958. The propaganda content of the movement was ambiguous, reflecting both developmentalist concerns about the professional performance of teachers and radical criticisms of the political dangers of professionalism.[51] Certain radical themes emerged then which were to find more virulent and unalloyed expression during the Cultural Revolution. According to the radical critique, policies which stressed the prestige of teachers created "bourgeois" professionalism. For the Maoists, a teacher's role only took on symbolic significance in relation to the larger political issues dominating the period of socialist transition. The social prestige of an individual teacher was to derive less from the specific nature of his occupation, more from his general political commitments.[52] Teachers at all levels, but most notably older teachers in middle schools and colleges, were identified as a conservative and elitist group who kept themselves aloof from the masses by exaggerated pretensions to "expertise." They tended to be seen as a practical and psychological obstacle to the mass movement during the Great Leap. The masses were called on to lose their "inferiority complex and blind faith in old experts"; teachers were criticized for "underestimating the initiative and creativity of the masses." As in posters, the masses became

larger than life and the embattled elites dwindled in comparison. Teaching was redefined as an activity within the competence of ordinary, untutored people. To meet the needs of educational expansion during the Leap, moreover, people without
professional training were hastily recruited as teachers, including retired workers and cadres, demobilized soldiers, and
ordinary peasants or workers. In the new "people-run" schools,
teachers were paid by the local community or unit and were
responsible thereto, thus losing the special status accruing to
"regular" teachers on the state payroll. The purity of teaching
as a form of "mental" labor was sullied by the introduction or
extension of obligatory manual labor for both teachers and
students in the regular school curriculum. The circumscription
of the teacher's role in schools and the general decline in educational standards which accompanied the Leap also contributed
to an overall decline in the social prestige of the teaching profession during this period.

The same themes returned with far greater force during the
Cultural Revolution and led to a correspondingly serious decline in the social standing of teachers in the late 1960s and
early 1970s. They were the target of an overwhelmingly negative ideological barrage, and many — particularly older, more
politically vulnerable teachers — were subjected to verbal and
physical attacks by their own students and control by outsiders'
mass organizations, notably the Worker Propaganda Teams introduced in 1968. Their professional functions were reduced
to minimal levels, most of their time was spent on "reeducation" through manual labor, and their ranks were swelled once
again by new recruits from among the masses and the PLA.[53]
By the early 1970s, therefore, the prestige of the teaching profession had reached a new low ebb, and the by now familiar
symptoms of decline appeared in the press: poor morale among
teachers themselves, tension between teachers and educational
cadres, and official concern about the reluctance of the middle-
school students to consider a teaching career.

In two periods since the Great Leap Forward, on the other
hand, sections of the Party leadership have intervened to re-

store the prestige of teachers as part of a general program to
enlist their cooperation and to reestablish teaching as a career
option attractive to talented young people — from 1959 to 1963
and again from late 1976 onward. In the early 1960s, the general prestige of the teaching profession rose gradually along
with the rehabilitation of academic knowledge and study, the renewed emphasis on the importance of professional training and
experience, and public criticism of people who allegedly be-
littled the role of experts in the educational process.[54] The
honorific titles of the 1950s were revived — notably "engineers
of the human soul" — and model teachers were chosen who embodied the professional virtues of experience, ability, and application.[55] The teacher and the general public were once again
assured that teaching was a highly respected professional activity.[56] Primary school teachers, for example, still complained that, in the eyes of their friends and relatives (and,
worse still, prospective spouses), they possessed no recognized
skill (unlike construction workers or carpenters) and "earned
a living by selling their mouth." In response, official propaganda argued that teaching, even at the primary level, constituted a skilled and "scientific" endeavor, and thus merited the
respect due to expertise.[57] Similarly, graduating middle
school students were again told that teacher-training was to
education as the steel industry was to economic development,
or the machine-tool sector was to the machine-building industry.[58] These measures were apparently not a very effective
incentive for young people since Mao himself was informed by
an educational official in early 1964 that "the worst students
are presently attending normal schools while the good students
attend physics and engineering colleges."[59]

Likewise, teachers were one of the groups to gain practical
and symbolic redress after the removal of the radical Shanghai
group in October 1976. In Deng Xiaoping's speech at the National Educational Work Conference in April 1978, for example,
he proposed new measures to raise the "social status" of
teachers.[60] Once again, national and provincial newspapers
called for "a social atmosphere of respecting teachers and en-

hancing their social status" and criticized radical leaders for "persecuting revolutionary teachers and maliciously condemning them as 'stinking scholars.'"[61] Honorific cartoons and illustrations once again appeared in the newspapers; teachers were now described as "master sculptors of the new people of the future"; competent and efficient teachers were singled out as models; art works glorifying the role of "people's teachers" were rehabilitated (for example, the Hunan opera Song of the Gardener* allegedly quashed by the Shanghai radicals in 1974) or commissioned anew; and outstanding teachers were dignified by a special grade to denote their excellence. To a person who remembered the policies of the mid-1950s and the early 1960s, these measures and themes were familiar indeed.

In sum, the constantly changing policies of the last three decades have had a fluctuating impact on teachers' social image among the population. Whenever Party policies damaged their social standing, they caused a drop in teachers' morale and in the enthusiasm of young people for a teaching career. Clearly the social prestige of the teaching profession could not be allowed to drop beyond a certain national level without severe costs for the modernization program. These costs have imposed limits on the capacity of Party leaders, notably the Maoists, to reform the educational process. Thus teacher discontent and passive resistance have contributed to changes in educational policy by thwarting the Maoists and by strengthening the hand of their opponents.

---

*For the official post-Mao "internal" CCP materials on the struggle over this opera, see Chungfa (1977), No. 37, part VIII, translated in Issues & Studies, Taipei, Vol. XV, No. 3. An associate of the radical Shanghai group criticized the opera for overpraising the role of teachers as "cultivators" of "peaches and plums" (i.e. good students). Jiang Qing is alleged to have said: "The gardener should be the Party. How could they be the teachers, the intellectuals?" Clearly, in the eyes of radical leaders, the opera was a disingenuous attempt to rehabilitate "bourgeois" teachers in the eyes of the public. For an article which rehabilitates the opera and defends it against the "Gang of Four" criticisms, see "Stifling the Song of a Gardener Is Also for Usurping Party and State Power," Renmin ribao (People's Daily), November 29, 1976 (translated in SPRCP, No. 6250, pp. 9-16).

   This picture of radical fluctuations in policy should not lead
one to exaggerate the degree of change in the social image and
motivations of teachers. Although systematic corroborative
evidence is lacking, elements of continuity seem to outweigh
elements of change. Lack of change can be attributed to material differences in the division of labor, variations in political
influence between different strata of teachers, the self-cancel-
ing nature of fluctuating policies, or the pertinacity of prerevolutionary social habits. There is little evidence to suggest, for
example, that — except for a minority of younger teachers —
the Party has been successful in replacing teachers' traditional
sensitivity to considerations of professional prestige with a
more altruistic, egalitarian commitment to the socialist cause.
   The Party has also been unsuccessful in significantly reduc-
ing prestige differentials between levels of teachers, which remain firmly rooted in levels of skill and ability. College
teachers seem to have maintained a consistently high social
status — in the case of professors, positively exalted — in the
eyes of the general community in spite of variations in their
political fortunes. Greenblatt recounts, for example, that when
Feng Youlan, professor of philosophy at Beijing University, was
criticized by his younger colleagues during the Cultural Revolution, they stood out of respect and read from prepared statements. [62] The Party has also been largely unsuccessful in
raising public esteem for primary school teachers. This is
probably connected with the fact that a high proportion of primary school teachers are women and thus a gender-based prestige differential is superimposed on their lowly occupational
status.* They have remained a highly problematic group, very
sensitive to social slight and political insult. Though white-

_____

   *According to figures collected by Cheng, 51 percent of primary school
teachers in 1960 were women, as compared with 18 percent for middle school
(1956) and 20 percent at the college level (1956): Chu-yuan Cheng, "Scientific
and Engineering Manpower in Communist China," in Joint Economic Committee of the U.S. Congress, An Economic Profile of Mainland China (Washington,
D.C.: U.S. Government Printing Office, 1967), p. 539.

collar employees and "intellectuals" of a sort, their skills are
relatively easily acquired and they have found themselves increasingly overshadowed and outranked by manual groups whose
status had traditionally been lower, notably skilled industrial
workers. Some primary school teachers thus appear to have
felt socially "boxed in": unable to achieve the symbolic attributes of the higher ranks of the intelligentsia on the one hand
and yet unwilling to bridge the psychological gap by accepting a
manual job on the other. It is not surprising that they have proven
a consistently discontented group. The status of middle-school
teachers is more ambiguous, but as of the late 1970s it does
not seem to be a popular career outlet among college graduates.
The propaganda of this latter period recognized the existence
of wide status differentials between the three levels and argued
that "it is necessary vigorously to create public opinion that it
is glorious to become a (middle and primary school) teacher"
and "the toil of a good primary school teacher is by no means
less important than that of a good university professor and they
should share equal honor." [63] Given the obvious differences in
skill and training, it is unlikely that this will prove convincing
to anyone.

2. Teacher-Student Relations

Now we turn to the status of the teacher in the classroom, the
prestige and moral authority of the teacher in the eyes of his or
her pupils. Judging from the literature on the subject since
1949, this relationship has been most problematic in middle
schools, and we shall focus mainly on this level.

The romantic Confucian ideal of teacher-student relations
continued to be very influential after 1949. According to this
notion, the relationship between the teacher and pupil was one
of moral example and emulation. It was hierarchical but emo-
tionally satisfying to both sides, an exchange of the teacher's
"love" (ai) for the pupil's "respect" (zun). In the classroom,
relations were regulated by strict rules of discipline and rituals

of obeisance and respect.* The satisfaction of the teacher was
enhanced by the academic success of his or her best pupils in
school and their achievements in higher education or in their
chosen careers after leaving school.[64] This latter idea finds
expression in a horticultural metaphor: "pupils (lit. "peaches
and plums") filling the earth" (taoli man tianxia).

The policy oscillations outlined earlier have clearly made
their mark on teacher-student relations. During the early
years of the "first revolution" after 1949, the Party encouraged
progressive students, notably at the college level, to participate
in the process of "reforming" their more "backward" teachers.
An article in the very first issue of the magazine Renmin jiaoyu
(People's Education) in mid-1950, for example, notes "a special phenomenon: in general, the young students' enthusiasm
for and speed of (political) progress are greater than their
teachers."[65] The latter were instructed to learn from their
students and accept their criticisms. The Party tried to keep
this role-reversal within bounds but, to the extent that it occurred, it undermined the idea of unidirectional professional
authority in the classroom. In the mid-1950s, it was discour-
aged by developmentalist policies which stressed the need for
teachers to wield more unqualified authority in the classroom and
for students to respect their teachers and observe strict standards
of discipline. This was seen as necessary in order to strengthen
both the moral and intellectual impact of teachers in the classroom.
In practice, this emphasis has, implicitly or explicitly, tended to
reproduce a muted version of the traditional relationship.

---

*In his article, "Rural Education in Transition" (loc cit, p. 42) T'ai-ch'u
Liao provides a fascinating description of teacher-pupil relations in a traditional rural sishu school during the Republic period:

> Every time a student wanted to go out he had to get the teacher's per-
> mission. The teacher might limit the amount of goings out by using a
> definite number of boards with the word "kung" on one side and the word
> "ching" on the other (both mean "respect").... Every time (a pupil)
> entered the room he had to bow to the teacher; and the first time he ap-
> peared in the room every day he had to bow first to Confucius' portrait
> and then to the teacher. This is a form of manner he was taught to do.

The "Rules of Conduct for Middle School Students," issued
in June 1955, are a good example of measures aimed at but-
tressing the teacher's position in the classroom. Take, for
example, rules seven and nine:

7. Stand up when answering the teacher's questions. Sit down when the
teacher permits you. When you want to ask the teacher a question, raise your
hand first.

9. Respect the principal and the teachers. Stand up and salute your teacher
when the class begins and again at the end of the class. When you meet the
principal or teacher outside the school you also salute them.[66]

During the same period, campaigns were launched to instill the
idea of "respect teachers, love pupils" (zunshi aisheng), a practice revived in the early 1960s to reestablish the proper relationship which "socialist modernizing" leaders felt had been
damaged during the Great Leap Forward. The early 1960s provide some excellent examples of the Party's willingness to allow partial preservation of the traditional relationship. For example, a prominent article "On the Question of Study" published
in the Guangming ribao (Guangming Daily) in 1961 emphasized
the "fine tradition in China's educational history" of students
honoring teachers and teachers loving students:

There were many rules laid down in ancient documents in regard to honoring
one's teachers. The chapter on "Minutiae of Etiquette" in the Book of Rites
said: "When you walk with your teacher, don't cross the road to talk with another person. When you meet your teacher on the road, you approach him,
stand erect, and salute him with your hands folded. When your teacher says
nothing, withdraw." It also said: "When you attend to your teacher, give answers only when you are asked questions." It also said: "Stand up when you
are instructed and stand up again when you ask for further information." These
rules appear to be complex and useless, but they also reflect how teachers
were honored in ancient China.

Confucius had warm affection for his students. When Yan Hui died, he wept
bitterly and arranged his funeral for him.

Descriptions above are traditions which reflect how teachers were honored and
students were loved in ancient times. In a class society, the relationship be-

tween teachers and students bore, of course, the class brand like other personal relationships. But it also left us a good deal of beneficial and rational
things.[67]

Similar sentiments were expressed in an article by a noted
educationalist in the authoritative Hong qi (Red Flag) magazine
that same year. The author lauded the "fine tradition" of student-teacher relations and cited certain Chinese classics on
the subject as worthy of study and emulation (notably a work by
Han Yu on teaching). The superiority of teacher to student was
defined as unambiguous since "the teacher, who 'has heard
truth earlier and has studied a specialized subject,' always
possesses greater and deeper knowledge than the student."[68]
 Ritual expressions of students' respect were also encouraged
in this period. Young Communist League branches in middle
schools, for example, were called on to "teach the pupils to
respect their teachers and learn humbly from them" by a variety of means: organizing receptions for new teachers, inviting
experienced teachers to lecture to the class about their teaching experience, and paying special visits to teachers in their
houses. Similarly, an interview respondent noted that in the
early 1960s students who had left middle school for universities
would return to Guangzhou in June or July for the holidays and
would hold honorific "teachers' meetings," either at the teachers' homes or at school. Primary and middle school students
were also encouraged to visit their teachers at New Year or
when they were sick at home or in hospital, or to display other
public signs of respect, such as surrendering seats on buses.
 During periods when the teaching profession came under political pressure, on the other hand, teachers' authority was
undermined and many students felt that they should not receive
automatic respect merely qua teachers. They had to earn respect through exemplary political conduct as well as professional excellence. Under the impact of the Anti-Rightist movement, for example, many "rightist" teachers lost face in front
of their pupils. An article in the magazine Zhongguo qingnian
(Chinese Youth) in early 1958, entitled "How to Deal with Your

Spouse or Your Teachers If They Are Rightists," illustrates
the change in relations between some teachers and their pupils
during this period.[69] The article noted that some pupils were
refusing to greet "rightist" teachers in the customarily respectful fashion when they entered the classroom, or were failing to stand up when answering the teachers' questions. The
article was somewhat ambiguous on the issue; such behavior
was politically understandable but should not be encouraged.
The correct way for students to deal with their "rightist"
teachers, it argued, was to "draw a firm ideological and political line" but "still treat them as teachers." Students who continued to respect and admire them for their learning alone, on
the other hand, were held to be "backward" in their thought.

During periods of Maoist policy dominance, however, this
type of ambiguity has been rejected, and there have been more
thoroughgoing attempts to revise the basic nature of teacher-
student relations. Mao himself had some radical ideas on
teacher-pupil relations, expressed most pungently during talks
with his nephew and with a visiting educational delegation from
Nepal in 1964.[70] He opposed authoritarian teaching methods,
encouraged the critical initiative of the pupil, and in general
favored a more democratic, reciprocal relationship. These
ideas found expression in the "educational revolution" of 1958,
the Cultural Revolution, and the abortive radical educational
campaigns of the early and mid-1970s. During the Great Leap
Forward, official propaganda urged that status distinctions between teachers and students should be minimized and asserted
that students were in fact superior to teachers in certain aspects, notably in their ability "to accept new things and new
thoughts."[71] A good deal of initiative was granted to pupils and
students, particularly those in the League or Party, who joined
in criticism leveled at their "conservative" teachers during
1958.

These policy fluctuations not only affected relations between
teachers and students as distinct groups, but also created different patterns of relationship between subgroups of each.
The "normal" relationship favored by "socialist-modernizing"

leaders tended to bring together the "professionalist" teacher
and the "talented" student. In the early 1960s, for example, the
official media called on teachers to learn from Confucius in
"teaching according to the aptitude of students and cherishing
the talented ones":

Students who strive to learn, attain good records, and show special skill,
ability or interest in certain fields should be given special guidance to develop
their special gift.... It is a good thing to have talented students in a class.
Instructors should pay attention to discovering them and giving them special
treatment beyond ordinary education.[72]

On the other hand, during periods of radical politicization, this
type of emphasis was seen as prejudicial and "bourgeois," designed to foster "the cultivation of intellectual aristocrats."
The political responsibilities of teachers to laboring-class students were emphasized — they were to receive privileged treatment, not their cleverer, sociologically more dubious classmates. Young teachers from "good" class backgrounds were
singled out as more suitable to this task. As a result, emerging
political distinctions between teachers were paralleled by differentiation within the student body — different segments would
react to the same political cues in different ways, and each successive political movement exacerbated these tensions.

It was the Cultural Revolution which brought the greatest push
toward the equalization and even inversion of status relationships between teachers and students. Although each group was
exhorted to treat the other as "comrades" and "class brothers"
engaged in the same political struggle, teachers tended to become political targets for their own students.[73] They were
also identified as agents of ideological corruption. One typical
example is the publicity given to a student from Beijing University who was cited as follows:

As soon as I entered the university, some of the teachers began to put into my
head the idea of working for prestige and authority. They wanted me to become a philosophy specialist and led me into the labyrinth of ancient books
while discouraging me in my study of Chairman Mao's works.

Later, they suggested I should take postgraduate courses in order to climb up
the professional ladder of instructorship and professorship instead of going
out to the workers and peasants. They used the position and high living standards of bourgeois professors to corrupt me.[74]

This type of analysis was spread abroad by radical leaders
such as Zhang Chunqiao and was reinforced by no less an allegedly "moderate" figure than Zhou Enlai who remarked as
follows to a meeting of Red Guards:

Many children of working-class families originally had strong feeling for
labor, but after studying in school for several years, their feeling is weakened.
This is because our schools are dominated by bourgeois intellectuals....
Though educated in our socialist society and graduating after 1949, a youth
will have his bourgeois world-outlook developed and even consolidated once he
studies under an old professor or an old teacher.[75]

It is hardly surprising, therefore, that throughout the whole
movement, teachers were fair game and student criticism was
regarded as a praiseworthy political act for both "conservative"
and "rebel" organizations alike.[76]

Official propaganda during the movement attempted to invert
the usual teacher-pupil relationship, citing Mao to the effect
that "because teachers are educators, they must receive education first." Given the fact that students were less influenced
by old ideas, argued the media, they could detect the deficien-
cies of their teachers relatively easily; in many cases, they
were more competent than their mentors. Teachers were thus
called on to "doff their superior airs and humbly accept criticism" from their students. Some of Beijing's Red Guard groups
responded by proclaiming that "all schools must abolish the
feudal rites between teachers and pupils and establish the relationship on the basis of equality."[77] The radical media praised
new modes of address as a reflection of the revolutionization
of teacher-student relations. Pupils in one rural primary
school, for example, no longer said "Good morning, teacher"
on entering the classroom but "We wish Chairman Mao a long
life."[78] In certain middle schools, the pupils were encouraged
to take over teaching responsibilities, former teachers acting

primarily as "guides" before and after classes.[79] Leading educators were accused of propagating "feudal" (i.e. traditional)
ideas about "the dignity of teachers," describing them as people
who "had learned the 'way.'"[80] Extreme variants of the "radical" line called for the abolition of the teacher-pupil relationship altogether to be replaced by new forms of education based
on equality of instructor and instructed.

The Cultural Revolution also politicized the tensions between
younger and older teachers with different class backgrounds
and between politically "reliable" students with "good" class
backgrounds and their "cleverer" classmates often from former
elite or middle-class backgrounds. To some extent, this structured patterns of alliance across the student-teacher divide
(e.g. young proletarian teachers joining Red Guard groups of
proletarian students or students of intellectual origins "making
revolution" against Party cadres to protect older, politically
vulnerable, teachers). However, I do not have enough information to trace these alliances in any detail. These more systematic patterns aside, moreover, the unfettered atmosphere of the
Cultural Revolution allowed the politicization of personal animosities, jealousies and inadequacies, both within the ranks of
teachers and students and between these two groups. So long
as attacks were couched in acceptable language, students were
able to vent their personal frustrations against their teachers
and could claim "revolutionary" legitimacy in so doing.

It is hardly surprising, therefore, that in many educational
institutions, particularly middle schools, the Cultural Revolution created a legacy of ambiguity and tension in teacher-
student relations. This was clearly an obstacle to official attempts, beginning in early 1967, to restore order to the schools.
One report by a teacher in a Shanghai middle school in March
1967 throws the problem into sharp relief:

The bad influence exerted by the bourgeois reactionary line has estranged the
students from the teachers. During the early period of the movement, a handful of power-holders incited the students to struggle against the teachers. At
that time all the students personally took part in that struggle. When the
teachers rose up to criticize the bourgeois reactionary line, most of the stu-

dents had already left the schools to go elsewhere.

Now, they are in school again. Not knowing the conditions of the struggle going on in the school at an earlier stage, they still view the teachers in the light of the past. In feelings, teachers and students stand quite far apart. Most teachers give the students "a wide berth" for fear that any verbal mistake will get them into trouble. In work, they have become timid and flinching. When they see something bad, they do not dare to voice any criticism. As they are at present, relationships between teachers and students are unusually abnormal.[81]

Sections of the Party leadership viewed this degeneration in classroom relations as a source of educational inefficiency which was damaging to the development program and attempted to rectify the situation by reestablishing a more disciplined relationship after the death of Lin Biao in late 1971. The Shanghai radical group and their followers, however, continued to view the nature of this relationship as an important political issue, as a microcosmic expression of correct relations between mass and elite, subordinate and superior, junior and senior. Students were urged to become "active promoters of the educational revolution," to avoid "being satisfied with the status quo and only following behind the teachers": for example, middle school and college students were encouraged to play an autonomous role in the reform of teaching methods, curricula, and course materials.[82] "In the old-type universities," argued the radical media, "the teachers and students sat apart from each other; today they are comrades-in-arms fighting in the same trench."[83] A special attempt was made to rally solidarity on class grounds, i.e. between younger college teachers from "good" class backgrounds and the post-Cultural Revolution generation of "worker-peasant-soldier students." Middle and primary school students were praised publicly for resisting conventional tests and examinations and rebelling against forms of classroom discipline which, they felt, stifled their initiative.[84] In some middle schools, students were encouraged to substitute a system of self- and mutual evaluation for the previous system of evaluation by the form-master. The latter, maintained the students, was harmful because it made them fear the form-master and fet-

tered them within the old academic conventions.[85] "Hereafter,"
said the form-master in one such class, "I should discard my
haughty airs, trust and rely on the 'children's corps.'" The
radical leadership dramatized the issue in late 1973 by giving
nationwide publicity to the case of a twelve-year-old Beijing
primary school pupil, Huang Shuai. She wrote a letter to Renmin
ribao complaining that her teacher advocated "the teacher's
absolute authority" and viewed all criticism from pupils as
"damaging to his prestige." The media hailed her as a "young
pathbreaker" who "dared to go against the tide" by refusing to
submit to the traditional teacher-student relationship like a
slave or a sheep.[86] She was cited as a model for emulation
throughout the nation. Huang's letter provoked a critical response from a PLA political cadre in Inner Mongolia who argued that this kind of attitude meant that "students confront
teachers as if they are enemies" and damaged teachers' "dignity":

At present, teachers in many schools have become timorous, punctilious, and
tame people while their students are in the habit of putting up wall posters.
They call this "going against the tide" and want to be trailblazers in the educational revolution. In fact, this is not a very good tide.[87]

The radical media dismissed this type of argument as tantamount to "bourgeois restoration" and integrated criticism of
the "feudal" idea of the "inviolable dignity of teachers" into the
campaign against Confucius and Confucian vestiges which gained
pace in early 1974. Confucius, it was argued, had maintained
that students should "keep themselves under the restraint of
the rules of propriety" and that "if the teacher is not strict, his
teaching will not be respected and the learning (he imparts) will
not be solid." The teacher-student relationship was seen as a
microcosm of the modal form of authority relationship in traditional (and contemporary) society:

(According to Confucius), the teacher should be one grade higher than the student. The student was required to show absolute obedience to the teacher.
The slightest sign of disrespect would be considered a "transgression." The
relationship between the teacher and the student was the relationship between
the ruler and the ruled.[88]

For the radicals then in charge of educational policy, the attack
on this relationship thus served at least two main purposes:
ideologically, it aimed to disrupt the continuity of traditional
practices and, politically, it was part of their attempt to piece
together a power base by mobilizing social underdogs against
powerful and strategic groups in society who stood opposed to
radical innovation. To their opponents, on the other hand, they
were mischievous extremists who, consciously or uncon-
sciously, were bringing the educational system into disarray
and disrepute by opposing an efficient and mutually beneficial
pattern of teacher-student relations. To a considerable extent,
the realities of the early and mid-1970s corroborated this analysis. Student autonomy too easily degenerated into indiscipline
and troublemaking, and the educational process suffered in consequence. This was reinforced by other reforms of the period,
notably the requirement that all middle-school students were
to go to factories and farms after graduation and subsequent
university selection was to depend on nonacademic criteria.
This meant that middle-school students had little incentive to
study and cooperate with the teacher in the educational process.
The media of the period attempted to counter the resulting notion that "study is useless" (du shu meiyong), but it was a natural product of the post-Cultural Revolution educational program. When leaders of "socialist modernizing" persuasion
seized the reins of power in late 1976, therefore, they brought
about an abrupt about-face in official policy. The incident of
Huang Shuai was dismissed as a ruse devised by the "Gang of
Four," certain good elements were rediscovered in Confucius'
educational ideas and, though allowing that students had the
right to criticize teachers, official propaganda once again called
for a restoration of order and discipline in the classroom.[89]
In essence, this marked a return to the themes and policies of
the mid-1950s and early 1960s.
     In sum, there has been considerable fluctuation in official
policies toward the authority possessed by and respect due to
teachers in the classroom. Although a minority of teachers
seem to have accepted or at least coped with the Maoist revi-

sion of the teacher's role, most teachers appear to have resented such notions as personally distressing and educationally
injurious. In consequence, Maoist policies led to a decline in
teacher morale. The radical critique seems to have provoked
most response among middle school students. They have posed,
particularly during the Cultural Revolution, the sharpest challenge to their teachers' authority in the classroom, primary
students being too immature (pace Huang Shuai) and college
students too "mature" to shake their teachers' position fundamentally.

Though the pressure of radical policies has been intense in
certain periods, however, evidence from a variety of sources
— notably visitors to China and former residents — suggests
that their impact was uneven and, in most cases, superficial.
Though in some cases they caused a breakdown of discipline
and efficiency in schools — most notably in the decade from
1966 to 1976 — the traditional teacher-student relationship
seems to have been remarkably resilient, even at times when
radical pressures were at their peak. Recent reports suggest,
moreover, that where the "normal" relationship had been undermined to some extent, it was quickly resurrected in the conservative environment of the late 1970s. This is a vivid testa-
ment to the ability of the older generation of teachers to maintain their traditional modes of operation, transmit them to the
new generation of teachers, and make them one condition of
their cooperation with the Party in the modernization program.

Issues of Income and Material Welfare

3

The nature and level of teachers' material conditions have
been a recurring bone of contention between the teaching profession and the Party since 1949. In their desire to increase
their wages and welfare provisions and improve their working
conditions, teachers have faced political authorities whose decisions on such matters have been constrained by egalitarian
scruples and concern about the political implications of material relativities between occupational groups. Moreover, the
desire to reserve state funds for high priority sectors, notably
economic construction and the national defense, has imposed
strict limits on educational spending.*

The Chinese concept "material treatment" (wuzhi daiyu) in-
cludes basic salaries and a wide range of welfare benefits:
teachers' medical treatment, welfare subsidies (fuli buzhu)
(such as supplements for large families, old age pensions, sickness benefits and burial expenses, known collectively as "sheng,
lao, bing, si"), job security, working conditions, nurseries,
housing, vacations, spare-time cultural activities and trips,
sanatoria, and clubs.[90]

We should first consider the specific problem of teachers'
"material treatment" in the context of the Party's general

---

*Expenditure on "Social Services, Culture and Education" was 15.5 percent
of the State budget in 1957, 10.6 percent in 1958, 11.1 percent in 1959 and 12.3
percent (projected in 1960).

policy on economic distribution since 1949. Take wage policy
as a convenient analytical focus: it has passed through several
major stages since 1949, each of which has influenced the economic position of teachers.[91] In the early and mid-1950s, wage
levels for the existing corps of higher intellectuals were pitched
relatively high in order to retain their services. During the
First Five-Year Plan, the Party attempted to integrate wage
policy with the new modernization program by matching higher
rewards to superior skill. This was the basic rationale of the
overall wage reform in 1955-56. In 1957, however, certain
pressing economic and political constraints led to the adoption
of a "rational low wage policy" for the urban sector, a policy
which remained in force over the next two decades along with
the complex framework of wage-grade differentials established
in 1956.

Given the financial limits on wage policy and its potentially
explosive quality as a political issue, central leaders have apparently been reluctant to open a Pandora's box by attempting
major policy changes in spite of clear ideological differences
on incentive policy. "Socialist modernizing" leaders have
shown greater willingness to use material incentives to motivate the intelligentsia, advocating salary differentials as a reward for skill and stimulus for effort. Radical leaders, on the
other hand, have been reluctant to pander to material motivations and have sought where possible to reduce differentials.
Their political influence, as well as the pressure of financial
constraints, kept wage rises marginal between 1957 and 1976
and restricted them mainly to lower-paid strata, thus com-
pressing the actual distribution of wages within the wage-
scales.

The urban wage structure in operation over the past twenty-
five years bears the imprint of the developmentalist policies
of the mid-1950s. During this period, incentives policy was
seen as a means to win the cooperation of teachers at all levels. Certain sectors of the teaching force, notably senior university faculty members, were granted high salaries and, for
the more distinguished, special "expert subsidies" (zhuanjia

jintie).* From this initial period on, therefore, we find discontent over issues of economic distribution mainly at the middle and primary levels, particularly the latter, and among younger junior faculty at the tertiary level.

There was a recurrent dialogue over questions of material distribution between the Party and teachers in the early 1950s, culminating in the wage reform of 1956. Many teachers were discontented with their material position in the early post-Liberation years. This discontent was particularly pronounced among primary school teachers who considered themselves to be an economically underprivileged group. The CCP made an early promise to raise their absolute economic position and to reduce economic differentials between them and their counterparts in middle and higher schools.[92]

While Party leaders committed themselves to improve the material lot of teachers, scarce resources and competing financial priorities meant that their promises exceeded their ability to deliver tangible material progress. Official propaganda in this early period attempted to create an image of material improvement by stressing teachers' impoverished position in pre-revolutionary society, where they were portrayed as plagued by job uncertainty and ruined by inflation. Glowing accounts of the material privileges of teachers in the Soviet Union were also

---

*According to interview information compiled by Ezra Vogel of Harvard University, the wage situation among college teachers at Lingnan University in Guangzhou in the early 1960s was as follows:

	Grade 1	Grade 2	Grade 3
Professor (jiaoshou)	¥ 265	¥ 249	¥ 234
Assistant Professor (fujiaoshou)	¥ 234	¥ 199	¥ 165
Lecturer (jianshi)	¥ 138	¥ 112	
Assistant (zhujiao)		¥ 97.50	
Probationary Assistant		¥ 42.00	

The salaries paid there to the top two ranks (professor and assistant professor) are very high compared both to their younger counterparts and to other occupational wage-grade systems, notably that of manual workers. I am indebted to Professor Vogel for allowing me access to this information.

published which carried implicit promises of similar treatment
for Chinese teachers in the not-too-distant future. Some of the
publicized privileges seem rash in retrospect (for example, the
claim that the wages of Soviet teachers had been raised to the
level of engineers). Such eulogistic accounts often seemed
self-deceptive and blindly optimistic about China's ability to
repeat rapidly the Soviet experience. They encouraged unfavorable comparisons with the current Chinese situation and unrealistic hopes for the future.

At the same time, the Party set about rationalizing teachers'
salaries and increasing their real incomes. The Government
Administrative Council decided in mid-1952 to readjust the
salaries of teachers throughout the country, and the Ministry
of Education issued a set of wage guidelines for all educational
workers.[93] The major beneficiaries of this readjustment were
primary school personnel: their average wage in 1952 increased
by 37.4 percent over 1951, compared with 15.5 percent in middle schools and 18.6 percent in higher institutions. Rural primary school teachers were seen as the main beneficiaries:
they were guaranteed a minimum wage of 200,000 (old) yuan a
month, and the method of payment was changed from grain (grain
prices were relatively low in the countryside) to cash, thus
raising their living standards. Reports on the readjustment admitted, however, that many problems remained unsolved:
teachers in rural "people-run" schools were still poorly off,
and a minority of state teachers had earned more before 1949
than in 1952, in spite of the salary increase.

Basic salaries apart, a number of transitional measures were
taken to solve the immediate difficulties suffered by many
teachers, particularly those with large families or plagued by
ill health (for example, union-organized consumer cooperatives
and mutual-aid societies to help pay for medical expenses).[94]
In these early years, a good deal of the responsibility for improving teachers' living and working conditions was entrusted
to branches of the newly established Educational Workers'
Union.[95] As the new state apparatus was constructed, moreover, teachers became eligible for its welfare programs, nota-

bly the system of socialized medicine (gongfei yiliao).

Provincial and municipal governments were also involved in
the work of improving teachers' material welfare. Primary
school teachers in Fujian Province, for example, enjoyed several wage increases between 1949 and 1952, and their average
wages rose nearly threefold during these three years.[96] In
Guangzhou, a battery of material improvements for primary and
middle school teachers was announced in 1952: wage increases
ranging from 19.4 percent for senior-middle schools to 23.5
percent for primary schools and 33.5 percent for junior-middle
schools; the establishment of a medical plan for teachers; an
increase in supplementary allowances; day-care facilities and
education for teachers' children.[97]

In spite of this sensitivity to the economic difficulties of
teachers, teachers' demands far exceeded the Party's ability
to satisfy them. This contradiction was particularly acute with
the launching of the First Five-Year Plan, and the Party took
pains to counter teachers' demands with the argument that funds
had to be concentrated on industrialization and the educational
sector would have to practice frugality.[98] Teachers who "made
a fuss" (nao) about material treatment, it was stated, were influenced by "bourgeois ideology."[99] There was a second national wage readjustment in 1954, but the increase was relatively modest — total wages for all educational workers rising
5.8 percent over 1953. In the area of welfare benefits, considerable official attention was devoted to making sure that the
limited funds available were used efficiently and fairly.* There
was criticism of administrative cadres who used the national

---

*For example, see the decree issued jointly by the central Ministries of Fi-
nance, Health, and Education in September 1953 ("Several Fundamental Decisions Concerning the Appropriate Solution of the Welfare Problems of Primary
School and Kindergarten Teachers and Employees"), another issued jointly in
September 1954 by the central Ministries of Education and Finance and the national committee of the Educational Workers' Union "On Dealing with the Welfare Funds of Primary School Teachers and Employees" and the relevant part
of the Government Administrative Council's "Decree Concerning the Readjustment and Improvement of Primary Education" issued in 1953. For the texts,
see Xiaoxue jiaoshi 12 (1954), 2-3.

economy drive as a pretext to avoid spending welfare funds, or
who diverted them for other purposes and ignored teachers'
problems. Yet at the same time, cadres were urged to solve
teachers' problems without spending money if possible.

Scarcity of welfare funds led to various types of discrimination and abuse at the basic level. While welfare funds were
supposed to be allocated according to economic hardship, many
administrative cadres based their decisions on teachers' political attitudes, or politico-administrative position, such as an official in the educational workers' trade union. This kind of discrimination created antagonisms among teachers, or between
teachers and cadres.[100] Moreover, many teachers in real need
were reluctant to apply for welfare funds in case they were
called "individualist" or accused of "taking the economic viewpoint."

With the beginning of the new policy on intellectuals and the
atmosphere of economic optimism in 1956, however, purely
economic demands and complaints from all sections of the intelligentsia, "progressive" or "backward," were given the
stamp of legitimacy. A sweeping program was initiated to rectify abuses in the welfare system, and greater resources were
earmarked to improve the material livelihood and working conditions of teachers at all levels. There was widespread criticism of the previous lack of attention to problems of middle
and primary school teachers' livelihood, and provincial and
local governments issued regulations to improve the situation
with dispatch. For example, regulations issued by the Guangdong Provincial Department of Education in mid-1956 included
the following provisions: new measures to ensure that wage
funds actually reached teachers without diversion by basic-level
cadres; criticism of a previous "egalitarian" tendency to narrow
wage differentials by arbitrarily lowering the wages of higher
paid teachers; more attention to welfare amenities and no diversion of welfare funds; simplification of procedures for access to welfare funds; appropriate use of trade union welfare
funds; special allowances for rest leave and convalescence; and
rapid improvement of health services, dormitories and mess

halls.[101] The educational workers' union branch in Zhejiang
Province announced the allocation of funds for the establishment of a Soviet-style "teachers' house" (jiaoshizhi jia) in
beautiful Hangzhou and a recuperation home in comparably de-
lightful Moganshan. Guangdong's Department of Education and
Guangzhou's Education Bureau issued a request for school administrations to help teachers clear long-standing debts. The
Guangxi provincial newspaper castigated a county-level cadre
for taking it upon himself to curb what he regarded as the "economic viewpoint" of teachers by arbitrarily docking their wages
and retaining the surplus in the county treasury, citing the need
for national economy as an excuse.[102]

To meet the complaints of married primary and middle
school teachers who were separated by their work, the Ministry
of Education ordered a systematic program of transfers both
within and between provinces. The ministry also admonished
educational administrators who ignored such problems, and, in
some cases, even deliberately blocked the reuniting of separated spouses.[103]

A particularly concerted effort was also made to improve the
living and working conditions of higher intellectuals in universities and colleges, with particular emphasis on the "old specialists" and the higher ranks (from lecturer through to professor). This policy was defended as follows:

> At a time when the state is in a position to better the life of every teacher, to
> have only those teachers of lecturer level and above better taken care of by
> granting them preferential treatment is both essential and entirely consistent
> with the spirit of the principle of "remuneration according to labor."

Cadres, students, and junior colleagues who regarded this as
unfair and potentially divisive were dismissed as "victims of
the retrogressive notion of egalitarianism."[104]

But the major change in the economic position of teachers in
1956 was the State Council's decision on a comprehensive wage
reform for all those on the state payroll (in the case of "educational workers" the relevant directive was issued by the Ministry of Education on July 9).[105]

The new wage system reflected the high priority assigned to the virtues of professionalism and technical competence in determining inter- and intra-occupational differentials. In relative terms, wage increases for educational personnel (28.7 percent) were above the average for all state employees (14.7 percent): the average wages of educational workers rose from 33.93 yuan to 43.67 yuan a month.[106] Primary school teachers were singled out as a previously underpaid group (along with rural administrative personnel and workers in supply and marketing cooperatives). Press accounts pointed out that their salary increase exceeded those in enterprises (qiye), business organizations (shiye), and state organizations (jiguan) by about 10 percent.[107] Their wages rose by an average of 32.8 percent (from 30.2 yuan to 40.13 yuan).

However, average wage increases were to be implemented in a "rationally" differentiated way:

(The) increase should be rational. In concrete cases, there are possibly larger increases and smaller increases and possibly cases where there is no increase. When things are made rational, the nation will be able, through the wage form, to unify the social benefit of educational workers with their personal material interest in the results of their labor. In this way, educational workers will be stimulated to improve their professional ability and raise educational quality.[108]

Commentaries on the new wage system alluded to previous injustices when competent teachers had not been rewarded by wage increases, or where "practice" teachers were not given an appropriate salary raise after their period of apprenticeship was over. The previous grading system, it was stressed, had too many levels (dengji) but too narrow differentials (jicha).[109] "Egalitarian" practices were criticized for obstructing teachers' professional initiative and the raising of educational standards. Cases of unequal pay for equal work (for example, salary differences between male and female teachers) also came in for criticism.

In general, the new grading system was based on the specific criteria of educational background (xueli), seniority (jiaoling),

work load (gongzuo liang) and work quality (gongzuo zhiliang)
with the result that the older, more experienced teachers came
out at the top of the salary ladder.[110] Each layer of teachers
had its own salary ladder, but there was significant overlap between the three scales. The highest wage standard for primary
school teachers was equal to the fourth and fifth grade of middle school teachers, while the latters' highest wage standard
equaled the highest rank of lecturer (jiangshi) in the tertiary
system.*

In sum, the overall impact of the wage reform was to increase
absolute and relative levels of teachers' income, particularly
in the case of primary teachers, and give economic recognition
to experience, formal training, and skill. There still remained
two sectors of the educational system where teachers were particularly poorly off — in private schools and "people-run"
schools, particularly at the primary level — their incomes being
variable and outside the standardized salary system.[111] Many
state-employed teachers, however, particularly in primary
schools, still complained that wage levels were too low both
absolutely and in relation to other occupations.[112] Many teachers took advantage of the flexible political atmosphere of the
Hundred Flowers to press material demands left unsolved by
the wage reform — housing, traveling expenses, welfare supplements — making invidious comparisons with other sections of
the work force such as industrial and office workers. In Heilongjiang, for example, they spoke at meetings of the provincial
People's Consultative Conference.[113] With the onset of the
Anti-Rightist movement, these complaints were silenced.
"Bourgeois rightists," said CCP spokesmen, had made use of
this discontent to stir up trouble and provoke violent incidents.
They recounted the concrete improvements in the material lot

*Renmin ribao, July 9, 1956. We can compare these equivalences with those
estimated by Vogel in Guangzhou schools in the early 1960s: of the eight wage-
grades for middle school teachers, grade 4 was equivalent to a university assistant, grade 3 to a lecturer and grades 1 and 2 to an assistant professor; of
the nine wage-grades for primary school teachers, the top four grades (1-4)
corresponded to the middle school salary scale.

of teachers since 1949 and argued that the "rightists" had been
distorting facts and blackening the situation.

With the Anti-Rightist movement, the dialogue between the
Party and teachers over questions of material treatment ceased
at the public level. The wage scales established in 1956 continued in force, but substantial salary increases were out of the
question given the new long-term "rational low-wage policy."
Economic bargaining between teachers and the Party over economic questions was also inappropriate to the mobilization politics and ideology of the Great Leap Forward. As Party leaders
strove to readjust the educational system in the post-Great
Leap period, they found it difficult to return to the policies of
the mid-1950s, given the general decline in the amount of dis-
tributable material resources during the "three hard years."
They responded in two ways. First, senior intellectuals, including senior middle school teachers and college professors,
were singled out for special treatment during the period of food
shortages, receiving, for example, extra rations of pork, oil, or
sugar. A former resident of Guangzhou told the author that
during this period there were special rooms reserved for higher
intellectuals in some of Guangzhou's better restaurants. They
gained entry by showing a special privilege card and could then
partake of better-than-average food. Second, steps were taken
to increase where possible the facilities available to teachers
for recreation and study, notably various types of "clubs."
Third, a series of steps were taken to improve the lot of teachers without significant cost. The latter strategy included, as
we saw earlier, measures to increase the social respect accorded to teachers by cadres, pupils, and the general public to
provide more professional autonomy and study time, to allow
greater cultural freedom, and to slacken some of the political
requirements introduced in 1958. As the economy began to re-
cover by 1963, more resources became available to improve
the welfare of teachers at the middle and primary levels: seniority bonuses for experienced teachers, promotions up the
wage scale for excellent teaching performance, raises for long-
term service, improvement of dormitories and food facilities,

and an increase in supplementary allowances and rations.[114]
With the increasing politicization of the teacher's role from
1963 on, and the fact that teachers were on the political defensive during the Cultural Revolution, the question of teachers'
material treatment became increasingly illegitimate as a public
political issue, either in the official or the Red Guard press.
It was seen as a form of "economism," a bourgeois ploy. The
legitimacy of public dialogue over issues of material distribution was not reestablished until after the removal of the Shanghai radicals in late 1976. This conversion of economics into
economism may have driven problems of material distribution
underground, but it did not solve them. Many teachers, notably
at the primary and middle school levels, continued to feel during the 1960s and 1970s that their status as skilled intellectual
workers in an avowedly crucial sector of society merited
greater financial reward. They have also felt they should be
compensated in economic terms for the particularly arduous
nature of their job. Others, notably younger teachers at all
levels, have chafed against the restrictions on opportunities
for promotion imposed by the economic austerity and egalitarian politics of the last two decades.

The lack of wage raises and promotions from 1957 onward
led to considerable "bunching" in the lower grades of each
wage-scale. Vogel reports that in the early 1960s most middle
school teachers in Guangzhou were in the lowest three grades
(6-8) of an 8-grade scale, and very few were in the top three
(1-3). Similarly, in the 8-grade scale for primary school
teachers, most teachers were in the lower grades 5-8.[115]
"Bunching" in the lowest grades was intensified by recruitment
patterns during the Cultural Revolution when, most visibly at
the college level, many young teachers were appointed, often
for political reasons. Lewis' data illuminate this pattern of
distribution in the mid-1970s. In Shanghai's Fudan University
in 1974, the 1956 12-grade pay scale for university teachers
was still in force (grades 1-6 for professors and associate professors) (360-157 yuan), grades 7-9 for lecturers (down to
92 yuan), and grades 10-12 for assistants (down to 60 yuan), the

ratio between the highest and lowest grades being 6:1. In fact, however, the great majority of teachers were on the lower grades
(1,331 out of 1,772 — 75 percent — were only assistants).[116]
A 1978 report on the same institution reveals that 1,000 out of
the then faculty total of 2,200 (45 percent) had been recruited
during the Cultural Revolution.[117]   Given this concentration in
the lower grades, the low statistics of 70 yuan as the average
wage for university teachers in Jiangsu Province as a whole,
given to Lewis by the head of the Provincial Education Bureau,
is understandable. The post-Mao leadership was thus faced
with a backlog of frustrated mobility and took steps, most visible at the college level, to rectify the situation. By early 1980,
it was reported that over one-third of all teachers in higher
institutions (61,300) had been promoted to professor (1,000),
associate professor (6,000), and lecturer (54,000).[118]

Egalitarian political pressures since 1957 also seem to have
constricted income differentials between teachers at different
levels. For example, the average salaries of the three layers
of teachers in Jiangsu Province in 1974 were not far apart: college
70 yuan, middle school 50 yuan, primary school 40 yuan.[119]
Though inter-level differentials may have narrowed, significant
economic differences persisted between teachers in rural and
urban areas, in part-time and full-time schoools, and in state-
run and "people-run" schools. Egalitarian pressure also reduced or even eliminated differentials between the average
wages of teachers and other occupational groups. Evidence began to appear in 1979 to suggest that teachers, particularly at
middle and primary levels, were concerned about this decline
and were demanding redress. For example, a report by
branches of the National Educational Workers Union in seven
middle and primary schools in Beijing claimed that "the
wages and material benefits for teachers are lower than in
other fields" and singled out housing and childcare facilities as priority areas for improvement.[120] Similarly, a
research team from Shanghai's Fudan University reported
that people who became factory workers in 1953 after graduating from junior middle school earned 20 yuan more per

month in the late 1970s than their contemporaries who had gone
on to senior middle school and college and become teachers.
Similarly, among junior middle graduates in 1965, industrial
workers now earned 20 yuan more than their classmates who
became teachers. The Union's national committee wrote to the
national organ Guangming ribao (Guangming Daily) requesting
that the Party leadership should pay more attention to these
anomalies.

Thus the post-Mao leadership will be under considerable
pressure to raise the absolute level of teachers' incomes and
restore differentials — within and between layers of teachers,
and between teachers and other occupational strata. Given the
continuing constraints on educational spending, the desire to
concentrate funds in directly productive sectors, and the prospect of discontent among competing social groups (notably
manual workers), the Party will find it hard to meet teachers'
demands in the short run. Many teachers will continue to consider themselves underpaid — in relative and absolute terms.
Issues of material distribution are thus likely to be an important source of tension between teachers and the Party throughout the 1980s.

The Political Status of Teachers

4

In this chapter I intend to examine the power relationship between teachers and the Party-state. I shall discuss two aspects of their "political status":* first, their <u>functional</u> power, viz. the amount of autonomy they have enjoyed in their professional work and, second, their access to <u>formal political power</u> as measured by their access to the key political institution, the CCP. In the next chapter, I shall focus on the dynamic aspect of their power relationship with the Party in the public arena, i.e. the ways in which teachers have attempted to mobilize power resources to pursue their interests by political means.

1. Red and Expert in the Schools:
Politics and Professional Autonomy

One of the most consistent issues dividing the Party and teachers since 1949 has concerned the amount of autonomy teachers enjoy in defining and managing the educational process. In practice, this is a question of the distribution of power

---

*In Chinese usage, the term "political status" (<u>zhengzhi diwei</u>) refers to the relationship between an individual or group and the Party-state. It is a composite concept, combining the ideas of formal authority (from a cadre position), formal political power (from membership in a political organization), and informal political influence. The process whereby the Party-state confers or denies political status is referred to as "political treatment" (<u>zhengzhi daiyu</u>)).

60

in schools and colleges between teaching staffs on the one hand
and nonprofessional groups on the other, notably political and
administrative cadres, Party and League organs, students, and
various "mass" groups of workers and peasants.

The competing sets of ideological commitments and policy
priorities outlined in Chapter 1 have different implications for
the question of professional autonomy versus political intervention. In the context of the "first revolution," the Party viewed
teachers as politically unreliable but professionally indispensable. Accordingly, it attempted to establish a vigilant political
control apparatus in the schools which would free education
from "bourgeois" distortions, yet at the same time leave
teachers adequate space for their professional work. In the
early and mid-1950s, a network of political and administrative
cadres was set up in the schools, its personnel recruited overwhelmingly on the basis of their reliable class background and/
or Party affiliation.* This led to a system of parallel hierar-
chies, one based on "redness" or political "virtue" (de), the
other on expertise, with little overlapping of personnel. This
situation was often symbolized in the relationship between a
"professional" school principal in charge of teaching and a "political" vice-principal, often an officer transferred from the
PLA, exercising political control (these roles could also be reversed).

Party-state cadres, often in cooperation with progressive
students in middle schools and colleges, were charged with the
tasks of supervising teachers in their professional work, and
bringing about their "ideological transformation" through formal political study and obligatory social and political activi-

---

*All employees of educational institutions, including all categories of per-
sonnel from janitors to teachers to Party administrators, are known as "educational work personnel." According to Emerson's calculations, in 1955 nearly
one quarter of the 2.2 million educational workers in state-run schools were
"administrative" personnel, many of whom were service personnel working in
canteens, dormitories, and the like. The ratio between "administrative" and
teaching personnel varied from level to level, reaching 61 percent "administrators" in higher institutions and only 22 percent in middle and primary
schools together (Emerson, op. cit., p. 20).

ties.[121] This structural dualism gave an "us and them" quality
to mutual perceptions and relations between teachers and administrators during this period.

But the Party's success in establishing a system of political
control and "transformation" was uneven. The task was particularly difficult at the tertiary level, where poorly educated
worker-peasant Party cadres came face to face with the intellectual elite of prerevolutionary society. As a result, supervision was often perfunctory and "leadership" often faded into
deference. Mao was to refer to this retrospectively in a 1958
speech, when he declared: "We've been afraid of professors
ever since we came into the towns. We did not despise them,
we were terrified of them."[122]

As China entered the First Five-Year Plan in 1953, there was
growing awareness among Party leaders of the tensions arising
from the ambiguous relationship between "redness" and "expertise" in the schools and of the obstacles this posed to a program of rapid modernization. Official directives affirmed the
central role of professional teachers through the slogan "the
central task of schools is to teach."[123] Political personnel and
administrators in schools were instructed to minimize their
direct interference in pedagogic affairs and, to the extent that
this was necessary, make it constructive by acquiring at least
a smattering of the necessary expertise. The focus of pressure
changed from making experts "red" to making "reds" expert.
Increasingly systematic measures were taken to free teachers
from excessive political demands in order to improve "teaching
efficiency and professional development." These policy changes
were a response in part to widespread complaints by teachers
about arbitrary and excessive interference by the new school
administrations. They claimed that Party cadres ignored or
made light of their professional expertise, monopolized power
and interfered too readily in professional matters beyond their
ken, and ordered them around at will without concern for their
professional responsibilities.[124]

The new policies, characteristic of the "socialist modernizing" position, found their clearest expression in the new deal

for the intelligentsia in 1956 and early 1957. The central Party
leadership publicly rebuked educational cadres for their unreasonable encroachments and introduced measures designed to expand the area of teachers' professional discretion and stream-
line the teaching process. This effort to develop the "precious
scientific strength" of teachers was most visible at the tertiary
level, as one would have expected given the scarcity of advanced
expertise during this early period and the contemporary stress
on higher-level training to meet the needs of the First Five-
Year Plan. In an April 1956 editorial, for example, Guangming
ribao instructed educational cadres to improve the working conditions of college teachers in a variety of ways: rectify shortages of books and other research materials; increase the supply of assistants for teaching and research work; restrict the
number of meetings and obligatory social activities; improve
library services and tighten up general administrative efficiency
at all levels.[125] Cadres and students were warned not to en-
croach unduly on teachers' time. The administration of Tianjin
University, for example, attempted to "protect" their academic
staff by decreasing standard office hours and only accepting
visitors with prior appointments. Similar measures were taken
in other colleges, while in middle and primary schools cadres
were accused of "sectarianism" and intolerance toward
teachers and were instructed to devise special methods for
safeguarding their time and improving their professional productivity. [126]
   Despite these gains during the mid-1950s, the professional
autonomy of teachers suffered a major setback during the "first
revolution" backlash of the Anti-Rightist movement. Their previous complaints were equated with the idea that "outsiders
(i.e. Party cadres) cannot lead insiders (i.e. teachers)" (wai-
hang buneng lingdao neihang) and were dismissed as "rightist"
propaganda. In the aftermath of this movement, Mao himself
declared that "the nonprofessional leading the professional is a
general rule." [127] The educational revolution of 1958 opened a
new period of encroachment on teachers' professional autonomy. Official propaganda during the Great Leap attacked the

"expert line," i.e., the belief that "education and scientific work
is just the business of a few experts, and the Party and masses
do not understand it," and the "mass line can be applied in military, political or economic work, but not in educational and
scientific work."[128] Underestimation of the practical role of
both Party and masses in educational work was condemned as
a "bourgeois viewpoint," as were alleged distinctions between
"simple" and "complex" labor, theoretical and practical knowledge, "talented" and "stupid" people.[129] Teachers came under
pressure from two sources: from politico-administrative
cadres and ordinary Party members on the one hand and the
"masses" on the other, including students, nonteaching personnel in schools and colleges, and various outsider groups such
as activist workers, peasants, and serving or demobilized soldiers. The main trend during the Leap was toward the consolidation and extension of the Party's supervisory apparatus in the
regular educational system. Intervention by the "masses" during this period was supervised by the Party and was kept on a
tight leash. Though mass intervention was channeled, spotty in
incidence and impact, and in most cases short-lived, it was a
foretaste of intervention on a far larger scale during the Cultural Revolution. Outside the regular school system, moreover,
there was a massive "deprofessionalization" of teaching roles
in the burgeoning "people-run" schools, where pupils were instructed by hastily recruited local residents, often with no more
than primary or junior middle school education themselves.
     The educational costs of these innovations, stemming from
a decline in teachers' morale and a pressing shortage of qualified personnel in a context of rapid educational expansion, became apparent by late 1958. Beginning in early 1959, the Party
leadership responded with a series of measures designed to re-
instate the position of professional teachers, restore their area
of decisional autonomy, and develop their professional skills.[130]
The official media emphasized that, contrary to the notions of
many teachers influenced by their experience of the "educational revolution" of 1958, the application of the "mass line" in
schools did not in fact seek to ignore or minimize the role of

the professionals. Early in 1959, in fact, it was publicly re-
affirmed that teachers were to play "the guiding role (zhudao
zuoyong) in pedagogic work" because of their specialized knowledge and experience;[131] such a role, it was emphasized, was
not incompatible with "Party leadership and the initiative and
activism of the students."

These trends were strengthened during the period of "socialist modernizing" predominance from 1959 to 1963 when many
of the policies of the mid-1950s were revived. The scope of de-
cision-making authority of non-Party school and college principals was expanded, and basic-level administrative cadres were
once again instructed to reduce their political demands on
teaching staffs.[132] In some colleges, the authorities revived
their procedures for guaranteeing academics time for teaching
and research. The history department at Nankai University in
Tianjin, for example, took the following measures: administrative cadres were instructed to reduce the number of meetings
on nonprofessional topics, shorten the length of meetings
through better preparation and management, give teachers ample time for preparing as well as merely delivering lectures,
reduce teachers' prescribed extramural activities, expand their
own duties to alleviate the teachers' burden of work, and shield
the latter from unwelcome visitors through an armadillo-like
reception system. [133]

Similar measures were taken in middle schools. In Shanghai,
for example, middle school teachers were released for study
courses in the city's Normal College, while the latter institution's students took their places temporarily in the classroom.[134] In Beijing, more special spare-time courses were
provided for primary and middle school teachers (night school,
correspondence, or radio and TV) and a significant number were
admitted to short-term full-time courses for "advanced study"
on full pay.[135] Youth League branches in middle schools, which
had played a leading role in the criticism of "bourgeois" teachers in 1957 and 1958, were instructed to support the teacher in
the classroom by helping to maintain discipline, studiousness,
and respect.[136] These measures were symptomatic of a shift

in power and authority within the school, the teachers gaining
at the expense of cadres, the League, and their students.

   The stress on professional proficiency during this period
brought increased emphasis on the need to utilize the experience
and expertise of older teachers, irrespective of their political
attitudes or class backgrounds. Their younger counterparts,
regardless of their political virtues, were instructed to "learn
humbly" from them. [137] An internal document on urban primary
and middle schools circulated by the Beijing Municipal CCP
Committee in mid-1961 criticized the tendency for "some comrades to take the sweeping view that young teachers are obedi-
ent and progressive in thinking and old teachers have deep-
seated and backward thoughts; and to attempt to substitute young
teachers for old ones." The report urged that political pressures be relaxed and more professional scope be guaranteed
to senior teachers through a policy of "laissez-faire" and
"trust." [138] At the tertiary level, special chairs were established to enable middle-aged or elderly professors to present
special lecture series on key areas of their expertise. [139] The
propaganda of this period carried the general message that
teachers at all levels should seek to attain higher standards of
expertise and proficiency in their subjects and in their jobs. [140]
Far from being seen as a diversion from "redness," this heavy
concentration on expertise was redefined as an <u>expression</u> of
political commitment.

   Although the general political environment became increasingly
radical from 1963 on, the actual impact of Maoist policies varied
from area to area and unit to unit. Some educational cadres
who accepted the logic of the socialist modernizing position
continued to delegate considerable power to teachers and strove
to shield them from untoward political interference. For example, one particular target of the Cultural Revolution, Kuang
Yaming, who became Party secretary of Nanjing University in
1963, allegedly delegated a great deal of power to senior academics (for example, in decisions about research and promotions) and repelled any pressure to restrict their role. [141] Similarly, Yang Xiguang, Party head of education work in Shanghai,

was accused of allowing teaching personnel (branded as "demons and monsters") to occupy 80 percent of the leading bodies of the city's higher educational institutions before the Cultural Revolution.[142]   Other Party officials adopted the increasingly anti-intellectual themes of official propaganda and increased their political pressures on "bourgeois" teachers. To the extent that teachers retained any significant degree of professional autonomy during these years, however, this was shattered by the Cultural Revolution. Power in the schools was one of the major issues of the Cultural Revolution in the educational sphere. The alleged "domination of the schools by bourgeois intellectuals" and "the idea that teachers are the key figures" were condemned as "bourgeois" and/or Soviet-inspired heresies. Party cadres who had taken a "soft" line on teachers now became targets of mass criticism. Some stuck to their guns but others sought to deflect criticism by taking a tough line with the "bourgeois authorities," particularly older teachers who were politically vulnerable. Official directives identified teachers, particularly senior ones, as a suspect group in need of "reorganization and serious purification."

When some semblance of the educational process was resumed after the disruption of 1966 and 1967, moreover, teachers became virtual Gullivers, pinioned from many sides by a variety of political forces: PLA or worker propaganda teams, students, mass organizations, newly recruited or rehabilitated administrative and political cadres, and outsider mass management committees. Friction was exacerbated by the sociological differences between these groups, teachers' resentment at the encroachments on their professional prerogatives, and radical propaganda which tended to polarize issues and inflame animosities. This is visible, for example, in attempts to institute worker-peasant management over primary and middle schools. In the rural context, for example, the media accused professional teachers of attempting to sabotage the mass management of schools because they regarded peasants as "clodhoppers who are in no position to manage schools just as they are unable to reach the moon in the sky" and "boors who know only how to

use the hoe and are unequal to the management of teaching."[143]
No doubt these citations reflected the hidden sentiments of many
teachers, but their appearance in national propaganda could only
serve to polarize the relationship between them and the masses
and make the process of educational reform more difficult.

While many teachers withdrew to positions of passivity or
perfunctory performance, the new educational policies also
proved frustrating for those teachers who made an effort to implement them. Authoritative definitions of "correct" educational practice and "red" attitudes were vague and ambiguous,
often depending on factional or personal hostilities within each
school. Teachers attempting to carry out the reforms often
felt they were walking a political tightrope and were afraid of
falling off. This was a particularly acute problem in the pro-
longed process of rewriting textbooks and lectures after the
Cultural Revolution and figures prominently in the press during
the early and mid-1970s. For example, when history teachers
at the Normal University in Shanghai were called on to revise
their lectures on European history, they ran into the following
problems:

One teacher encountered a problem of how Petofi should be evaluated in the
Hungarian bourgeois revolution of 1848. Though Petofi was an influential
character in the revolution, the teacher was afraid that he might be accused
of the mistake of perpetuating the memory of the exploiting class and wanted
to ignore Petofi altogether.

Another teacher was writing a chapter on the English bourgeois revolution....
[When] he came to the role played by Cromwell, he dared not admit even the
fact that Cromwell was the leader of the revolution.[144]

As the general level of educational quality declined, moreover, professional teachers found themselves partially replaced
by newly recruited full- or part-time "worker-teachers" or
"peasant-teachers" without educational qualification. For example, in the city of Wuxi in Jiangsu Province, an estimated 30
percent of middle school teachers were worker-teachers in
mid-1971. By early 1976, there were 1.5 million part-time

"worker-peasant-soldier" teachers across the nation.[145] The
beneficial effects of this policy, claimed the Party journal Hong
qi [Red Flag] , were to change the class status of teachers in
a proletarian direction and allow the working class "to gain an
all-round hold on the school leadership." In turn, members of
the preexisting teaching staffs were to be organized for manual
work in factories and farms.[146] There were similar personnel
changes in rural schools where teachers were replaced or sup-
plemented by "poor and lower-middle peasants with proletarian
consciousness." Clearly many or most of the original teachers
must have felt these measures to be unnecessary and irrational.

The early 1970s saw an attempt by leaders of the "socialist
modernizing" persuasion to return to the policies of the early
1960s. There were moves in 1972, for example, toward a "re-
academicization" of school curricula and a partial rehabilitation of exams, notably in university enrollment. According to
contemporary accounts, many teachers were delighted and felt
that "if things go on in this way, there is some hope for teaching." But this precipitated a tug-of-war over educational policy
at the center and fluctuations and ambiguity in schools and colleges. The Shanghai radicals and their supporters sought to
protect the innovations of the Cultural Revolution: restraining
the initiative of the "old" (i.e. pre-1966) unreconstructed
teachers, curbing tendencies toward a revival of professionalism and academic values, maintaining the effectiveness of mass
propaganda teams as a supervisory agency and of "worker-
peasant teachers" as alternatives to "regular" teachers. [147]
The radical counterattack began in earnest in 1973 with the publication of a letter by a sent-down youth, Zhang Tiesheng, who
complained bitterly about the reinstitution of academic criteria
in university enrollment. This letter seems to have been received coldly by most teachers — some of their reactions were
listed in the press: "this letter is like a ladle of cold water.
It has completely dampened the glowing enthusiasm for teaching"; "if even the university does not attach importance to
marks, what is the object of teaching"; "with the universities
taking in people like Zhang Tiesheng, what guarantee is there

for quality; can we still orbit a satellite in space?" In one
middle-school singled out for attention by the national press,
reporters asked why it was that "only the minority of teachers
supported Zhang's letter while the majority laid so much emphasis on marks."[148] It was attributed to the deep-seated professionalism of teachers and their conviction that "intellectual
education comes first." The official response was to intensify
the "reeducation" of teaching staffs through political study,
manual labor, visits to the countryside, and greater involvement
of chosen members of the masses in the teaching process.
Though the media of the time claimed great success in transforming the ideology of teachers, evidence from other sources
(notably emigré interviews) suggests that this renewed campaign
merely drove a deeper wedge between a majority of teachers
on the one side and proponents of radical reforms at all levels
on the other. It is not surprising, therefore, that the removal
of the Shanghai group in late 1976 was popular among teachers.
It paved the way for a revival of the "socialist modernizing"
emphasis on the need to guarantee the teaching profession adequate autonomy and time to take educational decisions on the
basis of their professional skills and experience.[149] The ambitious developmental goals of the new leadership required a
rapid increase in educational efficiency, and this required official recognition of the integrity of the teaching profession. The
familiar themes of the mid-1950s and early 1960s were revived
with considerable vigor.[150]

In sum, the recurrent fluctuations in national politics and in
educational policy have brought with them a constant ebbing and
flowing of political control over the teaching process, advancing
and receding like waves on a beach. By the 1970s the tide had
gradually crept closer to shore, and teachers' distinct professional identity had been eroded and increasingly integrated into
the wider issues and alignments of Chinese politics. In their
attempt to exert political control, Party leaders have faced a
continual dilemma. To the extent that they recognize the func-
tional significance of teachers for the modernization program
and guarantee them ample scope for professional initiative,

they are forced to accept the teachers' own definition of the educational process. On the other hand, when they have attempted to extend their political writ beyond a certain minimal level, teachers have responded with passive resistance and refusal to cooperate in "crypto-strikes." In consequence, educational standards have dropped, and policy changes have been necessary to regain their cooperation. This is a clear example of the ability of teachers to impose limits on the transformative power of the Party-state.

The nature of the interaction and the resulting pattern of tension and conflict between teachers and cadres have probably varied from level to level. Primary school teachers have found it difficult to lay claim to the title of "professional," let alone "expert," and thus have in general been easier game for unit cadres. Political tensions have thus arisen from feelings of subordination and powerlessness. At higher levels, on the other hand, the walls of "expertise" have been more impenetrable, and cadres have found it more difficult to exert effective supervision and control. Political tensions have thus arisen as teachers have sought to protect and extend a more or less tolerated decisional space and frustrated Party cadres have struggled to assert their putative authority.

2. The Political Recruitment of Teachers

In the preceding section, we discussed relations between teachers and the Party-state in terms of a simple bipolar model: expert teachers vs. red cadres, teachers vs. Party, profession vs. politics. This model represents one consistent aspect of basic-level politics in schools and colleges since 1949 and is particularly accurate in certain key periods, notably the early 1950s, the Anti-Rightist movement and the Cultural Revolution. However, the clarity of this division became increasingly blurred as a new generation of younger teachers emerged in the 1950s and 1960s (many of them from "good" class backgrounds) and a significant minority of teachers joined the new political organizations. In this section we shall examine this

process of political recruitment. An exhaustive coverage of the
problem would require us to discuss a wide range of organizations, notably the people's representative congresses at various
levels, united front organs, mass organizations, and the Young
Communist League. In practice, however, these organizations
have had little political influence — the key path to political advancement led to the Party. We shall therefore confine our
discussion to Party recruitment.

From 1949 on, many teachers, particularly younger ones
trained after Liberation, have sought access to the Party for
reasons of both commitment and careerism. Although statistics
are sparse, it can be argued that teachers in general have not
found it easy to join the Party for a variety of reasons. The
initial impact and the heritage of the "first revolution" of 1949
to 1956 created a political context inimical to the large-scale
recruitment of intellectuals in general and teachers in particular. The Party branches in many schools and colleges, dominated by older pre-Liberation cadres from poor peasant backgrounds, viewed intellectuals as unworthy of Party membership.
They drew attention to teachers' "complex" class backgrounds,
their murky "political histories," or their dubious "social relations." They were also sensitive to the threat posed by the
countervailing power and prestige which intellectuals could
command. Recruiting teachers into the Party, in their eyes, was
like taking in a Trojan horse, and they resisted it. Large-scale
recruitment should be postponed until a new generation of
"working class intellectuals" had emerged, with the "right"
class backgrounds and a socialist educational experience. Given
this opposition in many basic-level institutions, the access of
teachers to the CCP has depended to a considerable extent on
pressures from the central leadership.

Predictably, these pressures have been fluctuating and ambiguous. Developmentalist leaders have sought to recruit
teachers of all types into the Party, notably at higher educational levels, relatively regardless of their social and political
backgrounds. The underlying assumption is that if the Party is
to supervise modernization effectively, it must incorporate spe-

cialized personnel into its ranks. Although the fitness of
teachers for Party membership is to depend theoretically on
their "political performance" (zhengzhi biaoxian), political
standards have often been relaxed. For example, a more flexible approach to the political recruitment of teachers was
adopted in 1956. In his "Report on the Question of Intellectuals,"
Zhou Enlai called for the recruitment of more intellectuals into
the Party. The change in Party admission criteria approved
by the Eighth Party Congress in September 1956 (which abolished previous restrictions on people from "bad" social backgrounds) also made things easier — in theory at least — for
teachers who wished to join the Party. In this period, the Party
leadership argued strongly that the national priority of rapid
modernization required the admission of more intellectuals into
the Party:

> Why is the Party now emphasizing the need to increase recruitment among in-
> tellectuals? It is because our country is riding the crest of a wave of eco-
> nomic and cultural construction. In other words, we aim to strengthen the
> Party's leadership in the field of scientific culture, to enable scientific cul-
> ture to advance rapidly beyond its backward situation and to catch up both
> with the requirements of socialist construction and with advanced international
> levels.[151]

In a speech in early 1957, Mao himself called for an increased
effort to recruit more intellectuals and suggested a timetable:
15 percent of intellectuals by the end of 1957, 25 percent by
1963, and one third by the late 1960s.[152]
    In 1956, Beijing instructed Party organizations in the prov-
inces to increase the rate of Party recruitment among teachers.
The Guangdong Education Bureau, for example, highlighted the
problem by revealing the fact that many middle and primary
schools had no Party members among their teaching staffs. The
bureau told educational cadres in the province that "it is a mistake to overemphasize the complex nature of teachers and thus
to refrain from actively recruiting them into the Party."[153]
Cadres particularly objected to teachers with "bad" class backgrounds, and many espoused "the theory of only (taking into ac-

count) class status" (weichengfen lun), the idea being that people's political attitudes could be deduced from their class backgrounds, thus allowing virtually no scope for personal political
reform or degeneration, and closing the gates of the Party to
nonproletarian strata.

During 1956, provincial authorities reported substantial progress in recruiting teachers. Shandong authorities reported, for
example, that all local Party committees in the province had
drawn up plans for admitting more primary school teachers to
the Party and training political "activists" among teachers. In
consequence, 1,313 teachers had joined the Party between
January and September 1956, of whom 850 were recruited in the
third quarter of the year.[154] In spite of such reports, however,
there was considerable resistance at the basic level and progress was slow. The professional organ Xiaoxue jiaoyu tangxun
[Primary School Education Bulletin] pointed out in early 1957
that although 961 primary school teachers in Zhejiang Province
had joined the Party during the previous year, many teachers
with "complex political histories and social relations" were
still finding it difficult to gain the trust of their unit cadres and
be considered seriously as suitable Party material.[155]

Although no overall statistics are available, however, it
seems that teachers at all levels did benefit to a limited extent
from the brief period of easier access to Party membership
granted to intellectuals between mid-1956 and mid-1957. The
percentage of intellectuals in the Party rose from 11.7 percent
(June 1956) to 15 percent (September 1957).[156] This seems to
have stopped abruptly with the onset of the Anti-Rightist movement, when large numbers of teachers at all levels came under
fierce political attack for "rightist" heresies, which were interpreted as the resurgent expression of their dubious class backgrounds and political histories. There was evidence of a miti-
gating trend in late 1957, when a number of teachers who had
distinguished themselves in attacks on their "rightist" colleagues were admitted to the Party.[157] It is likely, however,
that these new recruits were overwhelmingly "progressive"
young teachers from "good" class backgrounds trained after

1949, thus contributing to a trend of increasing political differentiation between new and old generations of teachers.

Similarly, in the two other major periods of socialist modernizing predominance, 1959 to 1963 and the late 1970s, there were concerted efforts to recruit more intellectuals qua intellectuals and thus more teachers qua teachers into the Party, downplaying questions of class origin and political history and relaxing criteria for evaluating "political performance." In 1960, for example, Renmin ribao renewed the call for an increase in the recruitment of middle and primary school teachers and noted that as of August 1960, 15 percent of teachers at these levels in Shaanxi Province were in the Party (i.e. nearly three years later than Mao's original target for the end of 1957). Of these, a large proportion had been recruited during the previous year. In fact, the number recruited in 1959 had been eight times that of 1958 and exceeded the total number recruited between 1950 and 1958, in spite of the alleged progress made during 1956.[158] Although precise statistics are not available, it is again likely that the bulk of this influx were younger teachers educated since 1949, and their recruitment was connected with their role in the "educational revolution" of 1958.

To summarize, the underlying structural implication of socialist modernizing policies was to bring about the gradual integration of the formal political hierarchy and the hierarchy of skills and expertise by recruiting increased numbers of technical and cultural intelligentsia into the Party. This process of incorporation is comparable to the change in the relationship between occupational and political structures which began in the Soviet Union in the mid-1930s. The evidence cited above suggests that, among middle and primary school teachers at least, this merging process was well under way by 1960, and if it had continued without interruption, the ratio of Party membership would soon have rivaled the 1968 Soviet level of 25 percent membership, and Mao's 1963 target of 25 percent.[159]

In the 1960s and 1970s, however, this merger appears to have been slowed by two political forces which have tended to repolarize the Party and the intellectuals. First, the legacy of the

first revolution continued to pit "proletarian" Party members
and cadres against "bourgeois" intellectuals; second, radical
policies summoned a motley array of "proletarian" forces
(both inside and outside the Party) against "bourgeois" intellectuals and their alleged allies "taking the capitalist road" within
the Party. Both these political tendencies found intense expression during the Cultural Revolution, which both resuscitated the
hostilities of the first revolution and mobilized fresh hostilities
in the "new class struggle." The Cultural Revolution checked
the gradual merger between Party and intellectuals by challeng-
ing the "socialist modernizing" rationale for incorporating
teachers into the Party and questioning the political quality of
new "red professionals" who had joined the Party. [160]
    Statistics on the Party recruitment of teachers after the Cul-
tural Revolution are not available. Although a certain number
of "revolutionary teachers" who distinguished themselves during the Cultural Revolution were admitted to the Party after the
movement ended and there was a recruitment drive in 1973
aimed at young intellectuals, it is likely that total intake was
numerically limited and mainly comprised young "progressives"
from "pure" class backgrounds. The hypothesis of a slowing
of the rate of recruitment between 1966 and 1976 is supported
by criticisms of the Shanghai radicals published after their de-
mise. These critiques allege that the "Gang of Four" had been
politically hostile toward teachers (branding them as a "rightist
restorationist" force with a "bourgeois world outlook") and had
exerted far too much political pressure on them. [161] This hostility, it is alleged, also extended to intellectuals who had joined
the Party: the latter were an object of suspicion because "they
were very difficult to distinguish" because they "wore red
caps."[162] These charges are polemical and purposely overes-
timate the anti-intellectualism of the "radicals" who had clearly
hoped to recruit suitable "revolutionary teachers" and other
"revolutionary intellectuals" into the Party. At the same time,
however, their standards for defining "revolutionary teachers"
were overly strict and narrow, thus restricting the intake in
practice. The policies of the late 1970s have consciously re-

vived those of 1956 and the early 1960s. Once again, intellectuals were redefined as "an important force in socialist revolution" and Vice-Premier Deng Xiaoping, in his speech to the
National Conference on Educational Work in 1978, included increased access to the Party as part of the "new deal" for
teachers.[163]   Once again, subject to certain flexible political
qualifications, teachers are encouraged to apply for Party membership because they are teachers, i.e., because they belong to
an occupational group whose inclusion among the Party's ranks
is deemed essential if the Party is to fulfill its role as a dynamic force in rapid modernization. The interrupted process
of structural merger has been resumed.

Teachers as a
Political Interest Group

5

In earlier chapters, we have described the political interaction between teachers and the political authorities on a wide range of distributive issues. In this last chapter, we focus on the specific forms which this interaction has taken, notably the means by which teachers have mobilized political resources to protect or extend their interests in a changing political environment. What channels of political communication and pressure have been available, and how have teachers made use of them? Have teachers acted as a unified political group with common interests, or are they internally divided? How much influence have teachers been able to exert on educational policy, and what are the bases of this influence? Have teachers been the malleable object of Party policies, or have they posed significant constraints on Party objectives in education? How does the social power of teachers compare with other sectors of the intelligentsia?

Changes in the general political environment and in educational policy specifically have structured the political opportunities open to — and constraints on — teachers. During socialist modernizing periods, Party leaders have instructed educational cadres to show "concern" (guanhuai) for teachers and sensitivity to their interests. The expression of distinct professional demands has been legitimized and, in certain periods, actively encouraged by the establishment and expansion of institutionalized channels of political communication. The Party

has attempted to reduce the political liabilities of many teachers
— for example, by downplaying questions of class background,
"social relations," or political "histories" — and have encouraged teachers to exercise their political rights qua teachers, in
effect as a professional interest group. Teachers have been encouraged to speak up and speak out, subject to certain general
conditions of "reasonableness" and loyalty to the socialist endeavor. Cadres have been instructed not merely to listen passively, but to solicit opinions actively and respond to them
speedily and effectively. Ideally, the political relationship between teachers and cadres is one of "mutual confidence and mutual consultation," give-and-take rather than unidirectional
pressure.

The mid-1950s provides the clearest picture of socialist modernizing attitudes toward teachers' participation in the political
process. During this period both the general and the educational media carried numerous letters from teachers about the
unresponsiveness of local governments or unit cadres, complaints which reflected the tensions engendered by the first revolution. These problems were visible at all levels of education,
but appear to have been most acute and widespread in primary
schools. One typical case concerns a teacher in Jiangsu Province who complained that although Chairman Mao and the Party
might care about primary school teachers, a lot of cadres did not:

In our district the cadres only devote their energies to the central task and
very rarely make inquiries about primary education. The district government has been set up for over half a year now, and its office is very close to
the school. But the district head only came over once, at the beginning of this
term, but then it was to talk about the problem of his grandson entering school![164]

The same source reported a case of suppression of criticism
in Shaanxi Province:

In June last year, I saw with my own eyes our (administrative) village-head
tear open a letter sent to me from the Masses Daily. I was very annoyed at
the time, and I let the newspaper office know about it. But who could have
guessed that he not only refused to admit his fault but, in a full meeting of the
village teachers, he slapped a great hat on my head for "insulting the people's

government," saying that the village government had the right to check letters.

The official media branded as "sectarian" those cadres who suppressed criticism and ignored reasonable opinions.[165] Too many cadres regarded primary school teachers as "ideologically problematic" or "indifferent to politics," treating them as passive political objects, not active political subjects. In 1956, such cadres were criticized for behaving like "royal ministers" and thinking that "teachers should follow our orders."[166] "Sectarian" cadres at all levels were ordered to accept and respond promptly to the "rational demands" of teachers and to reduce their political demands on them. For example, they were instructed to abandon a crude, impatient approach to "ideological reform" in favor of more gradual, "milder" methods. The Party now maintained that over 90 percent of teachers were "good people" — those with "historical problems" should now be given the benefit of the doubt and allowed "to seek progress in a happy mood." Similar policies were adopted in the "Second Hundred Flowers" of the early 1960s and again in the late 1970s.[167]

During developmentalist periods, moreover, Party leaders have sought to expand the institutionalized channels of political communication open to teachers. In the early 1950s, various political channels were established which to some extent bypassed the face-to-face relations between teachers and cadres in schools and colleges. For example, specialized media were established at both national and local levels, such as Renmin jiaoyu [People's Education], Jiaoshi bao [Teachers' News or Teachers' Journal], Xiaoxue jiaoshi [Primary School Teacher] and Xiaoxue jiaoyu tongxun [Primary School Education Bulletin].* These journals were vehicles of pedagogic information and debate and nurtured a sense of professionalism. They also

---

*Jiaoshi bao succeeded Xiaoxue jiaoshi. The former was designed to cover all aspects and levels of the educational system but was mainly aimed at teachers in teacher-training institutes and in primary and middle schools: see "Farewell Message to Readers," No. 42 (March 20, 1956), translated in ECMM, No. 34 (May 7, 1956), 46-47.

provided opportunities for teachers to air their social, economic, and political grievances in print.

Teachers' interests also found some limited form of repre-
sentation in the All-China Union of Educational Workers, established in 1950. The union cannot be seen as a simple instrument of the professional interests of teachers for two basic reasons. First, it was organized on an industrial basis to represent all "educational workers," i.e., teachers, clerical and
manual workers, caretakers, and the like. Second, its primary
function as a "transmission belt" was top-down rather than
bottom-up. Its main responsibilities were to inform, educate,
mobilize, and control educational personnel; its role as a guard-
ian of and spokesman for their interests has tended to be secondary.[168] In the context of these priorities, however, the union
did play a limited role in the early 1950s in meeting the material needs of teachers in distress and in transmitting their concerns and problems to higher authorities.

In 1956, however, existing channels of communication were
introduced to increase the amount of reliable information available to the authorities on teachers' concerns and to grant
teachers greater influence over processes of educational deci-
sion-making. For example, the Party directed cadres in
schools, colleges, and educational departments to "hold regular
forums of teachers to seek their views on their work and on
their livelihood so that improvements can be made."[169] The
Party also took steps to involve teachers in local governments
by facilitating their election as representatives at municipal
and provincial people's congresses, or as delegates to trade
union conferences. Speakers at meetings of local Political Consultative Conferences or People's Representative Congresses
during the Hundred Flowers period were allowed to voice the
sectional grievances of teachers.[170] Local branches of the
Educational Workers' Union were also encouraged to intervene
more effectively as guardians of teachers' interests. For example, the union's second national congress in August 1956
concluded that "when the personal interests and proper rights
of educational and scientific workers are encroached upon by

bureaucratism (i.e. cadres in schools and local education departments), the trade unions should rise to protect them."[171] The union, it was stressed, should "mirror the views and demands of teachers and represent them to the administration."[172] Union cadres were brought to task for their previous failings, notably their frequently undemocratic work style, the tendency to exclude teachers from union membership, and their indifference to the economic problems of many of their members. This national congress also committed the union to a series of measures designed to alleviate teachers' work loads, to raise their social prestige through mass propaganda, and to provide supplementary allowances to teachers with large families. In his speech to the congress, Lai Ruoyu emphasized the union's role as a political channel for the expression of teachers' interests and called on them to "regard these (union) organizations as dear organizations of their own."[173]

The expanded role of the "democratic parties" provided another channel for the expression of teachers' concerns during the Hundred Flowers period, notably through the Chinese Association for Promoting Democracy, whose membership included many primary and middle school teachers. At the association's second national congress in 1956, for example, one speaker criticized the CCP leadership for neglecting primary and middle education in favor of the tertiary level and allowing teachers at these levels to be the victims of discrimination by school and local government cadres.[174]

In sum, the new political atmosphere of 1956 altered the relationship between teachers and the Party. It let off some of the steam which had built up amid the tensions of the early 1950s and opened the way for a more symmetrical dialogue between professionals and officials. Given the Party's increased receptivity during this period, this political dialogue contributed to an amelioration of the social, economic, and political standing of the teaching profession.

Similar measures were reintroduced in the early 1960s. Local cadres organized "meetings of immortals" to solicit the opinions of teachers and non-Party school officials, and the ac-

tivities of the Chinese Association for the Promotion of Democracy were again allowed to expand.[175] But these activities
were more circumscribed and teachers more cautious than in
the mid-1950s, and they were soon submerged in the waves of
ideological "class struggle" in the mid-1960s.

During the early and mid-1950s, many teachers did in fact make
their demands known to the Party, either directly through the institutionalized channels available to them or indirectly through
sympathetic elements within the Party or spokesmen among
prominent higher intellectuals.* During the latter stage of the
Hundred Flowers movement, moreover, when political controls
were slackened even further to permit the "spontaneous" expression of individual or group interests, teachers were one of
several groups to press distributive demands by unorthodox
collective means. During this period, teachers or teachers-in-
training were directly or indirectly responsible for a number
of "disturbances." For example, in several cases of public agi-
tation by senior middle school students over the issue of college
enrollment, some of their teachers either stood by or actively
encouraged them in their attacks on Party and government organs.[176] In Guizhou Normal College (which trained teachers
for middle schools), some students set up an organization to
agitate for improvement in the political and material treatment
of teachers and allegedly "planned to mobilize normal college
and normal school students all over the nation in common action."[177] In Chengdu, a deputy director of the curricular affairs
office of the municipal Second Normal School (which trained
primary school teachers) was accused of playing a leading role
in an "incident" among students sparked off by a newspaper report that a primary school teacher in Anhui Province had been
beaten up. Students in the school mobilized, with tacit or open
support from certain instructors, to criticize the Party's atti-

---

*For an example of such spokesmanship by a leading figure among the in-
telligentsia, note the role of Luo Longji during the Hundred Flowers movement
(in R. MacFarquhar, The Hundred Flowers Campaign and Chinese Intellectuals, pp. 20-21). He complained about the working conditions of college professors and the work loads of primary school teachers.

tude toward teachers and demand increased pay and social
status for primary school teachers.[178] On an individual level,
teachers were among the most strident public critics of the
Party's policies regulating the distribution of social prestige,
political status, and economic benefits.[179] In consequence,
they were disproportionately affected by the Party's counterattack during the Anti-Rightist campaign when "rightist" teachers
or their spokesmen were accused of manipulating "contradictions" over distributive questions for their own political purposes. As one would have expected given their lowly status,
discontent was most pronounced among primary school teachers, and the ensuing political backlash hit them hard. In fact,
according to statistics reported by Mao Zedong in 1958, no less
than one-third of all "rightists" (100,000 out of 300,000) were
primary school teachers.[180]

Teachers were also on the political defensive during later
periods of radical policy predominance, when they were subjected to political pressure (zhengzhi yali) as a suspect occupational group. Any attempt to articulate their own professional
interests was dismissed as "economism" or "bourgeois" special pleading and subordinated to broader, "class" imperatives.
Political distinctions based on political attitudes or "history,"
age, and class background have been emphasized, thus splinter-
ing the political solidarity of the profession at each level.

These pressures were particularly heavy during the Cultural
Revolution, partly because of the radical rhetoric of the movement and partly because the actual dynamics of the movement
at the basic level went beyond the official ideology. Since the
process of mass politics was relatively unfettered, particularly
during 1966 and 1967, qualifications and cautions built into official statements (for example, about the danger of completely
ignoring the professional role of teachers) tended to be forgotten
in the heat of factional struggle.[181] Moreover, the movement
politicized a range of "contradictions" far wider than those defined as "correct" in official statements. Radical appeals
against "bourgeois academic authorities" and "revisionist" educators released the latent accumulation of frustrations, jealou-

sies, petty resentments, conflicting interests, and negative
stereotypes which had built up among and within the various
constituencies in schools and colleges during the early and mid-
1960s. Teachers came in for some very rough treatment both
as direct targets and as scapegoats cynically thrust forward as
a shield or diversion by other threatened groups. Older teachers were particularly vulnerable and tended to be fair game for
both "conservative" and "rebel" attacks. They came under
heavy pressure during the first "conservative" stage of the
movement in mid-1966, when basic-level Party cadres deflected
criticism onto teachers with "bad" class backgrounds, "complex
social relations," or "impure political histories."*

In spite of these pressures, however, many younger teachers
did join mass organizations. In the nomenclature of the Cultural Revolution, these teachers were usually mentioned together with students — as "revolutionary teachers and students"
(geming shisheng) — as components of the same organizations.
But many teachers formed their own organizations independent
of their students. Some younger antiestablishment teachers
joined "rebel" organizations, while teachers who were Party
members or League cadres, or who had jobs of a wholly or
partly political nature before the movement, were more likely
to join the "conservatives." Attempts to reconstitute the educational process during 1967 and 1968 were clearly hampered
by this factionalism among teachers.[182] Because the political
initiative in the schools rested more with the students and
cadres and because teachers carried the taint of "bourgeois"
professionalism and "white" expertise, however, activist teachers found it difficult to organize around questions of overt or
even covert sectional interests. There is evidence to suggest,
however, that sections of the stratum which has been the most

---

*For a dramatic and detailed account of this early stage, allegedly master-
minded by Liu Shaoqi himself, see "We Accuse the Top Party Person in Au-
thority Taking the Capitalist Road of the Towering Crime of Suppressing Our
School's Great Cultural Revolution," Guangming ribao, April 7, 1967, translated in
SCMP, No. 3924 (April 24, 1967). In this school, the Party work-team dispatched in
July 1966 chose 49 percent of the teaching staff as targets for political attack.

consistently discontented since 1949, primary school teachers, did in fact form their own "rebel" organizations in some cities to press grievances over prestige and pay.[183]

In sum, therefore, the polarizing logic of both the "first revolution" and "radical" ideology has tended to define teachers as an object of "transformation" and has proscribed the very notion of professional interests as a "bourgeois" category. To the extent that teachers have been able to exert power during these periods, it has been largely negative. Through their passivity and silent opposition, they have frustrated the intentions and reduced the impact of official educational policies. During modernizing periods, on the other hand, teachers have been allowed to exert positive power over issues of educational policy and professional status. In periods when they did so effectively, their relationship with the Party has been a form of "interest group politics." In short, teachers have been able to exert influence in different political contexts, but the direction and forms of power have varied over time. The base of their power — their professional skills — has remained constant.

Conclusions: The Political Nature of the Teaching Profession

6

The record of teachers' relationship with the Party since 1949 points to a certain ambiguity in their political character. On the one hand, they have certain common professional interests and perspectives which have found political expression in a relatively solidary way in certain periods, notably in the mid-1950s and late-1970s. They have faced the Party as an interest group with its own special needs, claims, and abilities. Developmentalist Party leaders have encouraged this stance and have been willing to consult with teachers on educational policy and bargain with them on distributive issues. On the other hand, certain important elements of political diversity have emerged which were reflected in the political movements of the late 1950s and 1960s. First, there are differences among various professional strata: among primary, secondary, and tertiary teachers in the state-run system; among teachers in "regular" and "people-run" schools, rural and urban teachers, Second, there are differences which stem from the impact of Party policies: the distinction between teachers of "good" and "bad" class origins; those with "historical problems" and those without; those with "good" political performance and those with "average" or "backward" performance; instructors in political studies and those teaching other subjects; and those in the Party or the League and those outside these key organizations. The fluctuating pattern of political events and educational policies since 1949 also created different "political generations" among

teachers. Younger teachers, notably those trained and recruited
during the heavily politicized atmosphere of the late 1950s and
mid-to-late 1960s were more likely to be favorably inclined
toward radical educational thinking.[184]

By the mid-1960s, therefore, although teachers did have common professional interests and concerns stemming from their
precise position in the social division of labor, these were interpreted in different ways by different sections of the profession. Teachers reacted differently, moreover, to the main issues of the Cultural Revolution. This political heterogeneity allowed radical forces to penetrate their ranks and gain support
for educational reform and can be seen as one source of political weakness for the profession as a whole in its relation with
the Party between 1966 and 1976.

We must not exaggerate this heterogeneity and its political
effects. It appears probable that a considerable majority of
teachers, both new and old, have perceived their interests and
responsibilities in professional terms. We can root this phenomenon in their "objective" position in the social division of
labor, arguing that this basic social fact has been more influential than the actions of the Party-state in determining the political orientations of teachers.[185] They have opposed attempts
to weaken their authority in the classroom, to interfere with
their definition and management of the educational process, or
to lower their public prestige or material status. They have
resisted any radical attempt to redefine their social role. In
effect, they have behaved in ways comparable to teachers in
very different sociopolitical contexts.

As such, they posed an insuperable obstacle to Maoist educational programs. Their resistance is vividly reflected in an
exasperated statement attributed to the radical Shanghai group.

Remolding teachers is like pressing a rubber ball under water. Press hard
and it goes under, but as soon as you let go, it pops up again.[186]

In the face of this political reality, Maoist leaders have found
it impossible to avoid a vicious downward spiral of policy failure: radical innovation leads to low morale, passivity, or re-

sistance among teachers which brings about lower educational standards, increasing difficulty in recruiting young people to meet the chronic shortage of trained teachers, increasing resort to politically reliable but professionally unqualified personnel which further lowers educational standards, thus annoying parents and agencies which depend on educated personnel, and so on.... Radical policies seem self-defeating, but the basic reason seems to lie in politics, not in the intrinsic merit or demerit of the policies themselves.

In general, therefore, the professional and political orientations of teachers have overlapped significantly with the ideologically developmentalist and institutionally conservative goals of Party modernizers. The latter have been aware of this fact and sensitive to its political potential. For example, Deng Xiaoping referred specifically to the plight of teachers in one of his programmatic documents written in 1975 which were partly responsible for precipitating the power struggles of 1976.

The status of teachers is a problem. They are always being scolded, several millions of them. How can you give scope to their enthusiasm? Didn't the Chairman say that negative factors should be turned into positive ones?[187]

The educational policies of the Dengist leadership after Mao's death were designed to restore this lost "enthusiasm," by providing more power, more prestige and, where possible, more money for teachers.

To summarize the argument, although much of the fluctuation in official educational policies over the past two decades can be attributed to competing tendencies within the CCP leadership, it was also in no small part subject to the political influence — negative and positive — of teachers. Teachers have not been an inert social force subject to unrestrained political manipulation. They have provided one weight in the political balance which has, over the long run, swung power away from the radicals toward the modernizers. We should not view their political influence in isolation. They are one part of a "grand coalition" of social forces which supported the removal of the Shanghai

group in 1976 and underpins the strategy of the post-Mao leadership. On this general issue, they share the views of other
skilled groups such as scientists, technicians, cultural intelligentsia and economic managers, and authoritative strata within
the Party and government administration. More specifically,
they are a major component of an antiradical coalition on educational issues (along with planners and economic managers
alarmed at the decline in standards of skill and knowledge,
sympathetic educational administrators, and Party officials and
worried parents). In exchange for their support and cooperation, modernizing leaders have acted to increase their distributive benefits, both psychological and material. In general,
therefore, teachers are one part of a complex interest-group
structure which underlies the surface manifestations of leadership conflict and policy fluctuation in contemporary China.[188]

Teachers have political resources at their disposal which
they have used to protect or ameliorate their social position.
The evidence surveyed in this monograph suggests that the
source of their power resides less in their use of formal modes
of political communication, or their resort to unorthodox "disturbances," or sectional political organizations. It lies rather
in the implicit power which accrues to them from their distinct
occupational role: as transmitters of the social values and expertise crucial to China's socialist modernization. As Apter
has argued, the process of modernization confers an increasing
amount of this "social bargaining power" on skilled groups.[189]
Mao Zedong has described this phenomenon using a market
metaphor:

Some people consider knowledge as their own possession and wait to get a
good price in the market. When the price is not high enough, they will refuse
to sell their knowledge.[190]

Clearly the "price" exacted is social and political, as well as
economic. This social power has imposed constraints on the
extent to which the political leadership can redefine teachers'
professional role and ignore their distributive interests. It is
a bargaining resource which can be used in the continuing po-

litical dialogue with and within the Party.

It also implies that the higher the level of teacher, the more power at his or her disposal and, in consequence, the lower the level of vulnerability to political pressures. There is a great deal of social distance between the humble primary school teacher, "the king (or more likely queen) of the kids," and the exalted university professor, lauded by developmentalist leaders as a jewel in the diadem of socialist construction. We can perhaps relate this and other distinctions to "left-right" variations among teachers. Those with more resources to trade on the political market (notably higher-level or more senior personnel) would naturally favor a more liberal (i.e., within the Chinese political spectrum, more "rightist") political process which is consonant with their ability to influence the political authorities. Those with less resources — notably primary teachers in particular and young teachers in general — seem to have been attracted by the "radical" alternative at some point or another.

How does the political influence of teachers compare with other sections of the intelligentsia? The new political order of the late 1970s and 1980s clearly involves a greater overlap of teachers' professional interests and the strategic priorities of the regime. However, it is important to note that teachers are less central to the Party's long-term priority of rapid modernization than those skilled personnel involved directly in production, notably professional managers, technicians, and engineers. As part of the "superstructure," teachers are important for modernization, but less directly so. One can argue, therefore, that teachers face the Party from a weaker position of power than these other strata and that this finds reflection in their limited capacity to extract distributive (notably material) benefits from the authorities. The Party will probably remain reluctant to divert substantial resources to improving their welfare, particularly at lower levels of the educational system. While the post-Mao leadership has decided to increase the flow of resources to education, they are concentrating on the tertiary and research sectors. Though academics at these levels should do well in the near future, for their counterparts in primary and middle schools there will be more promises and praise than concrete payoffs. For the foreseeable future, we may expect the Party to concentrate on improving their political and psychological rather than economic position: more autonomy in the educational process, more unambiguous authority in the classroom, greater access to Party membership, and a better public image.

Assuming that the present modernizing leadership retains power, tensions between teachers and the Party will decline in comparison with the decade from 1966 to 1976. But they will not disappear. The basic claims of Marxist-Leninist ideology and the characteristic pressure of a Leninist vanguard party system continue to limit teachers' professional autonomy. The relationship between politics, administration, and professional work remains problematic. The political and personal tensions which have built up coral-like — layer by layer, movement by movement — over the past three decades cannot be eliminated in the short run; nor can we discount the possibility of a radical backlash. Thus in the 1980s the role of teachers in school, politics, and society will continue to be ambiguous, a focus of debate and uncertainty, as the Party struggles to reconcile competing priorities and resolve the political heritage of the past.

Notes

1. In Ossowski's words, the socialist Party-state undertakes "the large-scale distribution of privileges and discriminations and the conscious shaping of the social structure": S. Ossowski, Class Structure in the Social Consciousness (London: Routledge and Kegan Paul, 1963), p. 3.

2. Z. Bauman, "Officialdom and Class: Bases of Inequality in Socialist Society," in Frank Parkin, ed., The Social Analysis of Class Structure (London: Tavistock, 1974), pp. 129-147.

3. For some clarification of this last point, see Bernstein's description of the role of schools and teachers in mobilizing urban youth to go "down to the countryside" in the 1960s and 1970s: Thomas P. Bernstein, Up to the Mountains and Down to the Villages (London: Yale University Press, 1977), Chap. 3.

4. For example, see Martin K. Whyte, "Red and Expert: Peking's Changing Policy," Problems of Communism XXI:6 (November-December 1972); Dennis Ray, "'Red and Expert' and China's Cultural Revolution," Pacific Affairs XLIII:1 (Spring 1970), 22-23. For the case of Shanghai, see Lynn T. White III, "Leadership in Shanghai, 1955-69," in Robert A. Scalapino, ed., Elites in the People's Republic of China (London: University of Washington Press, 1972); Sylvia Chan, "Political Assessment of Intellectuals Before the Cultural Revolution," Asian Survey XVIII:9 (September 1978), 891-911.

5. For previous accounts of policies toward teachers, see Theodore Hsi-en Chen, Teacher Training in Communist China (Washington, D.C.: Office of Education, 1960); Marie Sieh, "The School Teacher: A Link to China's Future. Notes on Professional Tensions in the Educational System," Current Scene 3:18 (May 1, 1965); Charles K. S. Wang, The Control of Teachers in Communist China: A Socio-political Study (Human Resources Research Institute: Technical Research Report 36), January 1955. I found Glassman's article on primary school teachers particularly instructive since he uses a systematic political perspective and argues a strong thesis: Joel Glassman, "The Political Experience of Primary School Teachers in the PRC," Comparative Education 15:2 (June 1979), 159-173.

6. For general analyses of educational policy since 1949, see R. F. Price, Education in Communist China (New York: Praeger, 1970), Chap. 6; Suzanne

Pepper, "Education and Political Development in Communist China," Studies
in Comparative Communism 3 (July-October 1970), 132-157; Funi Kobayashi,
Education in Building Chinese Socialism: Theory and Reality in the Transitional Period (Tokyo, Institute of Developing Economies, Special Paper No. 1,
1976).

7. Government Administration Council, "Decisions Concerning the Differentiation of Class Status in the Countryside," People's China II:8 (October 16,
1950), supplement, 11-12. If they had worked independently (duli yingye), they
counted as "free professionals"; if they had worked for a private or public institution, they were "employees." Teachers in public schools in the pre-
Liberation revolutionary base areas were granted the special chengfen of
"revolutionary employees" (geming zhiyuan). Their period of service thus
counted as part of their "revolutionary work seniority" (geming gongzuo nian-
ling), which was important for job assignments after 1949. (See "Questions
and Answers," Renmin jiaoyu (People's Education) October 1950, p. 74, and
March 1951, p. 61.)

8. For the political role of the intelligentsia in general, see Michel Oksenberg, "Occupational Groups in Chinese Society and the Cultural Revolution,"
in Oksenberg et al., The Cultural Revolution: 1967 in Review (Ann Arbor:
Center for Chinese Studies, University of Michigan, 1968), pp. 12-14. For
the cultural intelligentsia, see James P. Harrison, "The Ideological Training
of Intellectuals in Communist China," Asian Survey V:10 (October 1965),
491-501; Mu Fu-sheng (pseud.), The Wilting of the Hundred Flowers: The
Chinese Intelligentsia under Mao (New York: Praeger, 1963); Merle Goldman,
Literary Dissent in Communist China (Cambridge, Mass.: Harvard University Press, 1967). For the technical intelligentsia, see Cheng Chu-yuan,
Scientific and Engineering Manpower in Communist China, 1949-1963 (Washington, D.C.: U.S. Government Printing Office, 1965).

9. Zhang Tengxiao, Xiaoxue jiaoshi yewu xuexi jiangzuo (Professional
Lectures for the Professional Study of Primary School Teachers), Beijing:
Great Masses Bookstore (revised ed.), February 1952. "Counterrevolutionary"
teachers were also "uncovered" in the various political campaigns of the
early and mid-1950s. For one example (a primary school teacher), see "Chen
Dongyao, a Counterrevolutionary Element Hidden among the Ranks of People's
Teachers," Xiaoxue jiaoshi (Primary School Teacher), January 1956, p. 11.

10. Documents of the time suggest that many teachers were reluctant to
learn from the Soviet precedent: see, for example, "Summary Report on the
Cultural and Educational Activities of Local Organizations of the China Demo-
cratic League," Guangming ribao (Guangming Daily), Peking, April 9, 1953
(translated in Survey of China Mainland Press, Hong Kong: U.S. Consulate
General [hereafter SCMP], No. 560 [April 29, 1953], 24-31). For a typical
critique of Dewey's educational theory, see Chen Yuanhui, "The Reactionary
Political Design of Pragmatic Education," Xin jianshe (New Construction),
September 1955 (in Extracts from China Mainland Magazines, Hong Kong: U.S.
Consulate General [hereafter ECMM], No. 14 [November 14, 1955], 39-46).
Dewey had visited China in 1919 and stayed for over two years. He exerted

considerable influences over liberal Chinese educational circles during the Republican period.

11. For information on the latter campaign in Shanghai, see Educational Workers Revolutionary Rebel Joint Committee of Middle Schools, Shanghai City, "Opinions concerning the Clearing up of Teachers' Ranks," Dongfanghong dianxun (East-Is-Red Telegraph), Guangzhou, No. 2, July 1968 (in SCMP 4227, pp. 4-5). In certain schools in the city, the political complexion of the teaching staff was "complicated" indeed. In the Shanghai Foreign Language Vocational School, for example, Red Guards estimated in 1968 that the teaching staff included the former Guomindang ambassador to Sweden, the former secretary and vice-minister of the (pro-Japanese) puppet government's Ministry of Foreign Affairs, the former director of a division within the puppet Ministry of Finance and of the puppet Economic Research Department and the former secretary of the Central Bank! See "No Mischievous Acts Will Be Allowed!" Shanghai hongwei zhanbao (Shanghai Red Guard Combat Bulletin), August 15, 1968 (in SCMP-Supplement 235 [September 23, 1968], 14-15).

12. This shift in priorities was detailed in a series of authoritative pronouncements: for higher education, see Ma Xulun (Minister of Higher Education) "The Policy and Tasks of Higher Education," Renmin ribao (People's Daily); for middle school education, see "National Secondary Education Conference Closes," New China News Agency (hereafter NCNA) Beijing, February 1, 1954; for the primary level, see "Government Administration Council Directive concerning the Reorganization and Improvement of Primary School Education" (November 26, 1953), NCNA, Beijing, December 14, 1953. Steps were taken to expand the system of "normal" (i.e. teacher training) education and improve its quality: for the tertiary level, see "Government Administration Council Directive concerning the Improvement and Development of Higher Education for Teacher Training" (November 26, 1953), NCNA, Beijing, December 14, 1953; for the secondary level, see "Central People's Government Ministry of Education Issues Directive concerning Establishment, Development and Reorganization of Normal Schools," NCNA, Beijing, June 19, 1954. All of these documents are translated in S. M. Hu and E. Seifman, eds., Towards a New World Outlook: A Documentary History of Education in the PRC, 1949-1976 (New York: AMS Press, 1976).

13. For a discussion of this issue, see Ding Xin, "Some Questions concerning Intellectuals," Zhengzhi xuexi (Political Studies) 5 (May 13, 1956), translated in ECMM, No. 47 (August 13, 1956), 13.

14. Zhou Enlai, Report on the Question of Intellectuals (January 14, 1956) (Peking: Foreign Languages Press, 1956), pp. 10-11.

15. For a discussion of the class status and ideological complexion of primary school teachers in this period, see "Is It the Case That Primary School Teachers Have Complicated Class Statuses, Are Backward in Thinking and Have Unimportant Jobs?" Jiaoshi bao (Teachers News), November 2, 1956 (translated in the Appendix IVaiii); "Lead Well the Ranks Two Million Strong," Renmin ribao, editorial, August 16, 1956, translated in SCMP, No. 1360 (August 29, 1956), 12-14. For college teachers, see Wang Sisong, "Learn from Veteran Teachers with an Open Mind," Zhongguo qingnian (Chinese Youth) 4 (February 16, 1956) (in ECMM 34 [May 7, 1956], 26-28).

16. Zhou Enlai, op. cit., pp. 10-11. Similar claims were made during later periods when modernization was the main priority. For 1960-62, for example, see Kuang Yaming, "A Brief Discussion on the Teacher-Student Relationship," Hongqi (Red Flag) 17(September 1, 1961 — in Selections from China Mainland Magazines [Hong Kong: U.S. Consulate General] [hereafter SCMM], 279 [September 18, 1961], 20).

17. For a recent authoritative restatement of these ideas and their implications for educational policy, see Deng Xiaoping, "Speech at the National Educational Work Conference," Peking Review 18 (May 5, 1978). The years 1963-66 and 1971-76 were periods of struggle between opposing factions and platforms. In the latter period, commentaries published after the fall of the Shanghai group suggest that "modernizing" educational policies gained temporary predominance in 1972 (under Zhou Enlai) and 1975 (under Deng Xiaoping), with the Shanghai group's "radical" policies regaining influence in 1973 and 1976.

18. For a discussion of these debates, see Peter J. Seybolt's introduction to his Revolutionary Education in China, Documents and Commentary (White Plains, N.Y.: International Arts and Sciences Press, 1973). For a recent discussion of educational policies and their fate in the post-Mao era, see Suzanne Pepper, "Education and Revolution: The 'Chinese Model' Revisited," Asian Survey XVIII:9 (September 1978), 847-890; Susan L. Shirk, "Educational Reform and Political Backlash: Recent Changes in Educational Policy," Comparative Education Review, June 1979, pp. 183-217. For a post-Mao critique of Maoist policies, see "Meeting of the Ministry of Education Exposes How the 'Gang of Four' Tried to Wreck the Educational Revolution," NCNA, Beijing, December 30, 1976.

19. Mao Zedong, "Talks with Mao Yuan-hsin" (1964-1966), in Stuart R. Schram, ed., Mao Tse-tung Unrehearsed: Talks and Letters, 1956-71 (Middlesex: Penguin, 1974), p. 248.

20. "To Be a Teacher Is to Make Revolution," Wenhui bao, Shanghai, editorial, May 25, 1965 (Appendix IVaiv); Yao Peikuan. "Be a Revolutionary Educational Worker," Shanghai jiaoyu (Shanghai Education) 6 (June 12, 1965) (in SCMM 491).

21. For an illustrative case study of such "leftist" pressures on teachers at the tertiary level during the Great Leap Forward, see Mao Zedong, "Reply to Article 'Tsinghua University Physics Teaching and Research Group Inclines toward the 'Left' Rather Than the Right in Handling Teachers'" (December 22, 1958) (in Miscellany of Mao Tse-tung Thought [1949-1968] Arlington, Virginia, Joint Publications Research Service, February 1974 [hereafter Miscellany], Part I, pp. 149-150). This article identified four main problem areas:

(1) It is felt that the intellectuals are the objects of revolution in the socialist revolution period, and even more so when entering communism, because the absolute majority of them are bourgeois intellectuals and belong to the exploiting class. Even League member assistant professors are considered the objects of revolution.

(2) It is felt that to start from the interest of the working-class the class line should be followed, but not the mass line, as it is not suitable in the school. In clarifying the dividing line, they incline toward the "left." They feel that "bringing out the role of old teachers" will confuse the class line and relax the struggle.

(3) It is felt that all high-level intellectuals are fundamentally opposed to the Party's education policy; that they set up a formation to attack us, that we must counterattack....

(4) It is felt that Party prestige and mass consciousness have been raised and that the time has arrived for replacement by Party members.... The leaders of all organizations should be replaced by Party members.

22. Zhongfa (1977) No. 37, Part VIII, translated in Issues & Studies, Taibei, XV:3, p. 112.

23. In their celebrated study of rural Yunnan in the Republican period, for example, Fei and Chang reported the common belief that "to be a scholar is a way to enter government, become socially important and become rich as well"; see Fei Hsiao-tung and Chang Chih-yi, Earthbound China: A Study of Rural Economy in Yunnan (Chicago: University of Chicago Press, 1945), p. 273. For a general analysis of the sociopolitical implications of education in Imperial China, see C. T. Hu (ed.), Chinese Education under Communism (New York: Columbia University Teachers College, 1962), esp. pp. 1-16. In Hu's view (p. 8), "The true value of education was in the belief that education provided the only avenue to moral superiority which, in turn, was regarded as the sole qualification for participation in government and social leadership."

24. For example, Ping-ti Ho discusses the lowly role of shengyuan degree holders as village teachers or family tutors: The Ladder of Success in Imperial China (New York: Wiley, 1964), pp. 35 et seq.

25. For an illuminating discussion of stratification and mobility in the Republican period, see Yichu Wang, "Western Impact and Social Mobility in China," American Sociological Review, 25 (1960), 843-55.

26. For an interesting description of teachers in traditional rural schools during the Republican period, see T'ai-chu Liao, "Rural Education in Transition: A Study of the Old-fashioned Chinese Schools (szu shu) in Shantung and Szechuan," The Yenching Journal of Social Studies IV: I (August 1948), 19 et seq.

27. For example, see Song Jianming, "Any Job That Benefits the People Is a Glorious Occupation," Xiaoxue jiaoshi, November 1953, p. 13 (Appendix IIai). According to Song, "some people" said to him: "What a pity for a young fellow to live a life of chalk."

28. For an excellent analysis of these problems over the whole decade, see Ding Haochuan (acting president of Jilin Normal College), "The Students Who Plan to Sit for Entrance Exams of Institutions of Higher Education," Guangming ribao, June 18, 1959 (in SCMP 2054, July 14, 1959).

29. "A Meeting to Discuss the Question of Whether or Not Primary School Teachers Have a Future," Xiaoxue jiaoshi, October 1953, p. 15.

30. For an early example of this approach, see Ding Haochuan, "How

Teachers Should View Their Work, Their Students and Themselves," Renmin jiaoyu, May 1950, pp. 34-37 (Appendix Ii).

31. Cui Jieping, "Just What Is the Social Status of Teachers Like?" Jiaoshi bao, Beijing, December 10, 1957.

32. Sun Shuzhi, "One Should Not Distort the Happy Life of Teachers," Heilongjiang ribao (Heilongjiang Daily), August 29, 1957.

33. Zhang Tengxiao, op. cit., Lecture 5: Section I, pp. 103-4; compare "The Livelihood of Primary School Teachers in Fujian Is Constantly Improving," Dagong ribao (Impartial Daily), Hong Kong, December 17, 1952.

34. Ding Haochuan, "Apply for Normal Schools, Prepare to Shoulder the Sacred Responsibility of Training the Motherland's Next Generation," Guangming ribao, August 8, 1953. For Ye Shengdao's novel, see Schoolmaster Ni Huan-chih (Beijing: Foreign Languages Press, 1958).

35. M. I. Kalinin, On Communist Education (Moscow: Foreign Languages Press, 1950).

36. For the shortfall between planned and actual graduates in education, see J. P. Emerson, "Manpower Training and Utilization of Specialized Cadres, 1949-68," in John W. Lewis, ed., The City in Communist China (Stanford: Stanford University Press, 1970), p. 202. The number reported was 93.1 percent of the target while the targets for engineering (103.5 percent) and economics-finance (115.2 percent) were overfulfilled.

37. Liu Shi, "Be an Engineer of the Human Soul," Zhongguo qingnian bao (Chinese Youth News), May 20, 1956 (Appendix Iiii).

38. Mofande renmin jiaoshi (Model People's Teachers), Educational Materials Compilation Company, 1951; "He Works at a Glorious Post," Xiaoxue jiaoshi, March 1955, pp. 13 et seq.; "How to Implement the Spirit of the National Advanced Producers Representative Congress in Educational Departments," Xiaoxue jiaoyu tongxun (Primary School Education Bulletin), No. 9, 1956.

39. "Why Are We Launching a Movement for Respecting Teachers?" Qingdao ribao (Qingdao Daily), January 24, 1952; "A New Atmosphere after Launching (a Movement) to Esteem Teachers and Respect the Truth," Jinzhou ribao (Jinzhou Daily), January 10, 1957; Shiqian, "Educate the Peasants to Respect Teachers," Nanfang ribao (Southern Daily), Guangzhou, March 5, 1957 (Appendix IIaiii); "Jinzhou and Luda Launch Propaganda Activities to Encourage Respect for Teachers," Jiaoshi bao, February 12, 1957.

40. Xiaoxue jiaoshide qiantu wenti (The Question of Primary School Teachers' Future), Beijing: People's Education Publishing House, September 1954, p. 90.

41. "A Shaanxi County Ought to Raise the Political Treatment of Primary School Teachers," Guangming ribao, June 18, 1952; Zhou Yanye, "Our Country's Educational Workers' Union Pays Attention to the Work of the Pedagogic Profession," Xiaoxue jiaoyu tongxun, No. 19 (November 1956), 22; "This Is How I Realized the Noble Nature of the Teaching Profession," Zhongguo qingnian bao, June 16, 1955; "People's Teachers Should Enjoy Social Esteem and Respect," Jiaoshi bao, June 29, 1956.

42. For example, see Zhang Qing, "Teachers — Engineers of the Human

Soul," <u>Zhongguo qingnian bao</u>, July 3, 1954; Yang Dongxun, "Educational Work
Is a Glorious and Difficult Undertaking," <u>Changjiang ribao</u> (Yangtse Daily),
June 28, 1955. On the social position of Soviet teachers, see Nigel Grant,
<u>Soviet Education</u> (Middlesex: Penguin, 1964), p. 150.
    43. Zhang Lianfeng, "The Soviet Teachers I Have Seen," <u>Xiaoxue jiaoyu
tongxun</u>, No. 5 (April 20, 1956), 7-8 (Appendix Iii).
    44. <u>Xiaoxue jiaoshide qiantu wenti</u>, p. 97.
    45. "A Discussion Meeting on Whether or Not Primary School Teachers
Have a Future," <u>Xiaoxue jiaoshi</u>, No. 10, 1953, p. 15.
    46. "Respect and Love Primary School Teachers," <u>Zhongguo qingnian bao</u>,
editorial, April 10, 1956 (in <u>SCMP</u>) 1279 [May 1, 1956], 8).
    47. "A Discussion Meeting...," <u>Xiaoxue jiaoshi bao</u>, No. 11, 1953, p. 14.
    48. "Respect the Work of Primary School Teachers," <u>Liaoning ribao</u> (Liao-
ning Daily), editorial, January 12, 1957 (in <u>SCMP</u> 1497 [March 26, 1957],
16-17) (Appendix IIaii).
    49. For example, see Wu Wenyin, "We Should Pay Sufficient Attention to
Middle and Primary School Education and Teachers" (speech at the Second
National Congress of the China Association for the Promotion of Democracy),
<u>Guangming ribao</u>, August 16, 1956 (in <u>SCMP</u> 1380 [October 1, 1956], 12-15);
Shen Yang, "You Cannot Treat Primary School Teachers That Way," <u>Gongren
ribao</u> (Workers Daily), July 14, 1956 (Appendix Vi).
    50. This is cited in R. MacFarquhar, <u>The Hundred Flowers Campaign and
Chinese Intellectuals</u> (New York: Praeger, 1960), p. 95.
    51. This ambiguity is reflected in the appeal to teachers by Zhang Jichun,
"Develop a Great Leap Forward in People's Education and a Great Leap Forward by People's Teachers in Becoming Red and Expert," <u>Renmin jiaoyu</u>, 1958,
No. 4, pp. 4-5.
    52. For example, see the articles on the educational revolution in <u>Guang-
ming ribao</u> and <u>Renmin ribao</u> on July 15, 1958 (in <u>SCMP</u> 1831), and in <u>Hong qi</u>
September 1, 1958, translated in <u>Current Background</u> (Hong-Kong: U.S. Con-
sulate General), No. 516.
    53. Rather than attempt to survey the voluminous literature for this period,
the author refers interested readers to Stewart E. Fraser and Hsü Kuang-
liang, <u>Chinese Education and Society: A Bibliographic Guide. The Cultural
Revolution and Its Aftermath</u> (White Plains, N.Y.: International Arts and Sciences
Press, 1972), esp. sections V to VIII. For general discussions of the impact of the
Cultural Revolution on educational institutions, see Marianne Bastid, "Economic
Necessity and Political Ideals in Educational Reform during the Cultural Revolu-
tion," <u>The China Quarterly</u> 42 (April-June 1970), 16-45; Ellen K. Ong, "Edu-
cation in China since the Cultural Revolution," <u>Studies in Comparative Com-
munism</u> (July-October 1970), 158-176.
    54. For an example of this reevaluation, see "Bring up a Force of Red and
Expert Teachers," <u>Fujian ribao</u> (Fujian Daily), editorial, June 21, 1959 (in
<u>SCMP</u> 2076 [August 14, 1959], 18-20).
    55. The role of older teachers was emphasized: see "Foster the Advisory
Function of Old Teachers and Actively Train Young Teachers," <u>Guangming</u>

ribao, February 22, 1963, p. 2.

56. For official regulations emphasizing the need for social respect for the teaching profession during this period, see Susan Shirk, "The 1963 Temporary Work Regulations for Full-time Middle and Primary Schools: Commentary and Translation." The China Quarterly 55 (July-September 1973), 520-529. For an article reemphasizing the importance of professionalism, see "Do a Good Job of Inculcating a Sense of Professionalism among Normal School Students," Guangming ribao, March 9, 1962, p. 2 (Appendix Iiv).

57. "To a Youth Who Has Taken up the Post of a Primary School Teacher," Zhongguo qingnian 18 (September 16, 1963) (in SCMM 390 [November 1, 1963], 1-5).

58. Chen Yuan, "Train Red Successors to the Revolutionary Cause — A Talk with Forthcoming Senior-Middle School Graduates on the Work of Teachers," Guangming ribao, June 29, 1961 (in SCMP 2547 [July 28, 1961]).

59. Mao Zedong, "Minutes of Spring Festival Talk" (February 13, 1964), in Miscellany, part II, p. 333.

60. Deng Xiaoping, "Speech at the National Education Work Conference," Peking Review 18 (May 15, 1978), 11-12. Compare "Vice-premier Wang Zhen Praises the Role of Teachers," NCNA Beijing, August 19, 1979 (translated in Foreign Broadcast Information Service, Daily Report: People's Republic of China [hereafter FBIS] August 20, 1979), and "The Entire Society Must Respect Teachers and Love Students," Renmin ribao, editorial, May 5, 1980, p. 1.

61. "Provincial Paper Calls for Respect for Teachers," Shanxi provincial radio, October 9, 1977 (translated in BBC, Summary of World Broadcasts: The Far East [hereafter SWB], October 20, 1977).

62. Sidney L. Greenblatt, "Organizational Elites and Social Change at Peking University," in Robert A. Scalapino, ed., Elites in the People's Republic of China, p. 473.

63. Theoretical Unit of the Ministry of Education, "Start from the Primary School in Tackling a Fundamental Task Crucial for Generations to Come," Guangming ribao, September 3, 1977 (in Survey of People's Republic of China Press [hereafter SPRCP] [September 16, 1977], 194).

64. Price points out the close link between the traditional concepts of teacher and scholar. According to Mencius, for example, one of the "three things in which the Superior Man delights" was to "obtain the young men of finest talent in the empire and educate them": R. Price, Marx and Education in Russia and China, p. 122.

65. Ding Haochuan, "How Teachers Should View Their Work, Their Students and Themselves," Renmin jiaoyu I:1 (May 1950), 34-37 (Appendix Ii).

66. "Rules of Conduct for Middle School Students," June 1955, in Stewart Fraser, ed., Chinese Communist Education: Records of the First Decade (New York: Wiley, 1965), p. 208. For comparable regulations for primary schools, see "Rules of Conduct for Primary School Students," Wenhui Bao, Shanghai, February 26, 1955, translated in Hu and Seifman, eds., op. cit., p. 72 (especially rules 3, 6, 7, 8 and 11). Compare Chen Jian, "This Is No Ex-

cuse for Not Respecting the Teacher," Zhongguo qingnian bao, October 31, 1956 (Appendix IIbi); "Teacher Wang Enjoys the Respect of His Students," Jinzhou ribao (Jinzhou Daily), January 6, 1957; "Can One Not Respect Teachers?" Xiamen ribao (Amoy Daily), January 16, 1957.

67. Fu Chensheng, "Concerning the Question of Study," Guangming ribao, October 17, 1961 (in SCMP 2612 [November 3, 1961], 7-8); compare the similar message in the 1963 "Temporary Work Regulations for Primary and Middle School Teachers," in Shirk, op. cit., pp. 537-538.

68. Kuang Yaming, "A Brief Discussion on the Teacher-Student Relationship," Hong qi (September 1, 1961) (in SCMM 279 [September 18, 1961], 17ff).

69. Ji Feng, "How to Handle Your Spouse and Teachers If They Are Rightists," Zhongguo qingnian 8 (April 16, 1958) (in ECMM 134 [July 7, 1958], 15-17).

70. For his talk with the Nepalese delegation, see Current Background, No. 888; for his talks with Mao Yuanxin, see Schram, ed., op. cit., pp. 242-252.

71. "New Relationship between Teachers and Students," Beijing ribao (Beijing Daily), editorial, January 23, 1959 (in SCMP 1957 [February 19, 1959], 25).

72. He Dong, "Teach according to the Aptitude of Students and Cherish the Talented Ones," Guangming ribao, December 2, 1961.

73. For examples of the propaganda of the early Cultural Revolution, see Yong Wentao, "Sweep Away All Freaks and Monsters on the Educational Front," Yangcheng wanbao (Yangcheng Evening News), Guangzhou, June 12, 1966 (in SCMP 3728 [June 29, 1966]); "Students May Help Their Teachers to Make Revolution," Zhongguo qingnian bao, editorial, June 28, 1966 (in SCMP 3737 [July 13, 1966]).

74. "Peking University Students on Revolution That Touches the Innermost Soul," NCNA, Beijing, April 14, 1967.

75. "Central Leaders on Revolution in Education," Hong dian xun (Red Telegraphic Bulletin), March 1968 (in SCMP 4193, p. 3).

76. For an account of student maltreatment of middle school teachers during the Cultural Revolution, see Gordon A. Bennett and Ronald N. Montaperto, Red Guard: The Political Biography of Dai Xiao-ai (London: Allen and Unwin, 1971), p. 41.

77. Mao Zedong Doctrine Red Guards, "One Hundred Examples for Breaking the Old and Establishing the New," September 1, 1966, pamphlet (in SCMM 566 [March 6, 1967]), example no. 93.

78. "School Management by Poor and Lower-Middle Peasants as Shown by the Practice of Three Production Brigades in the Educational Revolution," Renmin ribao, October 28, 1968 (translated in Seybolt, op. cit., p. 123).

79. Guo Tong, "Taking a Joyous Step Forward in the Educational Revolution — A Visit to Peking's Shih-ching-shan Middle School," Zhongguo xinwen (China News), February 16, 1968, translated in Seybolt, op. cit., pp. 147-154. For comparable practices at the college level, see "Red Guard Young Fighters Ascend the University Platform," Renmin ribao, December 12, 1967 (in SCMP 4101) (Appendix IIbiv).

80. "What Is in Yu Xiu's 'After Reading Han Yu's Theory of Teachers,'"
Shandong jiaoyu (Shandong Education), Jinan, No. 7-8 (August 1, 1966), 41-42
(translated in Joint Publications Research Service [hereafter JPRS], Politi-
cal-Sociological Translations on Communist China, 379 [39, 476], January 10,
1967).

81. "How Should Middle and Primary Schools Resume Teaching and Make
Revolution?" Wenhui Bao, Shanghai, March 12, 1967 (in SCMP-Supplement
176, p. 18).

82. For example, see 10th Class, Hangchow Municipal No. 14 Middle
School, "We Resolve to Be Promoters of Educational Revolution," Renmin
ribao, April 1973 (in SCMP 5364).

83. "Revolution in Education Develops New Teacher-Student Relations,"
NCNA (English), Beijing, January 10, 1974.

84. For examples, see "Why Have I 'Degenerated' Both Morally and Academically in a Day?" Renmin ribao, January 10, 1974 (in SCMP 5547, February 6, 1974); "Northwest China Middle School Teachers and Students Criticize
Revisionist Educational Line," NCNA (English), Lanzhou, April 8, 1974;
"Northeast China Pupil Militant in Criticizing Revisionist Line," NCNA (English), Shenyang, May 8, 1974; "What Yardstick Should Be Used to Gauge the
Students," Renmin ribao, June 9, 1974 (in SCMP 5656).

85. The Second Middle School of Yiqing Municipality, Hubei Province, "Who
Should Write Comments on Pupils?" Renmin ribao, April 21, 1975 (in SPRCP
5879).

86. The letter was published in Beijing ribao on December 12, 1973, and
reprinted in Renmin ribao, under the title "Letter and Excerpts from the
Diary of a Primary School Pupil," on December 28, 1973 (in SCMP 5539
[January 22, 1974], 29-31) (Appendix IIbv).

87. This is quoted in Huang Shuai's reply to the criticism, "An Open Letter
by Huang Shuai," Renmin ribao, February 11, 1974 (in SCMP 5570, pp. 45-48).

88. Wang Qian, "Understand Clearly the Reactionary Essence of the 'Dignity of the Teaching Profession,'" Guangming ribao, April 24, 1974 (in SCMP
5621, p. 201) (Appendix IIbvi). Compare Xie Qing, "When Teachers Are Absurd, It Is Right to Repudiate Them," Jiaoyu shijian (Educational Practice),
1976, No. 7 (in JPRS 368 [January 18, 1977]).

89. For a reevaluation of Confucius, see Chen Zenghui, "A Tentative Evaluation of Confucius' Educational Concepts," Guangming ribao, July 18, 1978
(in FBIS, July 21, 1978). For the post-Mao attempt to reorder classroom relations, see "Respect Teachers and Love Students; Establish a New Atmosphere," Hong qi 1977, No. 7, pp. 55-59.

90. For information on the various dimensions of "material treatment,"
see Li Xin, "Who Says That the Political Status and Material Treatment of
Teachers Have Not Been Raised?" Guizhou ribao (Guizhou Daily), August 24,
1957.

91. For a synoptic account of wage policy, see Christopher Howe, "Labour Orga-
nisation and Incentives, Before and After the Cultural Revolution," in Stuart R.
Schram, ed., Authority, Participation and Cultural Change in China (Cam-

bridge: Cambridge University Press, 1973), pp. 233-256.

92. For example, see Zhang Tengxiao, op. cit., February 1952, pp. 106-107.

93. "New China's Concern for People's Teachers and Youth," Renmin jiaoyu, August 1952, pp. 4-5.

94. "Teachers in China Improve Their Living and Working Conditions," NCNA, Beijing, September 21, 1951 (in SCMP 179 [September 21-22, 1951]).

95. "Organization of Educational Workers' Unions Greatly Extended," Guangming ribao, April 30, 1953 (in SCMP 571 [May 15, 1953]).

96. "The Livelihood of Fujian Primary School Teachers Is Constantly Improving," Dagong ribao (Impartial Daily), Hong Kong, December 17, 1952.

97. Wenhui bao, Hong Kong, December 20, 1952.

98. For concrete examples, see "We Must Take Thorough Care of Teachers' Livelihood and Welfare," Xiaoxue jiaoshi (editorial) 12 (1954), 2. For authoritative sources on the need for economy in educational spending, see Zhang Xiro (Minister of Education), speech to the National People's Congress on July 22, 1955, reported in Renmin ribao, July 25, 1955, and Li Fuchun, "Report on the First Five Year Plan for Development of the National Economy of the People's Republic of China," July 5-6, 1955 (in Communist China, 1955-1959 [Cambridge, Mass.: Harvard University Press, 1962], esp. p. 55).

99. Xiaoxue jiaoshi 8 (1954), 7.

100. For example, see "Oppose This Kind of Neglect of Teachers' Livelihood," Jiaoshi bao, May 22, 1956.

101. Guangdong jiaoyu, June 1956 (in ECMM 47, pp. 16-18). For comparable measures in Zhejiang Province, see Xiaoxue jiaoyu tongxun, 16 (October 5, 1956), 10.

102. "This Province Will Establish a 'Teachers House' and a 'Teachers Recuperation House,'" Xiaoxue jiaoyu tongxun, 9 (June 20, 1956), 26; "Help Middle and Primary School Level Teaching Staff to Clear Their Debts," Guangzhou ribao (Guangzhou Daily), October 7, 1956; "Can Rural Teachers Be Treated Like This," Guangxi ribao (Guangxi Daily), October 23, 1956.

103. "Let Teachers Work in the Same Places as Their Husbands and Wives — The Ministry of Education Orders Transfers to Be Made After the Summer Vacation" (July 21, 1956), Jiaoshi bao, editorial, July 24, 1956 (in SCMP 1344 [August 7, 1956], 5-6).

104. "Positively Improve the Working and Living Conditions of Teachers in Institutions of Higher Education," Guangming ribao, editorial, April 17, 1956 (in SCMP 1279 [May 1, 1956], 3-6).

105. "The Wages of the Nation's Middle and Primary School Teachers Have Been Raised," Jiaoshi bao, July 10, 1956.

106. Feng Suhai, "A Talk with Teachers on Wage Reform," Jiaoshi bao, Beijing, July 3, 1956 (Appendix IIIi).

107. "The Wages of the Nation's Middle and Primary School Teachers Are About to Go up," Renmin ribao, July 9, 1956.

108. Feng Suhai, op. cit.

109. Shi Tianhe, "My Opinions concerning the Calculation of Teachers'

Salaries," Jiaoshi bao, July 20, 1956 (Appendix IIIii).

110. For a report on the implementation of the reform in primary schools, see "This Province's Wage Reform in Primary Schools Has Already Concluded; The Income of Over 60,000 Teachers and Staff Members Has Increased," Xiaoxue jiaoyu tongxun (Zhejiang) 18 (November 5, 1956), 14.

111. "Solve realistically the Wage Problems of Private and People-Run Primary School Teachers," Jiaoshi bao, December 21, 1956; "The Wage Problems of People-Run Primary School Teachers Must Be Solved," Neimenggu ribao (Inner Mongolia Daily), February 12, 1957.

112. Wu Wenyin, "We Should Pay Enough Attention to Middle and Primary School Education and Teachers" (speech at the Second National Congress of the Chinese Association for Promoting Democracy), Guangming ribao, August 16, 1956 (in SCMP 1380 [October 1, 1956], 12-15).

113. Zhao Guangyu, "Do More to Solve Several Practical Problems of Teachers," Heilongjiang ribao (Heilongjiang Daily), June 8, 1957; Yin Sinan, "A Demand for Attention to the Livelihood of Primary School Teachers," ibid.

114. "Temporary Work Regulations...," in Shirk, op. cit., p. 539. For tertiary institutions, see the retrospective remarks in " 'Sixty Points on Higher Education' — A Black Outline Concocted by Liu Shaoqi for Counter-revolutionary Restoration," Jinggangshan (Beijing) 47 (June 14, 1967), 4.

115. Ezra Vogel, "Salary Systems for Non-farmers," mimeo.

116. I am indebted to Professor John W. Lewis of Stanford University for this information.

117. Pierre M. Perrolle, "Engineering Education in China: A Report on Observations of the U.S. Engineering Education Delegation to China" (September-October 1978), mimeo, prepared for the workshop on "The Development of Industrial Science and Technology in the PRC: Implications for U.S. Policy," St. George: Bermuda, January 1979, p. 16.

118. NCNA, Beijing, January 13, 1980.

119. I am grateful to John W. Lewis for this information.

120. NCNA, Beijing, September 19, 1979.

121. For an early discussion of the need for teachers to undertake political study, see Chang Jinwu, "On the Current Question of Teachers' Political and Theoretical Study," Renmin jiaoyu, 1950, No. 6, pp. 15-18. For college teachers, see Fang Zhi, "Launch a Study Movement for Ideological Reform among Teachers in Higher Schools," Renmin jiaoyu, November 1951, p. 9.

The "Three-Antis Movement" in 1952 focused on the political and ideological shortcomings of teachers at all levels. One report on the movement painted a dramatic picture of political recalcitrance among teachers:

> In very many schools, bourgeois ideology is still dominant in practice. In higher schools, it is maintaining an extremely obstinate position; it also has widespread impact in middle and primary schools.

See "Strive to Achieve the Leadership of Proletarian Ideology in Schools at All Levels," Renmin jiaoyu, July 1952, pp. 4-5; Chen Xuanshan, "Normal Education over the Past Three Years," Renmin jiaoyu, January 1953, p. 22. The problem remained a focus of official concern into the mid-1950s: for example, see Lian Jiansheng, "The Harm Caused to Students by the Bourgeois Ideology of Some Teachers," Renmin jiaoyu, April 1955, pp. 40-41, who accused teachers of spreading careerism, academicism, and "mammonism."

122. Mao Zedong, "Talks at the Chengtu Conference" (March 1958) in Schram, ed., Mao Tse-tung Unrehearsed, p. 116.

123. For example, see "Teaching Is the Overriding Central Task in Schools," Renmin jiaoyu (editorial) 1953 No. 3, pp. 4-5 (Appendix IVbi).

124. For a discussion of these tensions in Shanghai, see L. T. White III, "Leadership in Shanghai, 1955-1969," in Scalapino, ed., op. cit., pp. 317-318.

125. "Positively Ameliorate the Working and Living Conditions for Teachers in Institutions of Higher Education," Guangming ribao (editorial), April 17, 1956 (in SCMP 1279 [May 1, 1956], 3-6).

126. For a criticism of "sectarianism" (zongpaizhuyi) in primary education, see Wang Benqing, "Thoroughly Overcome Sectarian Sentiments," Xiaoxue jiaoyu tongxun, 1957, No. 1 (January 5, 1957), 14 (Appendix IVbii).

127. Mao Zedong, "Speeches at the Second Session of the Eighth Party Congress" (May 1958), in Miscellany, Part I, pp. 110-111.

128. For example, see "Does the Party Committee Lead or Do Experts Lead?" Renmin jiaoyu, 1958, No. 6, pp. 2-3; "A New Relationship between Teachers and Students," Beijing ribao (editorial), January 23, 1959 (in SCMP 1957 [February 19, 1959], 23-25).

129. "The Question of Whether or Not to Be 'Workers' Debated by Students at Northwest University," Renmin ribao, July 30, 1958 (in SCMP 1838 [August 22, 1958]); "Should Students Be Fostered to Become Workers?" Renmin ribao, July 25, 1958 (in SCMP 1830 [August 12, 1958], 9-11).

130. For example, see "Respect the Leading Role of Teachers in Pedagogic Matters," Zhongguo qingnian bao, (editorial), March 28, 1959; "Correctly Foster the Leading Role of Teachers in Pedagogic Matters," Guangming ribao, March 30, 1959.

131. "A New Relationship between Teachers and Students," loc. cit., January 23, 1959; cf. "Correctly Understand the Function of People's Teachers," Wenhui bao, Shanghai, March 21, 1959.

132. For example, see "Six Middle School Principals in Shanghai Successfully Hold Small 'Meetings of Immortals,'" Guangming ribao, March 15, 1961; cf. the Party committee of Yunnan University, "The Work of Schools Must Center on Teaching," Renmin ribao, April 14, 1961; Kuang Yaming, "A Brief Discussion on the Teacher-Student Relationship," Hong qi 17 (September 1, 1961) (in SCMM [September 18, 1961], 2).

133. "The History Department of Nankai University Adopts Diverse Measures for Assuring That Teachers Have Enough Time for Teaching," Guangming ribao, October 13, 1961 (in SCMP 2613 [November 6, 1961]).

134. Song Lanzhou, "Raise the Standard of Normal Education in Strict Accordance with the Needs of Middle Schools," Guangming ribao, May 25, 1961 (in SCMP 2515 [June 13, 1961], 18-22).

135. "Beijing Primary and Middle School Teachers Undertake Advanced Study," NCNA, Beijing, November 15, 1961 (in SCMP 2623 [November 21, 1961]).

136. For example, see "Actively Teach and Lead Students to Exert Efforts to Study and Do Their Lessons Well," Zhongguo qingnian bao, November 4, 1961 (in SCMP 2623 [December 11, 1961], esp. p. 6); compare the "Temporary Work Regulations...," paras 20 and 22, in Shirk, op. cit., pp. 533-534.

137. For example, see "Anhui University Pays Attention to Developing the Role of Old Teachers," Renmin ribao, July 7, 1961 (in SCMP 2539 [July 18, 1961], 11-12).

138. Yu Wen, " 'Some Views on Urban Primary and Middle School Educational Work' Advanced by the Education Department of the Former Peking CCP Committee Is a Revisionist Educational Program," Beijing ribao, June 21, 1966 (in SCMP Supplement 155, pp. 12-14).

139. "The Faculty of History, Nankai University, Sets up Professional Chairs on Basic Knowledge," Renmin ribao, August 23, 1961 (in SCMP 2573 [September 7, 1961], 23-24).

140. For example, Su Yun, "Continuous Progress," Renmin ribao, August 24, 1961 (in SCMP [September 7, 1961], 23-24).

141. Ju Hongqi, "Refute the 'Don't Be Afraid of Delegating Power to Your Aides' View," Renmin ribao, October 13, 1966 (in SCMP 3808, 3-5) (Appendix IVbiv).

142. Wenhui bao, Shanghai, May 20, 1968 (in SCMP 4197, June 13, 1968).

143. "New Changes Brought About by the Poor and Lower-Middle Peasants in School Management," Renmin ribao, April 21, 1974 (in SCMP 5619, pp. 105-106).

144. Report by the CCP General Branch Committee of the Department of History, Shanghai Normal University, Guangming ribao, February 20, 1973 (in SCMP 5325 [March 2, 1973], 161).

145. "Workers and PLA Fighters Teach at Chinese Middle School," NCNA, Shanghai, January 3, 1976.

146. CCP Jiangsu Provincial Committee Writing Group, "Strengthen the Building of the Ranks of Urban Primary and Middle School Teachers," Hong qi 6 (June 1, 1971), 9-13 (in Seybolt, ed., op. cit., pp. 157-158).

147. On the latter, for example, see "Workers and Peasants on the (Teaching) Rostrum Give Impetus to the Development of the Revolution in Education," Renmin ribao, January 7, 1974 (in SPRCP 5837).

148. "Zhang Tiesheng's Letter Has Given Impetus to the Revolution in Education," Renmin ribao, July 14, 1978 (in SCMP 5544) (Appendix Vvi).

149. For example, see Xu Changrong and Jian Zhixiu, "Reduce the Burden of Backbone Teachers Who Must Carry the Load on Both Shoulders," Renmin ribao, July 14, 1978 (in FBIS [August 8, 1978]).

150. For example, there was a renewed call for educational cadres to be skilled in pedagogic matters: see "Leading Cadres Must Know the Ropes of Teaching," Guangming ribao, May 1, 1978, p. 2 (in JPRS 432 [May 31, 1978]).

151. "A Discussion with Primary School Teachers on the Issue of Joining the Party," Xiaoxue jiaoyu tongxun 13 (August 20, 1956), 2-3 (Appendix IVbiii).

152. Mao Zedong, "Talk at the Hangzhou Conference of the Shanghai Bu-

reau," April 1957, in Miscellany, Part I, p. 69.

153. "Guangdong Provincial Bureau of Education Notification on the Implementation of Policy for Intellectuals in Schools," Guangdong jiaoyu, June 1956 (in ECMM 47 [August 13, 1956], 18).

154. "The Party and the Government Take Care of Primary School Teachers," Dazhong ribao (Great Masses Daily), Jinan, November 20, 1956.

155. Wang Kuige and Wu Yunlin, "Again Discussing with Teachers Some Questions of Joining the Party," Xiaoxue jiaoyu tongxun 1 (January 5, 1957), 13.

156. John W. Lewis, Leadership in Communist China (Ithaca, New York: Cornell University Press, 1963), p. 108.

157. "Many Middle School Teachers in Sichuan Honorably Admitted into the Party," Jiaoshi bao, October 4, 1957 (in SCMP 1642 [October 31, 1957], 41).

158. Liu Xianzeng, "Take Active Steps to Make a Good Job of Party-building Work among Middle and Primary School Teachers," Renmin ribao, August 22, 1960 (in SCMP 2329 [September 1, 1960]).

159. For information on the Soviet situation, see R. F. Price, Marx and Education in Russia and China, p. 137; and N. Dewitt, Soviet Professional Manpower: Its Education, Training and Supply (Washington: National Science Foundation, 1955), pp. 242-244.

160. For a discussion of the concept of "red professionals," see Dennis Ray, "'Red and Expert' and China's Cultural Revolution," Pacific Affairs XLIII:1 (Spring 1970), 22-23.

161. "How the 'Gang of Four' Stamped on the Party's Policy on Intellectuals," Peking Review 12 (March 18, 1977), 19-20, 24.

162. "More Scientists and Technicians Join the Party," Peking Review 30 (July 28, 1978), 21-22.

163. Xiang Chun, "Intellectuals Are an Important Force in Socialist Revolution and Construction," Peking Review 28 (July 8, 1977), 12-14; Deng Xiaoping, "Speech at the National Educational Work Conference," Peking Review 18 (May 5, 1978), 11-12.

164. Xiaoxue jiaoshi, 1953, No. 11, p. 14.

165. For example, see "Discrimination against Primary School Teachers Cannot Be Allowed," Renmin ribao (editorial), October 5, 1956 (in SCMP 1398 [October 26, 1956], 3-4).

166. "Respect and Love Primary School Teachers," Zhongguo qingnian bao (editorial), April 10, 1956 (in SCMP 1279 [May 1, 1956], 6-8).

167. For the early 1960s, see Gao Zhiguo (first Party secretary at Yunnan University), "The Work of Schools Must Center on Teaching," Renmin ribao, April 14, 1961.

168. For a discussion of the union, see Theodore H. E. Chen, op. cit., pp. 38-42.

169. Guangdong jiaoyu, June 1956 (in ECMM 47 [August 13, 1956], 18).

170. For Jiangxi Province, for example, see the speeches by delegates to the provincial People's Congress reported in Jiangxi ribao (Jiangxi Daily), November 9, 1956, and November 13, 1956; for the equivalent in Qingdao, see "Comprehensively Foster the Initiative of Intellectuals," Qingdao ribao (Qing-

dao Daily), January 15, 1957. For a comparable use of the Chinese People's
Political Consultative Conference in Qingdao, see "Difficulties and Worries
of Women Teachers in Primary Schools," Qingdao ribao, May 11, 1957 (Appendix Vii).

171. "Speech by Lai Ruoyu at the Second National Congress of China's Educational Workers' Union," Jiaoshi bao, August 7, 1956 (in SCMP 1358 [Au-
gust 27, 1956]).

172. "Lead Well the Ranks Two Million Strong," Renmin ribao (editorial),
August 16, 1956 (in SCMP 1360 [August 19, 1956], 12-14).

173. "Speech by Lai Ruoyu...," loc. cit.

174. Wu Wenyin, "We Should Pay Sufficient Attention to Middle and Primary
School Education and Teachers," Guangming ribao, August 16, 1956 (in SCMP
1380 [October 1, 1956], 12-15).

175. Merle Goldman, "The Unique 'Blooming and Contending' of 1961-3,"
The China Quarterly 37 (January-March 1969), 54-83. For an example of
such activities in Shanghai, see "Six Middle School Principals in Shanghai
Successfully Hold Small 'Meetings of Immortals,'" Guangming ribao,
March 15, 1961 (in SCMP 2481 [April 24, 1961], 1-3).

176. MacFarquhar, op. cit., pp. 145 et seq.

177. Li Xin, "Who Says That the Political Status and Material Treatment of
Teachers Have Not Been Raised," Guizhou ribao, August 24, 1957.

178. Chengdu ribao (Chengdu Daily), July 9, 1957 (in SCMP 1631 [Octo-
ber 13, 1957], 18-25).

179. See MacFarquhar, op. cit., pp. 26, 48, 85, and 156.

180. Mao Zedong, "Speeches at the Second Session of the Eighth Party
Congress" (May 8-23, 1958) in Miscellany, Part I, p. 108.

181. For the official attempts to define and direct the Cultural Revolution
in educational institutions, see "CCP Central Committee's Notification (Draft)
concerning the GPCR in Primary Schools" (February 4, 1967), in Hu and
Seifman, eds., op. cit., pp. 203-204, and "CCP Central Committee's
Opinion on the GPCR in Middle Schools" (February 19, 1967), in ibid., pp.
205-207; "CCP Central Committee's Regulations (Draft) Governing the GPCR
Currently Under Way in Universities, Colleges and Schools" (March 7, 1957),
ibid., pp. 207-208.

182. For example, see "Middle and Primary Schools Reopen Classes and
Make Revolution," Renmin ribao (editorial), March 7, 1967 (in SCMP 3900).

183. For example, there was a Primary School Teachers Red Rebel Corps
in Guangzhou, but I have been unable to locate any reliable information on its
goals and activities: see "The Case of August 1st Combat Corps in Canton,"
Current Scene VI:8 (May 15, 1968), 4.

184. For an interesting analysis of such "generations" among intellectuals
in general, see Renmin ribao, Special Commentator, "On Policy Toward Intellectuals," Beijing Review, 5 (February 2, 1979), 10-15. The newer generation of teachers, for reasons both ideological and practical (notably, their
relative lack of expertise and experience), are clearly a problem group for
the post-Mao leadership. Perrolle reports, for example, that in college-

level institutions this group was perceived as "virtually useless" for teaching purposes and would have to be retrained (Perrolle, op. cit., p. 16).

185. Compare the analysis of Hungarian sociologist Andras Hegedus concerning the role of the "technical division of labor" in determining "the particular interests and objectives" of different social strata: The Structure of Socialist Society (London: Constable, 1977), Chap. 1.

186. "How the 'Gang of Four' Stamped on the Party's Policy on Intellectuals," Peking Review, 12 (March 18, 1978), 19-20, 24.

187. "Comments by Teng Hsiao-ping on the Presentation of Hu Yao-pang's Report" (September 26, 1975), in Chi Hsin, The Case of the Gang of Four (Hong Kong: Cosmos Books, 1977), p. 294.

188. There is a good opportunity here for fruitful comparisons with the process of interest-group politics in the Soviet Union. For general discussions of this topic, see H. G. Skilling and F. Griffiths, eds., Interest Groups in Soviet Politics (Princeton, New Jersey: Princeton University Press, 1971), esp. the article by Skilling and Griffiths; for specific accounts of educational policy, see J. J. Schwartz and W. R. Keech, "Group Influence and the Policy Process in the Soviet Union," American Political Science Review 62 (September 1968), 840-851, and P. D. Stewart, "Soviet Interest Groups and the Policy Process; The Repeal of Production Education," World Politics XXII:I (October 1969), 29-50.

189. D. E. Apter, The Politics of Modernization (Chicago: University of Chicago Press, 1965), p. 131. For a similar argument in the Chinese case, see A. Eckstein, "Economic Development and Political Change in Communist Systems," World Politics XXII:4 (July 1970), 475-495.

190. Mao Zedong, "Reading Notes on the Soviet Union's 'Political Economics'" (1961-62), in Miscellany, Part II, p. 257.

Appendix

112

II. THE SOCIAL PRESTIGE OF TEACHERS

III. THE MATERIAL LIVELIHOOD OF TEACHERS

IV. THE POLITICAL STATUS OF TEACHERS

V. TEACHERS' DISCONTENT AND DEMANDS AND CCP RESPONSES

Appendix / I:i

How Teachers Should View Their Work, Their Students, and Themselves [Excerpts] *

Ding Haochuan

It is my opinion that today every teaching comrade, be he a primary school teacher, a high school teacher, or a university professor, should take serious consideration of the following three questions:

First, how should he view his work?

Second, how should he view his students?

Third, how should he view himself?

These, I believe, are the basic questions that every teacher of today ought to be clear about. A correct understanding of these three questions is the first prerequisite enabling us to become authentic people's teachers.

I would like to present my personal view as follows for the consideration of my comrades.

1. How Should We View a Teacher's Work?

In semifeudal and semicolonial China, workers, peasants, and other laboring people were, of course, "slaves suffering hunger and cold"; even the intellectuals were in general not guaranteed a livelihood. On the other hand, China was culturally a very backward country, and intellectuals made up a very small percentage of the entire population. At the same time,

---

*Renmin jiaoyu [People's Education], Vol. 1, No. 1 (May 1950), pp. 34-37. Translated in Chinese Education (CED) XII:4 (Winter 1979-80), pp. 9-18.

intellectuals were unemployed in large numbers, and it looked
as if China had a surplus of them. Under such circumstances,
to find a job and earn a living became primary concerns for all
intellectuals. It was even more so for workers, for peasants
who had lost their land, and for other laboring people. A
teaching job was by no means "sweet." (How many teachers
were there who did not feel they were a bit "miserable and
shabby" themselves?) However, in order to get hold of a job
like this, by which "one could somehow avoid starvation, but
nevertheless could not have enough to eat," people by the tens
of thousands experienced all kinds of hardship and humiliation,
in a tragedy of internal strife, jostling against each other, and
trying to squeeze out the others. This happened in the so-
called "pure and noble educational circles." Probably every
teacher, or anyone who had been a teacher before, had such an
experience. The longer one was in the profession, the more
and "richer" would be his experience of this.

Such was the social status of teachers that it yielded positive
results. Many teachers, especially teachers in primary
schools, leaned to the revolution and to the laboring people.
Among them there were a good many who played an important
role in the revolutionary movement, and who made great contributions. At the same time, this type of social position also
had its negative impact — the burden of making a living hung
so heavily on their necks that they were unable to raise their
heads. They lost the feeling for new things and events and
their courage and confidence in advancing forward.

With Liberation, there was a tremendous change in Chinese
history. The absolute majority of the teachers were conscious
of this change and experienced fully the joy of liberation. They
therefore studied actively and worked diligently, and they re-
covered the physical exuberance of youth. This was a great
event that merited joyous celebration. But, unavoidably, there
are also those teachers, who, because of the long suffering and
the heavy burden of making a living, and in addition, because of
our inability to improve our material life in a very short time,
are still not clearly conscious of this tremendous change, and

have not yet felt the joy of Liberation. These comrades are inevitably inclined to regard today's events with their old perspectives. They regard the task of the teacher simply as an "employment opportunity," or "a way to make a living." In the case of a number of teacher-comrades whose political consciousness is weak, when their personal gains are blocked, when they are psychologically bruised, or when they are unhappy for some other reason, the devilish shadow of their old thoughts and old cognition of long standing are likely to reappear. With a harsh wooden face, purporting to be worldly, they say: "What is this new society, old society; don't we still teach to earn a living!"

Therefore, what concerns us is that we must recognize precisely the change in the times. We must realize that in the past we were acutely concerned about our individual livelihoods and individual futures. This resulted from the oppressive shackles imposed upon us by the old society. Try to recall seriously your own attitude at the time when you had not yet been shackled by the burden of earning a living, or when you were only very recently shackled. You were full of the desire to pursue truth and freedom. Analyze seriously how this feeling became eroded and diminished; then you will understand concretely the harm and injury inflicted on you by imperialism, feudal forces, and the reactionary Guomindang clique. Then, you will realize concretely that today these shackles are no longer there. Today we are liberated. Today our fatherland and our people have demanded us to stand up to be proud people's teachers; we must not be timid mediocrities preoccupied with the conversion of hours of work into quantities of millet. Today, it is still essential to recognize fully this problem and to strengthen our courage and confidence when we go forth with our heads held high.

There is still another harmful perception, which is to regard teachers as brokers of knowledge [zhishi fanmaizhe]. This kind of perception was a product of the capitalist nations and was an import. In the past, China in fact paid much attention

to "teachers of men" (stressing the influence on the student of
the teacher's moral quality). In capitalist society, where everything is commercialized and controlled by the bourgeoisie, knowledge has become a merchandise and teachers have become merchants selling knowledge. The various kinds of knowledge have
their different markets and prices. Schools and other cultural and
educational institutions have also become enterprises in which
capitalists invest.

In China, which was a semifeudal, semicolonial country, the
transformation of knowledge into a commodity and the com-
mercialization of teachers were not as thorough as in capitalist
countries. Nonetheless, in big cities and in those schools which
had been deeply influenced by capitalist "culture," these phenomena were already in existence. This perception has already
become certain people's "faith." This "faith," when combined
with the ideology of the guilds and gangs of feudal society,
caused factional struggles in the past within China's educational circles, struggles of a particularly sickening nature.

Capitalist civilization is falling and in decay. Scientific
thought is being suffocated in all the capitalist countries. (We
only need to think of one fact — that nuclear energy in the
U.S.A. can only be used to manufacture weapons for the extermination of mankind — to realize that capitalism as a social
system can no longer tolerate the development of modern science.) In the socialist USSR [there is] progress by leaps and
bounds in all kinds of cultural enterprises and spectacular accomplishments in all kinds of sciences. After the elimination
of exploitation and oppression of men by men, mankind is in an
environment of boundless power and limitless glory, manifested
in the struggle against nature. Our China is following precisely
this road and advancing steadfastly. The first step is to consolidate the people's democratic dictatorship and complete
new democratic construction. The second step is to realize
socialism. Sober recognition of these facts should enable us
to discard resolutely the habits of the knowledge merchant and
arouse our enthusiasm for teaching and research for the sake
of the welfare of the broad masses and the true and free de-

velopment of science and technology.

Finally, certain segments of our young revolutionary comrades harbor another kind of incorrect perception of the task of teaching. They regard teaching as a nonpolitical task. Being a teacher, in their minds, is not sufficiently "revolutionary," or at the least, is lacking in [political] "spice."

These comrades have exalted revolutionary enthusiasm. They are willing to exert their greatest effort in the revolutionary undertaking. This is good. But they lack specific understanding of the revolutionary cause and the concrete content of political work.

The revolutionary cause becomes an empty idea without substance if it is devoid of concrete work of various kinds in various fields. Such concrete work for the most part is troublesome, tedious, and unspectacular. It is precisely the combination of these troublesome, tedious, and unspectacular concrete tasks of various kinds and fields that make the whole spectacular revolutionary undertaking possible.

In the people's cause, any single task has its political meaning. The task of the teacher is of course no exception.

According to the reasons stated above, we have reached this conclusion: today, we cannot regard a teacher's task as simply "a way to earn a living." We want to oppose "knowledge merchants" and the attitude of aiming for profit. The task of a teacher is one of those tasks that have decisive meaning in the the entire cause of people's liberation. We must view it with a serious and responsible attitude.

2. How Should We View Our Students ?

How should we view our students ? In my opinion there are two self-evident arguments that people often ignore or hastily glance at without paying much attention to their concrete content. This neglect is not necessarily in spoken or in written form; it is expressed in actual work.

The first argument: in most cases our students are pre-adults and youths, and they are still in the period of growth.

The second argument: they are our progeny. They will in-
herit the undertaking of our generation. Because they will be
living in an epoch still newer than ours, their epoch will make
greater demands on them. At the same time, owing to the fact
that they are our progeny, the lifestyle, thoughts, and consciousness of our generation unavoidably influence them tre-
mendously.

We can all agree with these interpretations. However, in
work situations we have often found phenomena deviating from
or diametrically opposed to them. . . .

The students are our progeny. What is the meaning of this
in the concrete condition of China today? In my view, they are
not only the builders of the New Democratic society, but they
must also shoulder the historical task of establishing socialism and realizing communism. Specifically, we the teachers
should use education and training to equip them with the abundant knowledge and high moral quality necessary for carrying
out their great historical tasks.

Because what we want to nurture is a completely new generation, we cannot mold the students according to the images
of our generation. On the one hand, we have to arm them with
distilled knowledge and accumulated experience; on the other
hand, we must remember not to let them walk along aimless
paths that we have already traversed. We must remember not
to let them suffer the kind of torture or pain inflicted upon us
by our elders. Most importantly, we must not influence them
with the various defects in our thought, consciousness, and
living habits.

In response to the demands of this task, we should naturally
think of the need for us teachers to reform our own thinking
and become personal examples.

When we talk about the thought reform of teachers and
teachers' having to be models for students, today in China,
especially in the original schools of the newly liberated areas,
there is a special phenomenon: in general the young students'
enthusiasm for and speed of progress are greater than their
teachers'. This phenomenon has been particularly obvious

in schools above the secondary level. In studying political
thought at many schools, the teachers are students and the students are teachers. This of course has its objective cause.
A person of advanced age, who has been subject to the influence
of the old educational system and the grind of daily life (more
correctly, we should use the term "torment") for several
decades is not capable of being receptive to new and fresh
events and objects as quickly and effortlessly as young students. When such a person had some sort of status in the old
society (in fact, this "status" was in general empty and un-
substantial), he'll have to overcome more psychological barriers on the road to progress. The young students don't have
such barriers, or their barriers are fewer. Therefore, this
kind of situation is in general unavoidable; moreover, it is not
a bad phenomenon.

However, if on the basis of this situation we conclude that
teachers cannot play the leading role in the study of political
thought or say that under such circumstances teachers cannot
be models for students, this is not correct in my opinion.

This is because there is another side to the picture. Until
we gain an understanding of our times and until we realize the
necessity of reforming ourselves, our old knowledge and experience of our old life will perforce remain "baggage" which
constitutes a burden on the road to progress. But the day we
understand our times and realize the necessity of reforming
ourselves, past knowledge and life's past experience can become intimate and rich study material. Through an analysis
and a critique of such material, we can strengthen and consolidate our progress. Young students have no way to enjoy
this kind of study material, and we cannot expect them to have
the same results in their studies. If we can openly criticize
our own ideas in front of the students, we shall not be met with
disdain, but with sincere respect and trust. This is because we
have set them a good example of self-criticism, and because
by criticizing our past knowledge, we can then transmit some
really nourishing knowledge to them.

How should we view our students? They are new lives in the

process of growth; they are our progeny. On them rests the
historical responsibility for the construction of the New Democracy, socialism, and communism. Let us nurture them.
Let us teach them well. Let us set a good example before
them, to enable them to shoulder the necessary historical task
bestowed upon them by the times.

3. How Do We View Ourselves?

In the old society most people looked down on the teaching
profession. We teachers also had a very low opinion of ourselves. In those days, only those few who were appreciated by
the reactionary ruling class were considered successful. The
great majority were depressed and endured life's pain and
mental torture. They lost faith in their future, and thus adopted
a slipshod attitude toward their lives. This was an extremely
prevalent phenomenon.

Since Liberation, there has been a fundamental change in the
teacher's position. Teachers have begun to serve the masses
of people with their brainpower. In some regions they have already established unions of educational workers. Such unions
will be formed everywhere in the country. As mental workers,
teachers are now ranked among the laboring people.

To the great majority of teachers, their being put into the
ranks of the laboring people is their greatest honor. Among
those who are blind to their times and retain much of their
old thinking and consciousness, there is the sense of "status
demotion." Among others who maintain a slovenly attitude
toward world and national affairs, their own jobs, and personal
lives, there is "indifference." They teach and draw a salary
and that's that. This is not strange. In general, the mind invariably trails behind reality. It requires a period of time and
a process of ideological struggle to emancipate the mind from
its age-old consciousness.

The fact is that teachers are people who earn their living by
selling their mental labor. Once unemployed, i.e., when there
are no buyers for their mental labor, then they face the prob-

lem of earning a living. On this point, teachers are no different from the janitors in the schools and the workers in the
factories and mines. The only difference is that the latter sell
physical labor whereas the former sell mental labor.

Then why is it that many of us — before Liberation, perhaps
the great majority — have not recognized this fact, and are convinced that we and the working class have nothing in common?
This was because we are intellectuals, because our knowledge
was gained through a feudal, semifeudal, and semicolonial education. This education served the landlords, capitalists, and
imperialism. It taught us to help control and exploit the laboring people. This type of education did not want you to look
downward to unite with the masses; rather, it wanted you to
look upward, "to rise above all else." At the same time, this
mental labor was for the most part individual labor — teaching,
preparing lectures, etc. — that gave us a mistaken and dis-
torted perception. We tended to feel that our own individual
cleverness and ability were the decisive elements. We distrusted the masses and were unaccustomed to collective life.
Although our lifestyle was not as affluent as that of the exploiting classes of landlords and capitalists, even a low-paid
primary school teacher habitually wore a long gown to distinguish himself from the laboring people. Our lifestyle was
modeled after that of the exploitative classes.

It is about time we liberate ourselves from this erroneous
consciousness and move resolutely closer to the laboring people. From our thoughts to our lifestyle, we should become
members of the laboring people. It is time we endeavor to
make ourselves into excellent people's teachers, to contribute
our energy to the construction of a democratic, independent,
rich, and unified new China.

In order to be teachers in the new China, to shoulder the
responsibility of the people's educational construction, we must
raise our thinking, consciousness, and work attitude to a proper
level. This is the task that we face.

First of all we must study Marxism-Leninism-Mao Zedong
Thought. There is no exception to this. To be a master of

one's own country, to be a member of the working class, and
to be a people's teacher in the new China — a person in charge
of leading the younger generation in the construction of the
great history of the new China — one cannot but study this.
Stalin once pointed out to the scientists and intellectuals of the
USSR the following:

There is no necessity for a medical specialist to be simultaneously a physi-
cist or a botanist. The reverse is also true. But there is one scientific discipline whose knowledge must be possessed by all the Bolsheviks in all scientific disciplines. This is Marxism-Leninism. It is a science of society, of
laws of social development, of laws of development of the proletarian revolution, of laws of the development of the undertaking of socialist construction,
and of the victory of Communism.

A Leninist can never be merely a specialist in his chosen science. He
should also be at the same time a politician and a social activist, actively
concerned with his country's fate, informed in the laws of social development,
and skilled in the application of these laws. Furthermore, he strives to be a
person who participates actively in the nation's political leadership work
(Stalin, Problems of Leninism).

These words can be similarly applied to us teachers. They
are equally pertinent.

The second point is that we must master our work. We must
continuously generalize our experience, elevate our thoughts in
teaching, improve our teaching method, and make our own work
truly lively and in coordination with the rhythms of the rapidly
advancing new China and the new epoch!

My opinion is that only by firmly establishing this direction and
actively striving in this direction can each of us become an
authentic people's teacher.

The Soviet Teachers I Have Seen*

*From the Notes Taken on
My Trip to Russia*

Zhang Lianfeng

After more than two months' visit and study in Soviet
Russia, I deeply understand that in socialist countries the profession of people's teacher is one of the most respected professions. The secondary school students we met, especially
girl students, were all willing to choose teaching as their profession. According to the headmaster of the First Normal
[Teacher Training] School in Moscow, each year during the
period of entrance examinations, he would personally conduct
interviews with each of the applicants. In the conversation he
would introduce the conditions of the school and ask the applicant's opinions. If he should discover that a student had not
applied to the normal school on [his or hers] own initiative,
or had no great interest in the education of young children, he
would dissuade the applicants from taking the entrance examination. Nevertheless, each year applicants who take the entrance examinations to the normal school are very numerous
even though these applicants all have the qualifications to apply to other schools. From this we can tell how much the
young people of Soviet Russia love the teaching profession.

We participated in the activities of the Young Pioneers at the
No. 702 Secondary School in Moscow. On that day we learned
how the Young Pioneers spent their Pioneers' Day and saw the

---

*Xiaoxue jiaoyu tongxun [Primary School Education Bulletin], 1956, No. 5
(April 20, 1956), pp. 7-8. Translated in CED XII:4 (Winter 1979-80), pp. 19-26.

happy childhood of working people in Soviet Russia. At the
same time we also felt deeply the tremendous friendship the
Soviet teachers and students had for us Chinese people. Let's
not talk about this. Let's talk about the time after we had
finished our activities and we were invited to the downstairs
dining room for a meal; we had never expected to have another
kind of warm reception.

In this not-too-large, rectangular dining room were arranged
three rows of tables covered with snow-white tableclothes. On
the tables were fruit, candies, refreshments, cigarettes, water-
melon seeds, and so forth. Many beautifully dressed female
comrades shook hands with us warmly and invited us to sit
down. Equally warmly, they shook hands with the Soviet teachers who had accompanied us and invited them to sit down too.
These hostesses filled the plates that were in front of us and
the Soviet teachers with candies, fruit, and refreshments. They
repeatedly urged us to eat. They also used a special kind of
small teapot to serve us tea (it was said that this was copying
the Chinese custom as we knew that our Soviet comrades did
not use small teapots when they drank tea).

Who were these hostesses? After the headmaster's introduction we learned that they were parents of the students.
The headmaster said that, after learning that the Chinese
guests were coming, they contributed money on their own initiative to have this reception with abundant refreshments, and
they personally came to entertain the Chinese guests.

This occasion moved us greatly. In a conversation [between
one of them and us], we not only felt their friendship for the
Chinese people, we also keenly felt the respect and love they
had for the teachers of the school. "We have entrusted to them
the future of our children. We believe they will not fail the
mission vouchsafed to them by the Soviet nation." From her
expression when she said this I could detect her respect for
the teachers.

While we were in Soviet Russia, no matter where we were,
no matter what occasion it was, whenever people mentioned
teachers, they all revealed a sense of admiration. We also

heard the story told by many teachers that when they conducted family visits they were received very warmly by the parents.

Speaking about the concern the Soviet nation has for teachers, I only want to describe the conditions of a "teachers' home" [jiaoshizhi jia] to explain the general concern, because I know that you are already familiar with how the Soviet nation has guaranteed an abundant material life for teachers, how it has given subsidies to teachers who have many children, and how it has emphasized helping teachers improve and elevate their education.

What I saw was a "teachers' home" in Leningrad. In 1918, shortly after the victory of the "October" socialist revolution, Comrade Lenin personally gave the order to donate the palace of a Czarist prince to teachers to be converted into a "teachers' home." We visited this place on a Saturday evening. It was not too cold this November in Leningrad. The snow melted as soon as it had fallen. The water in the city's rivers was still running. Since it was very close, we walked over. On the way we saw many pairs of people also walking toward that huge building. Among them, most of the females were teachers, and the males were their husbands or boyfriends. Many of the males were military officers in uniform. We followed the others and entered the gate, removed our coats and hats, and ascended the marble staircase to the spacious lounge on the second floor. Dancing music was being played and some young female teachers in finely woven dresses were already dancing. A comrade in charge led us on a tour of the place. Within this grand and elegant building there were many great halls, including a ballroom, a theater, a concert hall, a gallery, an exhibition hall, rooms for chess and ping-pong, and reading rooms. There were also many smaller rooms for teachers to use. The lounges and corridors all had sofas. On the walls of these halls were famous murals, sculptures, and oil paintings. In one of the corridors we saw huge portraits of the meritorious and superior teachers of Leningrad, some of whom we had already met.

We were invited to a concert hall which had a capacity of

1,000 seats. The host seated us in the front row. [That] was
the day when the most famous actors and artists of Leningrad
performed especially for the teachers. According to the Soviet
comrade who accompanied us, Soviet actors are all willing to
give free performances or performances at a reduced rate for
teachers. Teachers can see performances by some of the
best actors at the "teachers' home" every weekend. Sometimes
it is free of charge, sometimes the fees are reduced. Teachers
can come with their own partners.

That evening the performance included piano solos, soprano
solos, a female chorus, excerpts from plays and ballets, and
talk shows. The performers were all first-rate actors and ac-
tresses. Although we did not understand the Russian language,
we could still see how absorbed the audience was in the performance.

In every one of the big Soviet cities there are different numbers of "teachers' homes." We were also guests at a "teachers' home" in Moscow. There, the furniture and the decor
were even more beautiful than in Leningrad, and the building
had been newly constructed. It was more compact and convenient.

We also went to a resort city, Sochi, on the shores of the
Black Sea. This beautiful city is like a park, with a concentration
of all the tropical and subtropical flowers and plants. Many spot-
lessly white resort houses are built along the seashore. In
front of the houses are fountains and parks, and behind the
houses are bathing beaches. In these houses are all kinds
of recreational and athletic equipment and excellent medical
facilities. Rooms are of two kinds: singles and doubles. In
every room there is a private bath equipped with seawater
faucets and warm-water faucets.

Every Soviet teacher has the opportunity to go to such a
place every year for a rest, either free of charge, or at a reduced rate. All Soviet residents, whether young or old, enjoy
free medical care. Of course, teachers also enjoy all such
privileges. When we saw this, we could not help thinking of the
great economic strength of the socialist nation and the fact

that the socialist economy is for the welfare of the working people.

The spirit of the Soviet teacher at work and his socialist attitude toward labor are very impressive and moving. On this point, I would merely cite a few examples.

One afternoon when we were visiting the No. 711 Secondary School in Moscow, the lady principal gave us a guided tour to different parts of the school long after the students had left. On the fifth floor everything was quiet. The principal opened the doors of the classrooms one by one, and we followed close behind her. None of us had expected that there would be a female teacher standing on the platform and lecturing quietly to two students, a boy and a girl, in front of her in the first row of seats. On the left side of the classroom, close to the wall, sat a male comrade; he was the parent of one of the students and he had been invited by the teacher to come and listen in on the instruction. The female teacher told us that she was making up the lesson for the two students because they had for some reason missed a lesson in Russian the day before. In order to make up for the missed lesson for these two students, the female teacher conducted her instruction in exactly the same way as she would in regular class. She extended a special invitation to the parent to come and watch so that he might better help educate his child.

Later, the lady principal told us that the teacher was correct in what she was doing. This was because in Soviet schools whenever a student misses a lesson, the teacher has to make up the lesson immediately. When we were visiting the No. 321 Secondary School in Leningrad, the principal also told us that the Soviet school strictly requires the teacher to be responsible for the student's every lesson. The school will not change its curriculum for any reason; nor can the teacher make any excuses for failing to teach well.

Soviet teachers do their work in this serious spirit. In the past, some of our comrades had thought perhaps the teaching load of Soviet teachers was relatively light. This time, with our own eyes, we saw the opposite. Soviet teachers have a

heavy teaching load. The Ivanovsk Village Primary School in
the suburbs of Moscow was one of the primary schools to which
we paid particular attention on our visit. The lady principal,
Comrade Shahawa, is a mother of two children, a student at an
evening university and at the same time the head teacher of the
fourth grade with a weekly teaching load of twenty-four hours.
Of course, as principal, she has to be responsible for all matters concerning teachers and students. The primary-school
section of our delegation visited and studied her primary
school for six days. As always, Comrade Shahawa taught for
four hours in the morning, and then, at noon, she set up refreshments for our comrades in the delegation (because of the
school's small size, there was no dining room). In the afternoon, she analyzed the lessons with the comrades in the delegation and answered their questions until about three or four
o'clock. Then she would go home to take care of her house-
keeping chores, and in the evening she would attend an evening
university. This continued for six consecutive days. From
start to finish, Comrade Shahawa worked spiritedly and happily. Our comrades were very grateful to her, and we made a
special call on her family. Her home is beautifully furnished.
The beds have mattresses with steel springs; on the floor are
beautiful rugs; on the wall is a huge oil painting; at the win-
dows are snow-white curtains and dark blue velvet draperies.
There are complete sets of sofas and chests-of-drawers.
There is also a television. On the table there are many toys.
Her two children spend the days in the day-care center but are
brought home for the evening. She has to give them lessons,
and only after putting them to bed can she go to the evening
university to study. This Comrade Shahawa not only manages
the school very well, but she is also a methodical housekeeper.
She not only works well, but also lives her life well, and studies well.

Why does Shahawa live such a busy and happy life? Aside
from her love for educational work and her optimistic communist view of life, she has a more immediate hope, which is
that, when she completes her courses at the evening university,

she will be promoted to be a high school teacher.

When we were visiting the No. 204 Secondary School in Moscow, a young female teacher explained to us her work experience as a head teacher of the various grades. In the beginning,
when she graduated from normal school, she could only start
by teaching first graders. But as soon as she began teaching,
she joined a higher normal school's correspondence course in
the humanities. Because she was good in her studies, she
moved up, together with her first graders, year after year until the ninth grade (comparable to the second year of our senior
high school). Of course she already had the qualifications and
ability to teach her class of students up to their senior high
school graduation. She said, "I have taught them since they
were first graders to the time when they are nearly adults. I
understand every little peculiarity in the growth of each of
them. I love them. I'm happy, but I am also very tense from
beginning to end."

Now this young female teacher not only does her classroom
work well; she teaches courses in the humanities as well. She
spends all her energy and time on her students. In Soviet Russia, teachers like her are not scarce.

Are young teachers the only ones who work and study so
seriously? No. We met an elderly female teacher at the Moscow Teachers Institute. Her hair has already turned white,
but she is still vigorous. She gave us a report on her experiences in teaching composition. She teaches three literature
classes in a Moscow high school. At the same time she also
teaches classes at the Institute three days a week. She receives full pay from the high school, and she receives an instructor's half-time pay from the Institute. The students
taught by her are not only good in the humanities but also have
good marks in other subjects. For instance, among the sixty-
seven students of last year's graduating class, sixteen received
gold and silver medals. This, in Soviet Russia, is a rare
achievement.

This elderly teacher works an average of over eleven hours
a day. She has to teach three classes in literature, and every

day she has compositions to correct. Each composition takes about thirty minutes; some take as much as three times that. She needs three hours to prepare for her classes every day. She also goes to movies and plays quite often with her students, and afterward she has to guide the students in their analysis and criticism [of the movies and plays]. At the time, we unceremoniously asked her to explain how she managed her time. After repeated calculations, she gave the same answer as before — every day she works for more than eleven hours. She said to us with a smile: "It is a bit demanding, but I am happy. As we have chosen this glorious profession, we should wholeheartedly do our job well." When we heard her words we were truly moved.

We met another literature teacher. He is almost sixty years old. He has taught literature for twenty-seven years but is still taking correspondence courses on Marxist aesthetics. There was also a mathematics teacher who has been teaching for over forty years. She is very serious in preparing every lesson. We saw her lesson plans. Her neatness and seriousness put us to shame. We also met a high school geography teacher. He is a corresponding member of the Academy of Educational Science. There are also high school teachers who have already become candidates for a doctoral degree. Nevertheless, these comrades are still quite humble, and they exert great effort in their study and work. They characterized a teacher's work this way: he has to progress constantly, and he has to be continuously interested in his work. If you think that once you have taught a course many times you need not prepare it seriously, you'll lose interest, and of course you will not be able to teach your students well.

Soviet teachers have a good life and a boundless future. They work hard and study hard. They have the respect and concern of their people and their nation. These can only be achieved in a socialist country.

The call made by Lenin over thirty years ago — "We ought to raise the position of the public school teachers of our nation to a level beyond the reach of teachers in capitalist countries" — is being realized in Soviet Russia today. In our People's China, this beautiful prospect will also be realized in the near future.

Be an Engineer of the Human Soul*

Liu Shi

My young friends:

First I must congratulate you, because you have successfully completed your studies at the middle [secondary] level
and will soon graduate. After graduation, all of you will have
opportunities to receive higher education. This is also something worthy of celebration.

Today I want to introduce to you the higher normal colleges.
These colleges train a special type of engineer for our father-
land, the type that is respectfully called "soul engineers."
They are the people's high school teachers.

This year, aside from the forty-five thousand freshmen
scheduled to be admitted to the higher normal colleges, these
colleges will admit twenty thousand more, if there are too
many applicants. The total number to be admitted will constitute a sizable percentage of the total number of students to be
admitted this year to all higher educational institutions. This
is because in order to construct socialism and to realize the
cultural revolution, we must have large numbers of qualified
high school graduates. At present, there are not enough of
them. Why is that? The expansion of high school education
lags behind the requirements of the nation. Why don't we es-

---

*Zhongguo qingnian bao [Chinese Youth News] (Beijing), May 20, 1956. Trans-
lated in CED XII:4 (Winter 1979-80), pp. 27-31.

tablish more high schools? One of the principal reasons is
that we don't have enough high school teachers. Consequently,
this year the number of students to be admitted to higher normal colleges [where teachers are trained] is even higher than
those admitted to engineering colleges. This is because the
nation is urgently in need of trained teachers.

According to the current situation in the development of culture and education, higher normal college education is an important link in the entire educational enterprise. If we regard
basic education as an "industry," then higher normal college
education can be regarded as the "steel industry." The steel
industry manufactures a large quantity of steel materials to
supply the various machine industries for the manufacture of
all kinds of products; without steel, there is no industry. The
higher normal colleges train high school teachers. Only with
an adequate number of high school teachers can we train a
large number of high school students. Only with an increase
of the number of high school students and with the improvement
of their quality as well as quantity can we have a reliable
foundation for the development of higher education, science,
and technology. It is only with many more high school students
who are good in academic work and in citizenship can we tackle
the development of compulsory education at the primary level,
the people's cultural revolution, defense facilities, and the
agricultural and industrial productive enterprises.

The undertaking of building socialism in our fatherland requires all kinds of engineers, including the people's teachers,
the engineers of the souls of mankind. The present-day industrial revolution and cultural revolution are intimately related. Our country needs two different types of engineers;
they shoulder different responsibilities, but they work together
to build a great fatherland. This requires that each year among
high school graduates there will be many who will firmly dedicate themselves to becoming people's teachers and apply for
admission to higher normal colleges.

It is the responsibility of the people's teachers to train and
educate the new generations. The nation delegates this task to

the teachers and depends on them to train the new generation
to become fully developed persons and builders of a communist society. Is there any occupation which is more
glorious?

From your own living experience as young people you can
understand the honor associated with the profession of teaching. Haven't you been receiving training and education from
your teachers ever since you were very little? Haven't your
knowledge, thought, feelings, and behavior been influenced by
your teachers? Without these teachers, can you imagine that
you could walk into a college today? I have often thought about
many teachers from my high school days who commanded respect. The foundation for my knowledge and my study habits
was basically formed in my high school days. That was
around the time of the "May Fourth" movement [1919], when
schools were not so well run and cannot be compared with today's schools. Still, I benefited greatly. Now, as I write this
piece for publication, images of my many teachers float in my
mind — their faces, styles of speech, and mannerisms....
Although there has been an interval of thirty years, these
images have not faded. I think it will be the same with you.
Everybody has his or her favorite teachers. When you are
about to leave your high school, there will well up in your pure
heart a sentiment testifying to your reluctance to depart. Don't
you think this type of work, which cannot be forgotten after
many decades, is a worthy activity for us?

Today, however, there are still young people who lack enthusiasm in applying for admission to higher normal colleges.
Why? The main reasons are that in old China, teachers had
no social status and were poorly paid, and normal school education was not valued. The influence of the past prevents our
young friends today from seeing the new situation in normal
school education.

Today, the Party and the government value the people's
teachers and are concerned about their welfare. Teachers
have opportunities to participate in all kinds of political life.
Their material life and working conditions are improving step

by step. In the near future, our country will institute many
ways to give recognition to teachers, including the awarding of
honor badges, medals, and honorary titles. Teachers have ample opportunity to make great contributions to the nation. Just
as Lenin said, "We ought to raise the status of the people's
teachers in our country to the level that can never be reached
by teachers in capitalist societies." The honors and rights
that are enjoyed by teachers in the USSR today will also be obtained by our teachers one by one.

Maybe some will say: "The teachers' distant future will be
bright; but in today's higher normal colleges I can't acquire
the knowledge I need." This is because they do not understand
the state of development of today's higher normal colleges.

Now, I want to tell everybody, a new system of higher normal college education has fundamentally been established. The
facilities and regulations of higher normal colleges and technical normal colleges are basically the same as those in the nation's higher educational institutions. It is only because of different requirements that facilities differ somewhat. In the past
several years, the nation has spent a considerable sum in
building higher normal colleges. Each one now has gathered a
sizable teaching staff, including many nationally known instructors. We can learn a good deal from them.

More importantly, as of this moment, higher normal colleges
and technical normal schools have already begun to teach according to a newly devised teaching plan and teaching outline,
a new teaching organization, and new teaching methods. Science and knowledge in higher normal colleges have, in fact,
been raised to a high academic level. The content of the various technical sciences is also very rich and there are the
requisite laboratories for scientific research, now being used
by many of the students. The study of Marxist-Leninist theory
is especially emphasized in higher normal colleges. Other subjects, such as art and physical education, are also emphasized because these are necessary parts of a people's teacher's knowledge
and training. To sum up, today's higher normal colleges are able
to completely satisfy young people's thirst for knowledge.

My young friends, I'd better stop talking. The saying goes, "It is better to see it for yourself." Please go visit a higher normal college in your vicinity. Talk with the instructors there and the students you know. Go and chat. Then you'll be much better informed.

We and the sixty thousand students in the nation's higher normal colleges ardently welcome all of our young friends who have resolved to be people's teachers, to take the entrance examinations for higher normal colleges, and to contribute their strength to train the next generation for our fatherland.

Do a Good Job of Inculcating a Sense of Professionalism among Normal School Students*

Jinan Normal School

In strengthening its work in political indoctrination, our normal school has simultaneously paid attention to the inculcation of a sense of professionalism in order to make the students dearly love their educational careers and of a willingness to devote their entire lives to educational work. This is very important.

The following is a discussion on the methods for and experiences of carrying out the inculcation of a sense of professionalism among our students.

Carry Out the Inculcation of a Sense of Professionalism on the Foundation of Political Indoctrination

The inculcation of a sense of professionalism is an organic component of political indoctrination. In order to have a professional sense of "loving the children and loving the people's educational enterprise," we must first have the thoughts and feelings of loving both the Party and socialism, and also good moral quality. The inculcation of a sense of professionalism cannot be carried out alone, in isolation from the work of political indoctrination.

To inculcate in the students a sense of professionalism, we realize that we must first raise their political consciousness.

---

*Guangming ribao [Guangming Daily], March 9, 1962. Translated in CED XII:4 (Winter 1979-80), pp. 32-38. Jinan Normal is a school for training primary school teachers.

This is the principal content of political indoctrination in our school, and this is also the foundation for the inculcation of a sense of professionalism. The most basic reason some students are unwilling to become primary school teachers is that they have not yet embraced the viewpoint of wholeheartedly serving the people. We [must] carry out education among the students on the four viewpoints (the class viewpoint, mass viewpoint, labor viewpoint, and dialectical materialist viewpoint); raise the students' political consciousness; and gradually form a revolutionary philosophy of life. Along with this continual heightening of consciousness and the gradual solution of the problem of world outlook, if we firmly carry out the inculcation of a sense of professionalism and develop in the students a dedication to people's education, we shall reap even better educational results.

The next task is to develop in the students a communist moral character. The inculcation of a sense of professionalism is not merely required to solve the problem of whether students are willing to be teachers, but also the question of how to be a good teacher. Not only are we responsible for the sense of professionalism in the students while they are in school, but we must also be concerned about their work posts after they leave school. The nation demands a certain standard in the moral character and behavior of its teachers. We should educate the students to respect the nation's demand, to strengthen their moral cultivation, to love children, to be consistent in words and deeds, to be hard-working and frugal, to be exemplary persons in thoughts and activities, and to be worthy of the name of teacher. Strengthening communist moral education may stimulate in the student a sense of honor in dedicating himself to be a people's teacher and facilitate the establishment and consolidation of a sense of professionalism on his part.

Situational education [xingshi jiaoyu] is one important component of the school's political indoctrination work. A clear grasp of his situation has a direct relationship to the development of a student's sense of professionalism and the consoli-

dation of this outlook. When the student has a clear idea about
his situation, his political feelings will be exuberant, he will be
energetic in his studies, and his sense of professionalism will
be stable. Therefore, in our political indoctrination work we
pay a good deal of attention to situational education. Since
1958, we have successively carried out, among the students,
education on the Three Red Flags of the general line, the Great
Leap Forward, and the people's communes and the revolutionary tradition of hard struggle. This has enabled our students,
under the bright glow of the Three Red Flags, to maintain from
start to finish a correct attitude of "studying for the sake of the
fatherland," and has enabled graduates to accept happily the
posts assigned to them by their fatherland. They are willing
to go to work in the most difficult regions.

Permeate Your Teaching with the Inculcation of a Sense of Professionalism

Politics, Chinese language, mathematics, and professional
subjects constitute the main curriculum of the normal school
at the secondary level. By teaching these courses, we can not
only equip the student to be a people's teacher with cultural and
scientific knowledge and specialized technique, but we can also
help the student to develop a sense of professionalism and to
consolidate this sense.

In teaching political courses, we have emphasized education
in systematic basic theories to arm students with Marxism-
Leninism-Mao Zedong Thought, and to firmly establish the political direction of the proletariat. At the same time, we also
take into consideration the existing problems concerning the
students' sense of professionalism and have organized lectures
on special topics. Lectures such as "Vow to Be a Qualified
People's Teacher" and "The Purpose of Our Studies and the
Problem of Our World Outlook" have been offered to help the
students improve their understanding and to solve some concrete ideological problems arising from their studies.

Courses in Chinese are rich in ideological material. Many

lessons such as "Old Mr. Xu Is Not Old" and "Old Mr. Ren Ruiqing" are good teaching materials for the introduction of a sense of professionalism to our students. Focusing on these lessons, we have, in addition, selected and compiled Chairman Mao's "Letter to Comrade Xu Teli," "The Work of a Teacher Is Noble Work," and other excellent children's literature as supplementary teaching materials. We have had good results in the introduction of a sense of professionalism to our students through the teaching of Chinese courses. The grand and elegant sayings that have become popular among the students, such as, "teachers are engineers of the souls of mankind" and "teachers have the honorable mission of training communist successors" were, to a large extent, influenced by these lessons.

We can inculcate students with a sense of professionalism through professional courses. In the teaching of these courses, you can educate students on educational policy and strategy, teaching methods, and theoretical knowledge. This makes the students realize that education is a science and that teachers are not "without a future"; they have much to do.

Practice teaching should be conducted well. The courses on practice teaching are generally offered to students in their graduation year (the third year). For the students, practice teaching gives them the chance to put into practice what they have learned in school and their knowledge of teaching. It is also the stage during which they deepen their sense of professionalism. The common saying goes: "In all things, to begin is difficult." The difficulties that trouble them at the beginning and the rebuffs they experience will often damage their sense of professionalism. Therefore, we have to be all the more concerned about students who are taking courses in practice teaching, with respect to their ideological performance, the quality and quantity of their knowledge, and the improvement of their professional skills. We must carry out good preparatory work in practice teaching, in cooperation with the schools, to create good conditions for practice teaching, and to have a good impact on student teachers. Experience has proved that

the student teachers' love for children and love for teaching are
developed and consolidated through practice teaching.

Start from Reality, Give Educational Content
Different Emphases at Different Stages

The students' problems in their sense of professionalism
have different concrete manifestations according to their different stages of studies. Therefore, carrying out the inculcation of a sense of professionalism has to begin with practical
reality, and educational emphases may not be the same at all
times.

New students by and large lack understanding of the nature
and tasks of the normal school. Influenced by remnant ideas
from the old society that despised primary school teachers,
they feel inferior. Focusing on their attitude, in the first academic year we emphasize education on the purpose of their
studies. This makes the students understand the status and
function of the teacher in socialist construction and in the educational enterprise, and develops a sense of pride in being
specialized in normal school education. At this stage we should
emphasize solving the main ideological problems among most
students to make them feel at ease in their studies. Then we
can advance in an orderly fashion and deepen [their learning]
step by step. We must not be greedy or impatient, hoping to
summarily solve all the problems in a very short time.

When the students begin their second academic year, their
knowledge has increased. But they do not understand the requirements of primary school teaching. Therefore some students easily develop the idea that they are "doing work unworthy of their talents," or they adopt the attitude that they
will learn the skill first and leave everything else to the
future. On the surface it seems that the students' ideology is
more stable than the year before. In reality, there are problems which have yet to be fundamentally tackled. We think that
at its root, the problem of the sense of professionalism is one
of world outlook. The inculcation of a sense of professionalism

should be built on the foundation of the first year. It has to start by solving the problem of world outlook. It cannot be confined to questions of the moment.

After two years' education, the problem of whether the students are willing to be primary school teachers is basically solved. Nevertheless, you are still sure to find some students who are critical of the location and conditions of their future assignment, and even fuss over the pay. Some students with good marks show their self-satisfaction, while those with low marks are depressed. The substance of these problems is still the issue of attitude toward the teaching profession. Thus, we cannot slacken, in the slightest, in the inculcation of a sense of professionalism in the students. Aside from continuing education on their world outlook, in this stage we should unite education closely with practice and develop in the students thoughts and feelings of love for children. We should unite the task of assigning graduates to their posts with education on the need for more thorough obedience to the Party and the father-land's need for education. This makes students happy to accept allocation [of jobs] [fucong fenpei] and willing to go to their work posts with complete confidence.

Develop Extracurricular Activity Around the Inculcation of a Sense of Professionalism

Touring and visiting; inviting heroes, model personages, and superior teachers to give reports; conducting effective discussion sessions around some central themes; convening meetings of delegates representing superior workers among the graduates; maintaining correspondence with graduates on a regular basis; and organizing cultural and recreational activities are all good methods for inculcating a sense of professionalism. When we organize our students to visit primary schools, we receive an enthusiastic welcome and warm reception from the teachers and students. Our students are deeply moved. During the visits, the children raise many questions for our students to answer. For example, they ask: "How did Gargarin get into

space?" "Why should we aid Cuba?" and so forth. All this
stimulates and challenges our students to study harder and to
seek progress. After hearing a report by Comrade Chen
Changfeng, who had been Chairman Mao's bodyguard, and a report by the engineer Niu Fahe, who had started life as a common apprentice, the students received an indelible education.
They consciously criticized the individualistic thoughts expressed in fussing over status and pay. After listening to a
talk by Ma Xiuju, a teacher in the primary school attached to
the normal school, who introduced the history of the educational
transformation of naughty children into well-behaved ones,
our students reached a more advanced understanding of the important meaning of a teacher's work. After we organized a
number of class discussion sessions on themes such as "Being
a red and expert primary school teacher," and "how to deal with
status and pay," students were made even more aware of the
direction of progress and the relationship between the individual
and the nation. When we mobilized students in our school to
correspond with our graduates who had been assigned to work
posts in the Yimeng Mountains, our students were very encouraged. All these extracurricular activities can strengthen
the students' sense of professionalism.

(Manuscript furnished by [the magazine]
Shandong jiaoyu [Shandong Education].)

Learn from and Serve the Workers and Peasants*

Kang Jintang

I began my job as a physics teacher in 1957. At that time, while I was eager to make a good job of my work, the students were always dissatisfied with me. I thought that the trouble was due to the low level of my knowledge. I therefore spent almost all my energies on the study of theoretical books. But the result was that the lessons I gave were nothing better and were more abstract and pedantic. My students were bored and I was at a loss to know what to do.

I read some of Chairman Mao's writings and his appeal to the revolutionary young intellectuals to form one with the workers and peasants. However, I thought the appeal was made to the youths on the industrial and agricultural front, to the administrative cadres, or to the higher intellectuals and had not much to do with me.

In 1958 the school Party branch mobilized us teachers to take part in the three great revolutionary movements in factories and rural districts. The secretary to the Party branch led us to perform labor and carry out scientific experiments in neighboring factories and rural districts. Only then was I brought to the road of forming one with the workers and peasants.

Between 1958 and 1960 I threw myself into the class struggle

---

*Wuli tongbao [Physics Bulletin], No. 8 (August 18, 1966). Translated in Survey of China Mainland Magazines (SCMM) — Supplement, No. 13 (November 17, 1966), pp. 8-10.

and productive labor. I took part in the political movements,
fought against calamities and did harvesting jobs. I took an active part in the construction of the first hydroelectric power
station in our xian, and in the technical innovation campaigns
of some factories. In the big classroom of factories and rural
districts I learned from the worker and peasant masses many
revolutionary ideas and much practical knowledge not found in
books.

First, the worker and peasant masses taught me the revolutionary idea of "for whom I should work as a teacher." I saw
with my own eyes the pressing need for educated youths in the
rural districts. How the workers and poor and lower-middle
peasants expected the teachers to train red successors for
them! When I was at Tianbao hydroelectric power station a
commune member told me: "Tianbaoshan does not worry about
shortage of water or grain, but only about shortage of young
people who are capable of both mental and manual labor." To
bring up successors to the workers and the poor and lower-
middle peasants, to provide socialist construction with a group
of educated youths capable of manual and mental labor — such
was the honor of people's teachers. It also made made me
realize that my responsibility was heavy.

I therefore reversed my wrong way of thinking — "devote myself to teaching to the neglect of training of man, and concern
myself with what is happening in class and not with what is
happening after class." I then not only made a good job of
teaching in class but also interested myself in the thought and
life of the students after class. I was particularly interested
in the progress the children of workers and peasants made in
their studies and thought.

At the same time, I felt that the most important thing for me
to do in order to bring up revolutionary successors was to set
an example and play an exemplary role. To this end I took an
active part in the political struggles and seriously implemented
the Party's education policy in these years. When I taught lessons
or corrected students' work, I had a feeling that I was performing labor to produce grain and turn out new products for the

fatherland. I felt that when I was giving lessons and writing with chalk I was also working for the revolution. I made up my mind to work as a people's teacher and a revolutionary as long as I live.

Second, the "foolish old man's" spirit manifested by the worker and peasant masses who dared to fight and win encouraged me to break through the professional barrier. Whenever I ran into difficulties in my work and took a pessimistic view of my ability, I recalled to my mind how comrade workers of the machine plant and the woodwork factory worked hard to innovate machine tools day and night, how the poor and lower-middle peasants and commune members repaired the long embankment in heavy rain and storm. I gained confidence and made up my mind to learn from others right away, to learn the hardworking spirit of the workers and peasants. I learned bit by bit and continued to learn. In eight years I accumulated a definite volume of teaching data and my professional level was constantly raised. I was promoted from a teacher of junior middle two to a teacher of senior middle three.

Third, the worker and peasant masses taught me much practical knowledge and skill and made me find the direction of teaching reform. When I went to Tianbao to take part in the construction of a hydroelectric power station I brought with me many books on theories, being confident that the knowledge contained in the books would be enough to meet my needs. My first assignment was to survey the flow in the branches of the Baocheng irrigation canal so as to determine the location of the hydroelectric power station and the size of the generator to be installed. I adopted the "flotation method" found in the book, and the result was that I made mistakes in the survey. Later, comrades peasants helped us in the survey. They pointed out to us that the "flotation method" did not take into account the fall of water level in the canal and the different speeds of flow at the upper and lower strata. This matter gave me a great education.

Once, I gave lessons in "fuses." My head was full of theories but, lacking practical knowledge and skill, I was afraid of con-

tact electrification at the time of demonstrating the "connection
of fuses." My hands trembled and the electric light flashed.
Later, I worked with the power station workers to install circuits. I learned not only the real ability to prevent contact electrification but also much electrical knowledge not found in
books. Now, many students welcome the lessons in electricity
as given by me.

In agricultural and industrial production I have had many bit-
ter experiences in the use of only my theoretical knowledge.
"Once bitten twice shy." It was only after I experienced difficulty as a result of divorce from reality that I was conscious
of the sweetness of Chairman Mao's directive. Chairman Mao
said: "Man's knowledge comes mainly from material productive
labor...." "Not integrated with practice, the knowledge the intellectuals gained from books is not complete or far from being
complete." How true his directive is! It has occurred to me
that if a teacher has only theoretical knowledge, the knowledge
he imparts to the students can only be theoretical, knowledge
that is not applicable to production and is even likely to cause
trouble. If so, teaching would be a failure. For this reason,
integration of theory with practice must be stressed in the reform of physics teaching.

With this understanding I made up my mind to learn from the
workers and peasants regularly and according to plan.

How to learn from the workers and peasants? Chairman Mao
has taught us that one must study like a student before one can
teach. I began to step out of my office, acknowledged the workers and peasants as many teachers, and took three measures:

First, I went to factories and rural districts to take part in
labor, made friends with workers and peasants and learned
from them. I often went to the machine plant, the woodwork
factory, the power plant and the tractor station to learn. For
example, I learned from the power plant workers the general
knowledge of using electric power with safety, and the technique
of installing circuits; from the machine plant workers, the forging technique and the knowledge of machine tools; from the
tractor station workers, the knowledge of internal combustion

engines; from the cinema technicians, the knowledge of cinematography. I then applied such knowledge and techniques flexibly to teaching.

Second, I took an active part in the technical innovation of industry and agriculture and in scientific experiments. For example, after taking part in the innovation of the "thermal convection oven for drying timber" I began to appreciate the usefulness of the knowledge of "thermal convection" to which I had given no importance in the past. In the course of practice I tested the correctness of my theoretical knowledge and learned from the workers their method of putting knowledge to flexible use. I intensified and improved teaching of "thermal convection."

For further example, with the object of learning the new farming technique of "using plastic films for breeding seedlings," I went to Liming Brigade some ten li away from our school and sought the advice of the aged peasants. With the object of acquainting myself with the electrification of agriculture, I visited the rural district some 50 li away. Whenever I heard of a factory overhauling, dismantling and assembling agricultural machinery, I would take the opportunity to visit that factory and make an observation of the machinery dissected.

Third, at leisure time I went to the worker and peasant masses and learned from them while popularizing and publicizing scientific knowledge among them. On off days and festival days I used to go to the rural districts and factories and told the masses of the scientific and technological achievements made in our country, talked about the scientific and technological knowledge of interest to the worker and peasant masses, and conducted propaganda to break down superstitions. Over the past four years I talked about such topics as "the ABCs of atomic bombs," "congratulating the PLA on shooting down U-2 aircraft," "China's new scientific and technological achievements," "the ABCs of physics in agriculture," "revolution in the mechanics of industrial machines," and "random talks about the breaking down of superstitions."

At the same time, taking the opportunity of contact with the

broad masses I collected data on their life experience, lifelike
language and comprehension of difficult problems. This provided me with ways of improving the teaching method.

Now, workers and commune members from factories and
rural districts often come to our school to see me and ask me
questions. They often "exchange information" with me, letting
me know what innovations they have made. This makes me
very happy and I am more conscious of the need for learning.
My teachers are found among the worker and peasant masses
and my classroom is extended to factories and rural districts.
I begin to take the road of forming one with the worker and
peasant masses. This is exactly the royal road Chairman Mao
has charted for the revolutionary intellectuals and revolutionary
youths.

Training New-Type Teachers with Greater,
Faster, Better, and More Economical Results*

Investigation Group of Propaganda Team Stationed
in Guangxi Normal College and Revolutionary
Committee of Guangxi Normal College

To meet the needs of the proletarian revolution of education
in the countryside, rural middle-school teachers' training
classes have been operated for several terms since July last
year in Xiangan xian and Yongfu xian, Guangxi Zhuang Autonomous Region, and 460 teachers of junior and senior middle
schools have been trained under the leadership of the administrative district and xian revolutionary committees and with the
concrete help of Guangxi Normal College. Remarkable results
have been scored.

Importance of Running Rural Teachers' Training Classes

After the poor and lower-middle peasants took up the management of schools, revolution of education has developed very fast
in the countryside. In Xingan xian and Yongfu xian, the children
of poor and lower-middle peasants basically do not have to go
out of the commune to attend senior middle school, do not have
to go out of the brigade to attend junior middle school, and do
not have to go out of the village to attend primary school. The
development of education in the countryside has posed a very

*Guangming ribao [Guangming Daily], March 12, 1970. Translated in Sur-
vey of China Mainland Press (SCMP), No. 4624 (March 26, 1970), pp. 92-94.

important new problem: The teachers of rural middle schools
have fallen far behind the needs of development of the current
situation in number and in quality.

The training classes for rural middle school teachers have
been set up precisely to meet this state of affairs. Supported
and shown concern by the poor and lower-middle peasants, the
teachers' training classes have been run with better results
one term after another and have shown tremendous superiority:

1. Time required is short, only a small expenditure is necessary, quick results can be produced, and a force of revolutionized teachers can be brought up with greater, faster, better and
more economical results to meet the urgent needs of revolution
in the countryside. In Yongfu xian, during the summer vacation
last year, 40 days' time was used to train 119 middle school
teachers, this number being nine times the number of graduates
of Guangxi Normal College assigned to this xian in the past 16
years. This changed the condition of shortage of rural middle
school teachers.

2. This facilitates fast establishment of a force of revolutionized teachers with poor and lower-middle peasants as the
mainstay. The teachers' training classes take the road to
training technicians from among workers as adopted by Shanghai Machine Tools Plant. Members of these training classes
have been selected from cadres at the commune and brigade
levels, demobilized armymen, primary school teachers and educated youths who have practical experience. After their study
in the training class, they return to their communes or brigades
to take the posts of education. Most of the members of the
training classes are children of poor and lower-middle peasants who are good in political understanding, good in labor
training and good in work, and many others are backbone elements of the commune, the brigade and the school. Their participation in the force of teachers helps the poor and lower-
middle peasants directly grasp cultural power and facilitates
transformation of the former force of middle school teachers
and fast establishment of a force of new-type teachers with
poor and lower-middle peasants as the mainstay.

3. Revolution of education in the countryside is promoted.
In the teachers' training class, the teachers and the students
take Mao Zedong thought as the sharp weapon to criticize
incisively the "theory that cultural work is dangerous," "theory
that it is a misfortune to teach," "theory of studying in order
to be an official" and their variation, "theory that it is of no use
to study," which hinder the deep-going development of the revolution of education. They further eliminate the pernicious influence of these "theories." This promotes revolution of education in the countryside.

After studying in these classes, many members become activists in the revolution of education. For example, after this
study, a teacher in Rongtian Brigade, Sanhuang Commune, further heightened his thinking of serving the poor and lower-
middle peasants. After returning to his school, he pays close
attention to bringing proletarian politics to the fore in teaching,
integrates teaching with practice and often leads the students
to the fields and the power stations to learn lessons on the
spot. He actively allows the students to ascend the teaching
platform. He also pays attention to training the students in the
practical abilities to analyze and solve problems.

Methods of Opening Rural Teachers' Training Classes

The following methods have been adopted to open classes for
training rural middle school teachers:

1. In accordance with Chairman Mao's teachings, "In carrying out the proletarian revolution in education, it is necessary
to have working-class leadership" and "Form a revolutionary
three-in-one combination," a leading group comprising representatives of workers (poor and lower-middle peasants), representatives of revolutionary leading cadres (revolutionary
teachers) and representatives of members of the training
classes is set up in the form of "three-in-one" combination
which is revolutionized and is capable of linking itself with the
masses, so as to ensure that the working class and its most
reliable ally — poor and lower-middle peasants — may take up

management of the school and firmly seize the power of education. In the course of forming the "three-in-one" combination,
particular attention should be paid to developing the leading
role of the workers and poor and lower-middle peasants and
the representative role of members of the training classes.

2. The living study and application of Mao Zedong thought
is put in the first position and effort is made to tightly grasp
revolutionization of thinking of members of the training class.
Class education is tightly grasped and class struggle taken as
the main subject and the members are helped to continuously
heighten their consciousness of class struggle and the struggle
between the two lines and their consciousness of continuing
revolution.

3. The orientation of the "May 7 Directive" is followed perseveringly. Members of the teachers' training classes should
"take study as their main task and, in addition to their studies,
learn other things, that is, industrial work, farming and military affairs. They should also criticize the bourgeoisie."
Therefore, the teachers' training classes constantly take a
firm hold of revolutionary mass criticism and infuse revolutionary mass criticism into all tasks and all subjects of study.
They correctly handle the relationship between study as the
main task and learning of other things. The members not only
study Mao Zedong thought and their major subjects well, but
also take part in industrial and agricultural productive labor.
Meanwhile, they are organized regularly to apply Chairman
Mao's idea of revolution of education in summing up, studying
and exchanging experience in revolution of education.

4. Obeying Chairman Mao's teaching of "reforming the old
system of education and the old policy and method of teaching,"
the teachers' training classes adhere to the principle of learning fewer but essential things, implement the policy of integrating theory with practice and, taking society and productive
bases as the classroom, organize their members to learn things
in such productive bases as the factory, the farm and the power
station. The teaching methods adopted are diversified and
vivid, including the method of inviting people to teach and send-

ing out teachers to learn. Classroom teaching is integrated with on-the-spot teaching theoretical knowledge with practical work, and explanation with discussion. Mass activities of "officers teaching soldiers, soldiers teaching officers, and soldiers teaching one another" are carried out, so that the members can teach and learn things from one another, and those who are capable may teach.

5. A force of teachers with workers and peasants as the mainstay is organized. Old workers, old poor and lower-middle peasants and revolutionary cadres work as part-time teachers of the courses of class education and productive techniques.

Worker-Teachers in China's Education Revolution*

New China News Agency

Workers with rich experience in revolutionary struggles and production are teaching in institutions of higher learning throughout the country. This important aspect of the revolution in education has been a feature in all areas since the beginning of the Great Proletarian Cultural Revolution.

Some workers serve as full-time teachers, and a great number become part-time teachers. They give lectures in colleges at fixed times or give guidance to the students in the workshops.

There are 105 worker-teachers at Shanghai Teachers' University. Eighteen of them are full-time teachers and the rest teach part-time. Some 90 percent of them are veteran workers with 10 to 30 years of experience at the bench and have studied theory.

In Shanghai, there are 10,000 workers giving lectures in primary and secondary schools and in institutions of higher learning. More than 1.5 million outstanding workers, peasants and fighters of the Chinese People's Liberation Army are serving as part-time lecturers in schools all over the country. They are playing an important part in the current revolution in education.

Under the influence of Liu Shaoqi's revisionist line in educa-

---

*NCNA, Shanghai, October 28, 1975. Translated in SCMP (November 10, 1975), No. 5971, pp. 16-19.

tion before the Cultural Revolution, China's colleges used bourgeois school systems followed in foreign countries. On May 7,
1966, Chairman Mao issued the call "education should be revolutionized." After the inception of the education revolution,
Chairman Mao pointed out: "To accomplish the proletarian
revolution in education, it is essential to have working class
leadership; the masses of workers must take part in this revolution. . . ."

The worker-teachers give lectures by linking theory with
their own practical experience. Additionally, in collaboration
with the college teachers, they compile new textbooks, improve
teaching methods and conduct scientific research.

Under the old educational system before the Cultural Revolution, the colleges aimed solely at giving the students more book
knowledge with the result that education was divorced from
practice and from productive labor. Now the institutions of
higher learning have set up their own workshops on campus for
the students to do fieldwork. In addition, teachers and students
spend a period of time every year in factories outside the
schools as well as in rural people's communes where teaching,
study of theoretical knowledge, and practice are combined. In
China, this is known as "open-door education," and the worker-
teachers are central to it.

You Minfei became a teacher of Tongji University upon graduation in 1961 after six years study at the architecture faculty
there. In the fourteen years before 1968, she spent only 100
days at a building worksite. "As a student I used to watch my
teachers build houses on the blackboard. When I myself became
a teacher, I used to confine myself to textbooks too," said You
Minfei.

In the course of the education revolution, veteran building
worker Fu Xiaogen and I took a class of students to a construction site for on-the-spot teaching, she explained. "There, the
divorce between theory and practice in my work was fully revealed when I failed to solve the actual problems which arose
in designing and construction, but Fu Xiaogen, with dozens of
years of rich practical experience, was far more capable for

that than I. I learned a lot from him," she said. Since then we
have made a point of doing on-the-spot teaching and our knowledge has been greatly enriched through practice. We have
changed our textbooks accordingly. Our graduates are able to
design and construct ordinary buildings after a year and a half
of university study.

Reediting former textbooks is an essential aspect of the revolution in education in which many worker-teachers have taken
part. Fundamental Knowledge on Building Construction, written
after the faculty members and students had worked at construction sites, was edited with the participation of Huang Jinshong,
a worker-teacher with 33 years' experience in his trade and
the deputy head of the industrial and civil architecture teaching
research group. It is the first new texbook published by Tongji
University since the start of the Cultural Revolution in 1966.
Huang Jinshong collected all the teaching material used in five
courses and organized it into an integral whole covering the
order of building construction from foundation to roof. Huang
Jinshong wrote the two chapters on "foundation and basement"
and "finishing" and a part of the chapter headed "test for concrete mixing." He also drew 57 illustrations for the text. An
edition of several hundred thousand copies of the 350,000-word
book was put out by the Shanghai People's Publishing House
and is now in use.

Worker-teachers and other faculty members of Fudan University and the Shanghai Textile Engineering Institute edited
"The Curve and Curved Surfaces," "Basic Knowledge on Cotton
and Woolen Fabrics Looms" and a number of other textbooks.

A distinctive feature in lectures by worker-teachers is the
fostering of the students' socialist consciousness to replace
the old idea of schools as places only for "passing on knowledge" or "giving vocational training." While teaching "elements in fluidics," Liang Yougang, a worker-teacher in the
Shanghai Mechanical Engineering Institute, went beyond lecturing on the technical knowledge of fluidics, explaining to his
students how fluidic technology was applied and needed in
China's present-day socialist construction. His students began

to work hard, showing eagerness to meet the needs of the
country.

Worker-teachers in Shanghai universities are technical innovations experts, inventors or graduates of spare-time colleges
and specialized courses. They have raised their own ideological level and professional skills and learned from veteran
teachers, drawing fresh experience from their own factories
and worksites to enrich their teaching material.

They also help veteran professors improve their teaching.
Mathematics professor Su Bujing was invited to give a four
months' course of lectures in a tools plant. Worker-teacher Shi
Sibo was by his side and they soon became close friends. The
seventy-one-year-old professor said: "Shi Sibo has dealt seriously with my lectures. He helped me spot my shortcomings
and kept me informed about the reactions and demands of the
workers. My four months of lecturing to workers has in fact
been a period in which Shi Sibo and the workers taught me. I
learned how to give lectures, integrate theory with practice and
apply dialectics to analyzing questions. It gave me a good opportunity to study again professionally and receive ideological
reeducation from the working class." In the past few years,
the mathematics department in which Professor Su Bujing
teaches has carried to completion dozens of important scientific research projects.

Correctly Understand and Fully Bring into
Play the Role of People's Teachers*

Criticism Group of the Jiangsu
Provincial Conference on Writing

For the sake of usurping Party and state power, nothing was too evil for the Wang-Zhang-Jiang-Yao anti-Party clique on the educational front, and they in particular tried their utmost to discredit and hit hard at the broad masses of people's teachers. To thoroughly settle accounts with the numerous crimes of the "Gang of Four" in attacking the people's teachers and to correctly understand the standing and role of the people's teachers in the socialist cause is of great significance to the excellent situation for the development of the educational front.

People's Teachers Are Charged with the Glorious Task
of Training Successors to the Revolution

Our Party always attached importance to raising the standing of people's teachers and fully bringing into play their positive role in the cause of revolution. The great leader Chairman Mao taught that our country "needs a large number of people's educators and teachers." The esteemed and beloved Premier Zhou was most concerned with the progress of the teachers and he constantly instructed the departments concerned and people responsible for the schools to pay attention to the educating and remolding

---

*Renmin ribao [People's Daily] , June 28, 1977. Translated in Survey of People's Republic of China Press (SPRCP), No. 6378 (July 12, 1977), pp. 44-50.

the teachers, bringing into play their positive role, and improving their working conditions and wages and benefits. The brilliant and wise leader Chairman Hua is most concerned with the political treatment for people's teachers. He warmly guides them in work, takes good care of them in livelihood, and honors the hard toil of the teachers. He often said with deep feelings: "The teachers work very hard." The broad masses of workers, peasants and soldiers cherish the people's teachers and compare them to "gardeners" who carefully tend to seedlings.

The college, middle school and primary school students in our country make up more than one-fifth of the population of the whole country. They stand for the future of the motherland. How the younger generation behaves is a major question bearing on whether Chairman Mao's great banner can be handed down from generation to generation and held high forever, and whether there are successors to carry through to the end the revolutionary cause of the proletariat pioneered by the great leader Chairman Mao and the esteemed and beloved Premier Zhou as well as the revolutionaries of the older generation. The people's teachers are charged with the important task of bringing up and educating the next generation. Our Party and government as well as the broad masses of the people always highly praise, trust and support the broad masses of teachers who willingly serve the socialist revolution and construction and are resolved to carry the proletarian revolution in education through to the end as well as their cause.

A sinister clique made up of new and old counterrevolutionaries, the "Gang of Four" were extremely hostile to the broad masses of people's teachers, and vilified them in a thousand and one ways. They indiscriminatingly labeled all teachers as "bourgeois intellectuals." They babbled that "with the teachers now spreading poison on the rostrum every day," the students attending class were "food for jackals, tigers and leopards." They babbled that the students trained after liberation "are all for undermining the foundation of socialism" and "playing a subversive role toward the foundation of the socialist economy." That counterrevolutionary clown Zhang Tiesheng fed by the

"Gang of Four" even used all kinds of shameless vile ravings
to curse the broad masses of people's teachers.

The shameless slanders used by the "Gang of Four" to smear
the teachers were slanderous charges wantonly made against
Chairman Mao's teachings concerning the role of intellectuals
in frenzied opposition to his scientific analysis of the situation
of the intellectuals in our country. In 1957, Chairman Mao
pointed out in his brilliant "Speech at the Chinese Communist
Party's National Conference on Propaganda Work": "Socialist
society mainly comprises three sections of people, the workers,
the peasants and the intellectuals. Intellectuals are mental
workers. Their work is in the service of the people, that is,
in the service of the workers and the peasants." In this writing
Chairman Mao also pointed out: Those among the intellectuals
who are relatively familiar with Marxism and take a firm proletarian stand are a minority. The majority support socialism
and are willing to serve the people, but their world outlook is
basically a bourgeois one. The number of intellectuals who are
hostile to our state is very small. Chairman Mao's scientific
analysis of the role and situation of the intellectuals is based
upon the policy of uniting with, educating and remolding the intellectuals adopted by the Party. There is the question of transforming the world outlook of the intellectuals, but it is first
necessary to affirm that they are working people, that the majority of them support socialism politically and that their work
is to serve the people.

With ulterior motives, the "Gang of Four" equated the intellectuals with the bourgeoisie, vilified the intellectuals of "undermining the foundation of socialism" and "playing a subversive role," and described the majority of the teachers as "restorationist forces" hostile to the socialist motherland. Was
this not for deliberately transposing the enemy and ourselves?
Was this not for wantonly trampling upon the Party's policy
toward intellectuals?

The shameless slanders used by the "Gang of Four" to smear
the teachers were for maliciously attacking the socialist system of our country. The teachers who presently play a leading

role in various types of schools at different levels in our country were mostly educated and brought up by schools after Liberation. Although Liu Shaoqi and company seized control of
leadership in the educational sector and frenziedly pushed the
counterrevolutionary revisionist line in education at that time,
thus poisoning the broad masses of teachers and students, the
education they received was after all at variance in many respects with the intellectuals drawn from the old society. This
was because after Liberation sovereignty in education had been
recaptured from the hands of imperialism and the Guomindang
under the leadership of Chairman Mao and the Party Central
Committee, and the fascist system of school administration by
the Guomindang reactionaries and education for the enslavement
of students had been abolished. Under the guiding light of Chairman Mao's revolutionary line, the teaching of Marxist-Leninist
works and Chairman Mao's writings was stepped up in the
schools, and the broad masses of teachers and students actively
participated in various political movements led by the Party,
such as the agrarian reform, the suppression of counterrevolutionaries, the "movements against the three evils and the five
evils," the anti-Rightist struggle, and the criticism of the film
The Life of Wu Xun, of the "Studies of The Dream of the Red
Chamber," of Hu Shi and of the Hu Feng counterrevolutionary
clique. All these deeply influenced the ideological remolding
of the broad masses of the teachers and students.
    Twenty years ago, in the course of analyzing the intellectuals
from the old society, Chairman Mao also pointed out: "The
overwhelming majority are patriotic, love our People's Republic, and are willing to serve the people and the socialist state."
Over the past twenty years, after they spent a long time in the
study of Marxist theory and after they were educated and tempered in successive political movements, the majority of those
old intellectuals coming over from the old society have made
progress to varying extents. All this serves to show that it is
not possible to say that all students trained under the socialist
system are engaged in "undermining the foundation of socialism."
What is this if not a malicious vilification of the socialist society?

The shameless slanders used by the "Gang of Four" to smear the teachers were also basically for negating the Great Proletarian Cultural Revolution. After the Great Proletarian Cultural Revolution, led by the Party and guided by Chairman Mao's revolutionary line, the broad masses of teachers seriously studied Chairman Mao's thought on the revolution in education, deeply criticized the counterrevolutionary revisionist line in education of Liu Shaoqi and Lin Biao, and consciously made their way to factories, the countryside and armed force units to receive reeducation politically and to conduct study again vocationally. Profound changes were noticed in the spiritual outlook of both the teachers who came over from the old society and those who were trained after Liberation, and they made contributions to the revolution in education. Meanwhile, a number of workers, peasants and soldiers with practical experience were also selected for transfer by different places to serve as teachers, and part of the worker-peasant-soldier students were also sent after their graduation to schools at different levels to reinforce the teaching ranks with fresh blood. All these are facts obvious to all. Is it possible to say that the Great Proletarian Cultural Revolution has actually not brought any changes to the educational sphere and that the teaching ranks not only have made no progress but are on the contrary "daily engaged in spreading poison on the rostrum"? What is this if not a flagrant negation of the Great Proletarian Cultural Revolution personally initiated and led by Chairman Mao?

It can be seen from this that there are two diametrically opposite views concerning the standing and role of the people's teachers in the socialist revolution and construction. They reflect two fundamentally opposite lines. One is that it is meritorious and glorious to teach for the revolution and that the broad masses of people's teachers should be honored by the Party, the people and society. This is Chairman Mao's revolutionary line. The other line is that it is sinful and lowly to teach for the revolution, that the broad masses of the people's teachers form the target of the revolution, and that they must be "pressed down" "like pressing down the ball in the water."

This is the ultrarightist line of the "Gang of Four" seeking to transpose the enemy and ourselves in the socialist period. It exposes that they are a bunch of most vicious counterrevolutionaries who are hostile to the working class, the poor and lower-middle peasants and the broad masses of cadres and revolutionary intellectuals.

People's Teachers Play the Leading Role in the Education of Students

The people's teachers manifest an important leading role in the course of educating the students.

Throughout the historical period of socialism, the struggle between the proletariat and the bourgeoisie for winning over the young people will be protracted and acute. Adolescence is an important period which shapes the world outlook. This requires the teachers to assign the primary role to changing the thinking of the students under the leadership of the Party by vigorously conducting political and ideological education in conformity with the characteristics of the young people so as to foster proletarian ideology and liquidate bourgeois ideology in an effort to train the students as successors to the revolutionary cause of the proletariat.

Chairman Mao said that "the principals and teachers of schools should care more" for ideological and political work. This clearly points out the important position occupied by the teachers in conducting ideological and political education for the young people.

Young people are also at the age of physical growth to pick up knowledge. As they are heading from knowing nothing to knowing something and from knowing not much to knowing more, the guidance and help of the teachers are indispensable. Are the teachers able to put political work in command of vocational work? Have they relative comprehensive knowledge of the unity of theory and practice? Are they able to teach properly? All these directly bear on whether the students are able to make all-round development morally, intellectually and physically.

To bring up workers with both socialist consciousness and culture, it is imperative to see to it that "while the main task of
the students is to study they should also learn other things,"
and that while learning properly politics and culture, the students must at the same time be organized to learn industrial
work, farming and military affairs. It is also necessary to
make the school, society and family work in close coordination
in order to jointly strengthen the education of the young people.
All these require the teachers to conduct an abundance of meticulous propaganda and organizational work under the leaderhip
of the Party.

Affirming the leading role played by the teachers in no way
means that the students constitute the passive factor. Materialist dialectics holds that the fundamental cause of the development of a thing lies in the contradictory nature within the thing.
Both the transformation of thinking and the growth of knowledge
have to be consummated in the end through the students themselves. Therefore, bringing into play the leading role of the
teachers can never be interpreted as the monopoly of things by
the teachers. The leading role of the teachers should find expression in bringing into play the initiative of the students, enlightening their consciousness and fostering their capacity for
carrying out study and work independently. We also must perceive the reciprocal transformation of the educator and the
educated under given conditions. A teacher must have the
spirit of a willing pupil. He must humbly draw nourishment
from his students, warmly support the revolutionary spirit of
young people in daring to think, to speak out and to act, and encourage them to state their views and criticize his own ideas
and work. Only in this way can the leading role be better
brought into play in the course of educating the students.

For the sake of creating chaos in the school and sabotaging
the revolution in education, the "Gang of Four" entirely negated
the role of teachers in the course of educating students. They
fomented discord between the teachers and students and set
them against each other.

The "Gang of Four" advocated "the liquidation of teachers"

and "autonomy for students." This was the most reactionary
fallacy of the "gang of four" to negate the role of teachers and
to sabotage the revolution in education. A confidant of the
"Gang of Four" sent people to carry out experiments in selected
places in a middle school. He said that "bourgeois intellectuals
could not train successors to the revolutionary cause of the
proletariat." He wanted to create a "typical example" in the
liquidation of teachers and autonomy for students, and was prepared to send up a "satellite" at the National Congress of the
Communist Youth League. This view was reactionary politically and preposterous theoretically. Amid the hubbub of the
"Gang of Four" for creating such antagonism between the teachers and students, the riffraff and hooligans in society leaped at
the chance to carry out activities. The instigators were blatant
for a while, and as a result, the struggle for young people in
some places led to the emergence of a serious situation favorable to the bourgeoisie but unfavorable to the proletariat. To
tell the truth, "the liquidation of teachers" and "autonomy for
students" mean leaving the school to be run not by the proletariat but exclusively by the bourgeoisie.

The students were described as the natural administrators
and reformers of schools, while the teachers were described
as the target of administration and reform. This was another
reactionary fallacy of the "Gang of Four" for negating the role
of teachers and sabotaging the revolution in education. Since
the Great Proletarian Cultural Revolution, in accordance with
Chairman Mao's instruction that "students should be selected
from among workers and peasants with practical experience
and they should return to production after a few years' study,"
institutions of higher learning and secondary vocational schools
of all kinds have enrolled worker-peasant-soldier students.
Among them, the majority have definite political consciousness
and practical experience and are a new political force for the
proletarian revolution in education. Similar to the teachers and
students of the school, they also are the masters of the school.
Chairman Mao unequivocally pointed out: To carry out the proletarian revolution in education, it is imperative to rely upon

the broad masses of revolutionary students, revolutionary teachers and revolutionary workers in the school as well as the activists among them. Only when everyone fights in unity can a success be made of the revolution in education according to Chairman Mao's instructions.

With ulterior motives, however, the "Gang of Four" stood the worker-peasant-soldier students against the broad masses of teachers and fundamentally erased the teachers' role in the revolution in education. In this way, the call of the worker-peasant-soldier students for painstakingly transforming their own subjective world in the course of transforming the objective world was also negated. Lu Xun once said: To deal with a revolutionary, the reactionary forces "always adopted two methods — to press him down or to play him up." The "Gang of Four" also adopted these two methods of "abusing to death" the teachers and "flattering to death" the students toward the teachers and students. The tactics were different but they led to "death" just the same. They are the mortal enemy of the broad masses of teachers and students.

The cudgel of criticizing "the dignity of teaching" was brandished to impair the normal relations between the revolutionary teachers and students. This was the most vicious tactic used by the "Gang of Four" to negate the role of teachers and sabotage the revolution in education. The "Gang of Four" made use of the power they had usurped to insidiously and wantonly lay hold of "typical examples" and issue "instructions." They whipped up a gust of evil wind for criticizing "the dignity of teaching," thus creating great ideological confusion. What is "dignity of teaching"? "Dignity of teaching" looks upon the relationship of the teachers and the students as the relationship between the ruler and the ruled. The proletariat is always opposed to the promotion of "dignity of teaching" by the exploiting classes in the educational sphere. However, to fully bring into play the important role of the teachers in the course of educating the students under the leadership of the Party, to correctly manage the students and be strict with them, and to require the students consciously to obey management and education by the teachers, observe discipline in study and keep order in class — this is definitely not any "dignity of teaching," but a concrete manifestation of honoring the teachers and cherishing the students, and an important condition for consummating the task of education and teaching. The "Gang of Four" made every effort to publicize and disseminate that "going against the tide means opposing the teachers" and "opposing the teachers means opposing the dignity of teaching." They incited the students to fight against the teachers so as to create antagonism between the teachers and students. This was entirely for creating chaos on the educational front and serving their counterrevolutionary criminal goal of seizing power in the "chaos."

At present, the "Gang of Four" have been smashed, and all charges arbitrarily imposed by the "Gang of Four" on the broad masses of teachers must be toppled. Our glorious people's teachers must hold high Chairman Mao's great banner, and in response to Chairman Hua's call for "continuing to make a success of the revolution in education," insist on becoming both Red and vocationally proficient, actively bring their role into play in the revolution in education, train millions of successors for the revolutionary cause of the proletariat, and make contributions worthy of our great era.

(a) General Prestige in Society

Appendix / II:a:i

Any Job That Benefits the People
Is a Glorious Occupation*

Song Jianming, No. 3 General Primary School,
Xinhailian Municipality, Jiangsu Province

Having read Comrade Yuan Gongming's article "Is Teaching at a Primary School a Job of No Promise and No Future?" I would like to express some of my own opinions.

I am a young teacher. I joined in educational work in 1949 when I was only seventeen, and have always loved my job. Some people say to me: "What a pity for a young fellow to lead a life of chalk!" "To work in any factory or enterprise would be better than this." Of my former schoolmates and colleagues, one now works as a section chief in a hospital at Jinan, one serves as a secretary in a certain factory at Dalian, and there is yet another who takes part in the nation's vigorous construction work at the Anshan Iron and Steel Complex. However, none of these cases has ever shaken my faith in cherishing my work. I have always believed what I do is part of our fatherland's construction effort and is closely related to the entire cause of building our country.

During this year when our country has begun large-scale economic construction, I have grown to love my work even more, and at the same time, I feel the heavy responsibility on my shoulders. During the few days before the arrival of June 1, International Children's Day, I was so elated that I could hardly fall asleep at night. I wrote an article entitled "Spare

---

*Xiaoxue jiaoshi [Primary School Teacher], November 1953, p. 13. Translated in CED XII:4 (Winter 1979-80), pp. 80-81.

No Effort to Do a Good Job in Coaching the Young Pioneers"
and submitted it to Zhongguo qingnian bao [China Youth News].
After the newspaper reached Korea and was read by comrades
in the Chinese People's Volunteers, letters written by them
reached my hand one after another. They said: "You can conscientiously and responsibly cultivate China's younger generation. We are very grateful to you and extend heartfelt greet-
ings to you on behalf of the Chinese Volunteers! We hope you
can work even more carefully and patiently to educate the
children in following the road to socialist and communist society." What has been burned into my memory are the words
of Comrade Hu Derun of the Transport Company. He said:
"Today we are standing guard at the outpost, safeguarding
world peace; we are all glorious fighters for peace. But one
must know that among the great number of peace fighters
many have been brought up by your diligent efforts. Therefore
the glory of the contributions we make to the fatherland and to
the cause of peace also belongs to you."

Some students who graduated from the No. 3 General Primary School four years ago have now already been assigned
to fighting posts or taken on jobs in production. Zhou Zhen-
jiang, who joined the army when a grade 2 student of a junior
high school, is now a glorious fighter in the air force. He
rendered meritorious service in fighting and has been admitted
to the Party. Jin Zengxu went to work in the Huaxing Iron
Plant upon his graduation from the primary school and has now
become a skilled worker. They wrote me to say: "Our achievement must first be attributed to the teacher's patient cultivation." Who says that primary school teachers cannot take part
in building the country? Who says that primary school teachers cannot make great contributions to the fatherland?

Respect the Work of Primary School Teachers*

Editorial, *Liaoning Ribao*

We often receive letters reporting that some local cadres and masses discriminate against primary school teachers. This is a problem meriting attention.

Right now there are altogether more than 76,000 primary school teachers in the whole province of Liaoning, and they are responsible for the education of over 2.89 million children. During the four years from 1953 to the summer of 1956, primary school teachers in the province trained nearly 1.3 million graduates of higher primary schools for the nation. Children by the millions are now growing up in primary schools and becoming acculturated. Many of them will continue their studies at higher-level schools, learning different skills. They are a vital new force in building socialism. Primary school teachers who are responsible for the training of this new force have rendered meritorious service to the state and society. They shoulder a glorious task and their work ought to be respected. A great many teachers have devoted all their energy to cultivating the new generation. They have worked for several years and even several decades as if it were only one day. In the daytime, they teach in the classroom and organize the children's play. During lunch break or late at night, when others are resting, they either correct the children's home-

---

*Liaoning Daily, January 12, 1957. Translated in CED XII:4 (Winter 1979-80), pp. 82-85.

172

work or prepare new lessons. In their spare time, they visit
the children's families to find out how they are doing at home.
In rural areas, some teachers have to pick up the children in
the morning and see them home in the evening. If the water
level rises, they carry the children on their backs, wading
through the water to take them home, lest they get into danger.
As parents, each one of us should think it over: through their
diligent work and concern for the children, teachers share
much of the effort we spend on bringing up our children. Consequently, we can wholeheartedly devote ourselves to our own
work. Can there be any reason for us to look down on and
discriminate against primary school teachers.

The Party and the people's government have always attached
importance to primary school education. Compared with the
old society, the social status of primary school teachers has
now undergone a fundamental change. The overwhelming majority of cadres and masses hold teachers in high esteem.
However, there are still quite a few cases of disrespect for, or
even discrimination and insults against, teachers. Some cadres
call primary school teachers the "three petties," namely,
"petty teacher," "petty intellectual," and "petty bourgeois."
They describe them as "having nothing much to them," and
randomly assign them jobs beyond their teaching duties. They
are considered good if they are on call at any hour. Once they
are slightly late or fail to show up because they are occupied
with teaching work, they are accused of being "self-important,"
"resisting the leadership," and "failing to respond to the call
of the country." Some cadres at the district and township
levels would have primary school teachers suspend their
teaching and follow these cadres to the countryside to serve as
their "secretaries," sorting out their documents and notes.
When certain cadres of Linyuan County visit primary schools
and teachers say something polite to them, they attack these
teachers as being "able to make empty talk." If they fail to
address the cadres, they accuse them of being "conceited and
putting on airs." This really puts the teachers in an awkward
position. Some of the cadres even call the teachers names.

What the teachers resent most is that Party organizations regard them as being backward and take no notice of their desire
to become progressives.* Consequently they feel "there is no
way for them to become progressive and they are ill at ease."
    What is at the root of such phenomena? One cause is that
some people still entertain the sectarian sentiments of discrimination against intellectuals. Lacking an adequate understanding of the changes that have taken place among primary
school teachers and the progress the teachers have made in the
few years since Liberation, these people indiscriminately regard the teachers as having undesirable family backgrounds
and being ideologically backward and thus discriminate against
them. Not only is the assessment inconsistent with the actual
situation but the practice also violates the Party's policy on
intellectuals. Another cause of the disrespect for primary
school teachers is that some people do not fully understand the
importance of primary school education in the national effort
of construction. Having no understanding of the work performed by primary school teachers, they tend to think such
work is of little importance and negligible. Not to mention the
fact that primary school education exerts a far-reaching influence over the growth of the younger generation and the future of our country, we only have to consider the fact that the
overwhelming majority of our current state functionaries, engineers, and technicians have been educated by primary school
teachers, haven't they? Are our own children not now studying
in primary schools? Judging from this alone we can well understand the importance of the work being done by primary
school teachers. We should realize that in order to change the
economically and culturally backward condition of our country,
we simply cannot do without primary school education and primary school teachers.
    Of course, some primary school teachers have shortcomings,
and within their ranks there are a few bad individuals. How-

*This refers to the desire to join the Communist Party or the Youth
League. — Tr.

ever, if they have shortcomings, it is up to us to help them
correct them. Still less should we view the presence of a few
bad people as representative of the situation as a whole. They
cannot become reasons for disrespecting primary school
teachers. Esteeming the teacher and attaching importance to
learning are fine traditions in our country. Right now we must
pay more attention to and show more concern for the teacher's
work than at any previous time. We must help them in all ways
so they can be completely competent in fulfilling the glorious
task of bringing up the younger generation.

Educate the Peasants to Respect Teachers*

Shiqian

The lawbreaker Zheng Liangjia gathered together a number of peasants and [with them] tied and beat up the headmaster and teachers of Maqun Township Primary School. Zheng was recently sentenced to prison by the People's Court of Suiqi County. Such incidents merit our attention, and we should draw lessons from them.

That between two and three hundred peasants poured into the school at Zheng Liangjia's heels, tying up and beating people, and yelling was because, as a matter of fact, they did not understand the policy for culture and education; additionally they mistakenly thought the school intended to undermine the [local] theatrical troupe. Nevertheless, the root cause for this incident was that not a few peasants in rural areas hold an erroneous view of teachers.

In the past, intellectuals were heavily tied to the landlord class and the bourgeoisie, and quite a few intellectuals were themselves descendants of families of the exploiting classes. During the struggles of land reform, some of them even sided with the landlord class. Therefore, when class struggle became acute, the peasants were apt to regard them all as a part of the exploiting class, alleging that teachers did not do farm work and what they ate came by exploiting the peasants. This

*Nanfang ribao [Southern Daily], March 5, 1957. Translated in CED XII:4 (Winter 1979-80), pp. 86-88.

kind of attitude has more or less persisted among the peasants.
They do not understand that even when teachers are from a
family background of the exploiting class and although today not
a few ideas of the exploiting class still remain in the minds of
some teachers, teachers are nevertheless mental laborers.
Compared with manual labor in general, the mental labor of
teachers needs a basis of scientific and cultural knowledge and
therefore is more complicated. Besides, such mental labor is
indispensable for the building of socialism. We cannot confuse
the teachers' position as a laborer with their exploiting class
family background; nor should we confuse ideological problems
with political problems. The nation needs agriculture to boost
production and also must run the schools well to bring up our
younger generation, the builders of communism. If the peasants hope their children will become able people who are useful to the country and able to get married and start their own
careers, they must rely on the educational labor of teachers.
Therefore we can say that a teacher's labor is honorable and
a teacher's work is important. Furthermore, one ought to
realize that the present condition of teachers is greatly different from the early days after Liberation. They have undergone thought reform, they have made great ideological progress, and the overwhelming majority of them support socialism. In a nutshell, the relationship between the intellectuals
on the one side and the peasants and workers on the other is
one of fraternal alliance. The pity is that not only are many
peasants unaware of this change but a lot of rural cadres are
also unclear about it; they still insist on viewing today's teachers in the same light as during the land reform period. Consequently they show no respect for teachers, treat them in a
rude manner, and even commit the most serious mistakes of
breaking the law — like the events in Maqun Township.

In correcting the misconception that some peasants have of
teachers and in cultivating in the rural areas the practice of
respecting teachers, our rural Party members and cadres
shoulder a special responsibility. This is because it is up to
us to educate the peasants; they often model themselves on our

behavior. If we show respect for teachers, the peasants will
follow our example and change their attitudes. Of course, this
does not mean that teachers are immune from shortcomings
in their work. However, instead of discriminating against
them, we must adopt a comradely attitude to help them to continuously reform themselves and overcome their shortcomings
and the mistakes they commit in their forward movement. As
for the teachers themselves, it is imperative for them to foster
a fine work style in their job, life, and ethics. Moreover, they
must maintain close ties with the masses and parents of the
students so that they all can join hands in doing a good job of
educating the students. Thus when relations between peasants
and teachers become closer, not only will incidents such as
that in Maqun Township be averted but an even better job can
be done in the cause of education.

Appendix / II:b:i

This Is No Excuse for
Not Respecting the Teacher*

Chen Jian

A teacher should take good care of his students, and a student should respect his teachers. This is the normal relationship between teachers and students in the schools of new China.

Quite a few people have this to say: if the teacher's level of learning is high and if he teaches well, I'll respect him; otherwise, I'll not hold him in esteem. This viewpoint is open to question.

A student goes to school to acquire knowledge from the teacher. So long as he can gain knowledge from the teacher, he ought to respect the teacher. All the teachers in today's schools are recruited through a certain process of selection. The fact that they are appointed to teaching jobs indicates that they are qualified to teach the students. Even a teaching assistant newly graduated from the same school has had at least a few more years of education than the students he teaches. Particularly in terms of teaching, our teachers today work more conscientiously than those in the past; they make careful preparations before class starts, and some of the lessons even go through a collective discussion by the teachers beforehand. Therefore what they teach is sufficient for the students to take in. Thus we cannot regard any teacher as incapable of teaching

---

*Zhongguo qingnian bao [China Youth News] (Beijing), October 31, 1956, in the column "Sixiang yiritan" [Daily Ideological Discussion]. Translated in CED XII:4 (Winter 1979-80), pp. 89-91.

just because his knowledge is inferior to those even more
learned. As far as the method of teaching is concerned, it is
naturally an important problem, and all teachers should continuously try to improve their methods of teaching. However,
if a teacher's method leaves something to be desired, this only
means that the results of the students' study will be somewhat
unsatisfactory. By no means can we assert that the students
have nothing to learn from such a teacher. In view of this, we
are not allowed to show disrespect for a teacher because his
method of teaching is temporarily imperfect.

The students' acceptance of and response to a teacher's
lecture is a good criterion to judge his performance in teaching. Therefore a teacher should pay attention to the students'
opinions and strive to improve the method and contents of his
teaching according to these opinions. This is one side of the
problem. On the other hand, we must also not lose sight of the
fact that the views aired by the students are not necessarily
totally correct. It is often the case that a student's assessment is far from a teacher's actual capability. For example,
in a certain high school the students were very dissatisfied
with the physics course given by a young teacher. Later the
high school invited a university instructor to teach them. Without knowing that the new teacher was a university instructor,
the students were still dissatisfied after the first class. However, later when they found out who he was, they were very
attentive to his lectures. The response was unusually favorable
after class and everyone sang his praises. This incident
serves to illustrate that not all the students' dissatisfaction
with a teacher is formed on the basis of clear understanding.
Before they have delved deeply into any subject of study, it is
usually difficult for them to take an immediate interest in the
subject. Lacking an interest in the course, they are apt to accuse the teacher of being unable to give good lectures. Therefore we must first carefully differentiate and analyze our own
impressions of a teacher rather than blindly jumping to con-
clusions about his teaching ability and performance.

On a teacher's shoulders is the glorious task of bringing up

young people. Like a gardener watering flowers, he diligently
cultivates his students. A student's ability to develop intelli-
gence out of ignorance and acquire the capability of earning a
livelihood is inseparable from the education offered by the
school and the teacher. Moreover, the teachers of today
have the responsibility to train talented people for the construction of socialism. In order for the students to become
an outstanding work force for building socialism, they cannot
do without training by the school and the teacher. Therefore
we should hold teachers in particular esteem.

Respecting the teacher is also an important condition for a
student's being able to achieve good results in his studies. It
is hardly conceivable that a student can make good progress in
a course taught by a teacher whom he does not hold in esteem.
As for the teacher, if he is respected by all his students, he
will be encouraged and will work even harder on his teaching,
show more concern for the students' school work, and continuously improve his methods of teaching. Evidently we must
show respect for teachers if we want to study well.

Respect for teachers ought to be regarded as one of the fine
moral qualities we students should possess. It is part of a
good school spirit that each of our schools should display.

Equality and Respect*

Yang Yi

In our socialist schools we advocate the practice of respecting teachers and cherishing the students so that teaching can
benefit both teachers and students alike. The relationship between the teacher and the student should be one of equality and
democracy and of mutual benefit to both sides. The student
should respect the teacher, while the teacher should show concern for the student, so that they can be united, have a friendly
affection for each other, render mutual assistance, and improve together.

Some students, however, entertain certain misconceptions
about this new type of teacher-student relationship. They believe that since the relationship between the teacher and the
student is one of equality and democracy, there is no need for
the students to learn modestly from the teacher and accept his
guidance. In individual cases there are students who even commit the serious mistake of breaking classroom discipline and
showing no respect for the teacher's labor.

What is meant by an equal and democratic relationship between the teacher and the student? It means that, in the face
of political principles and scientific truth, a teacher is on an
equal footing with a student and they should be treated equally
without discrimination. The teacher plays a comradely role in

*Zhongguo qingnian bao [China Youth News] (Beijing), July 20, 1961, p. 2.
Translated in CED XII:4 (Winter 1979-80), pp. 92-93.

guiding the student toward being both red and expert. The student should have the right to speak up on scientific issues. In the field of teaching, however, the teacher always plays a leading role. It must be admitted that, amid the tremendous amount of culture and knowledge accumulated by mankind, it is precisely a teacher who has acquired a relatively systematic command of knowledge in a certain area. This is exactly what a student lacks. In a student's learning process, a teacher serves as the guide. In his article, "Shi shuo" [On Teachers], Han Yu once had this to say: "In learning the truth, some are early and others late; in pursuing academic studies some are specialized and others not." He also added: "A teacher is one who transmits truth, imparts knowledge, and resolves puzzles." In "learning the truth," a teacher is earlier than his student. A teacher is also more specialized than his student in "pursuing academic studies." Consequently, he is equal to the job of transmitting truth, imparting knowledge, and resolving puzzles," and capable of relaying the culture and knowledge of our ancestors to the younger generation. Therefore, a student must respect his teacher and learn from him all the useful knowledge [he can] with a most serious and conscientious effort. As for the fact that some students eventually surpass their teachers, this can only happen when the students have first learned from their teachers and then surpassed them on that basis. The old saying expressed it well: "Ice grows out of water but is colder than water; indigo is extracted from the indigo plant but is bluer than the plant it comes from." This is exactly the same argument. There is no such thing as a pupil surpassing his teacher without first learning from him.

In order to impart to the students the cultural and scientific knowledge he has at his command, a teacher has to put in a lot of hard work on his teaching. In the learning process, a student should respect the teacher's labor, submit himself to the teacher's instructions, and abide by the discipline of study. Only in this way can a good job of both teaching and studying be done and the quality of education improved.

On Drawing a "Dividing Line"*

Sheng De

Some comrades advocate drawing a line of distinction between "the sanctity of a teacher's right" [shidao zunyan] and
"respecting the teacher and abiding by discipline" [zunshi
shouji]. This is because, it is said, following the call to break
away from "the sanctity of a teacher's right," the students
"consider the teacher as being beneath their notice," and even
go so far as to "willfully make trouble and make fun of the
teachers." This is a very interesting subject, and I would like
to offer some opinions.

To begin with, we should make a basic assessment of how
things stand on the current relationship between teacher and
student. Because the revolution unfolded in the schools, an
excellent revolutionary situation has begun to emerge. Re-
sponding to the call to study for the revolution, the broad
masses of students have developed a revolutionary style of
study and have freed their thinking. They are becoming
daring in both thought and speech, neither entertaining super-
stitious beliefs in authorities nor blindly following their teachers. They have taken an active part in class struggle in the
ideological domain and also in the reform of education in the
schools. They have put forward a good many revolutionary
and beneficial views, forcefully attacking the idea of "the sanctity of a teacher's right," and helping to form a relation of

---

*Wenhui bao (Shanghai), April 30, 1966, p. 4. Translated in CED XII:4 (Win-
ter 1979-80), pp. 94-97.

equality and democracy between teacher and student. Some
students improved on the remarks the teachers had made on
the students' compositions; some students corrected the mistakes in the teachers' speeches; some students presented
views more profound and more advanced than the teachers';
and some students made teaching aids that were even better
than those made by the teachers.... All of these are phenomena unprecedented in the history of education, and constitute
the mainstream in terms of the relationship between teacher
and student. As a revolutionary educational worker, one ought
to keep in view the mainstream and essence of things and
applaud the students' revolutionary style of study. One should
support the students' revolutionary actions and modestly learn
from the students. As Chairman Mao has taught us, "one must
first be a good student before one can be a good teacher." A
revolutionary educational worker should guide the students in
the direction of becoming successors to the proletarian cause
of revolution. In regard to the influence of bourgeois ideas and
the force of habit among students, we must display a revolutionary spirit of winning over the generation of teenagers and
strive to foster proletarian ideology while eliminating bourgeois ideology in a strenuous effort to train every student to
be a successor to the proletarian revolution. In no way should
one only take notice of things which are backward and inessen-
tial among the students and shout: "How terrible!" But with
animated gestures, those teachers make frivolous remarks
about the students, demanding that a "distinction" be made
about this and a "dividing line" be drawn on that, in the hope of
imposing various restrictions on the students so as to put them
in fetters again. In fact such a move means [mis]taking the
branch for the root and reversing the order of importance.
   As a matter of fact, the so-called "respecting the teacher
and abiding by discipline" has different criteria for different
classes. What kind of "teacher" should be respected and what
kind of "discipline" should be abided by involve class analysis.
Respecting the proletarian "teacher" and abiding by proletarian
"discipline" call for a revolutionary and democratic relation-

ship between the teacher and the student. The so-called "respecting the teacher and abiding by the discipline" practiced
by the bourgeoisie means a buying and selling relationship
between the teacher and the student with all the power going to
the authority. And "respecting the teacher and abiding by the
discipline" exercised by the landlord class turns the teachers
into overlords and the students into slaves. Therefore indiscriminately advocating the practice of "respecting the teacher
and abiding by discipline" provides precisely an opportunity
for the landlord and bourgeois ideas of education to make an
incursion so that they can uphold "the sanctity of a teacher's
right" under the pretense of "respecting the teacher and abiding by discipline." Judging from the actual state of affairs, it
is not that too much destruction has been done to "the sanctity
of a teacher's right" and consequently that the normal teaching
order in school is affected and the quality of education lowered.
Rather, it is that the destruction is far from being sufficient,
and in certain areas no destruction has been carried out. It is
impossible to destroy the landlord and bourgeois superstructure at one stroke. Class struggle in the ideological sphere is
protracted and tortuous and can have setbacks. The same holds
for "the sanctity of the teacher's right." How can one set an
abstract demand for "respecting the teacher and abiding by the
discipline" when destruction of "the sanctity of the teacher's
right" has only just begun? Only when "the sanctity of the
teacher's right" has been thoroughly destroyed can a revolutionary and democratic relationship be established between the
teacher and the student. This is called "no construction without
destruction and no flowing without damming." It is a law of
ideological struggle.

If a dividing line must be drawn, the dividing line should first
be drawn between two different modes of educational thinking,
namely, between "the teacher's prerogative" and "equality and
democracy between teacher and student." In the final analysis,
whether this dividing line can be clearly drawn depends on
whether or not we can revolutionize ourselves, whether or not
we can remold our world outlook by applying Mao Zedong

Thought and embrace the concept of wholeheartedly serving
the people and the students. Without this, it is impossible to
thoroughly destroy "the teacher's perogative."

In a word, in drawing a dividing line we must have a clear
understanding of the situation and see things from a class
point of view. The division should be conducive to the destruction of "the teacher's prerogative" and must display a spirit of
self-remolding. It can only be this and not the contrary.

**Red Guard Young Fighters
Ascend the University Platform***

Revolutionary Students of First Class
of Third Political Grade of
Beijing Normal College

Renmin Ribao

In the course of resuming classes to make revolution, we
revolutionary young fighters of the First Class of the Political
Third Grade obey Chairman Mao's teaching of "making the
masses educate themselves" and have boldly ascended the
teaching platform of the university.

Chairman Mao teaches us: "In order to have a real grasp of
Marxism, one must learn it not only from books, but mainly
through class struggle, through practical work and close contact with the masses of workers and peasants." But, when bourgeois intellectuals dominated the schools, they monopolized the
platform of political theory classes. The content of the lessons
not only was divorced from reality, from the practical class
struggle and from the worker-peasant-soldier masses, but also
went all out to disparage and oppose our great leader Chairman
Mao and the great Mao Zedong thought. They freely peddled the
revisionist black ware of China's Khrushchev, and vigorously
created public opinion for capitalist restoration.

In the educational revolution, we acted contrary to the old
system of the course of political theory, resolutely opened, as
the most important course, the course of "Chairman Mao's the-

---

*Renmin ribao [People's Daily], December 12, 1967. Translated in SCMP,
No. 4101, pp. 5-6.

ory on the continuous revolution under the dictatorship of the
proletariat," which is most closely related with the class struggle at present, vigorously established the absolute authority of
our great leader Chairman Mao and the absolute authority of the
great thought of Mao Zedong.

At the time, the teacher of our class, who lagged behind the
current situation, lacked the ideological preparation for resumption of classes to make revolution, and dared not mount the
platform. In this situation, should we passively wait for the
teacher, or should we teach the lessons ourselves? This was
a test of whether we could closely follow Chairman Mao's great
strategic plan. Through study of Chairman Mao's works, our
classmates firmly gave this reply: "To resume classes to make
revolution is Chairman Mao's directive. We must quickly respond to it and resolutely carry it out!" What could they do
without their teacher? The revolutionary young fighters acted
as the teacher! With our incomparably deep class affection for
Chairman Mao, and with our incomparable loyalty to Mao Zedong thought, we definitely must do a good job of resuming
classes to make revolution and turn our classroom for the
course of political theory into the front for studying and propagating Mao Zedong thought.

The Cultural Revolution Group of our class assigned the task
of teaching the first lesson of the course of "Chairman Mao's
theory on continuous revolution under the dictatorship of the
proletariat" to the classmates of the third group.

Taking up this task of teaching, classmates of the third group
seriously studied the relevant writings by Chairman Mao and
Vice Chairman Lin Biao and met many times to prepare the
lesson. They unanimously held that to vigorously establish the
absolute authority of our great supreme commander Chairman
Mao and the great thought of Mao Zedong was the most fundamental task in the teaching of political theory, and that to creatively study and apply Chairman Mao's works, tightly grasp
the transformation of world outlook and promote the revolutionization of man's thinking was the most fundamental purpose of
the teaching of political theory.

Therefore, we specified the following content of the first les-

son, "Great Era, Glorious Task": Emphasis on expounding
Chairman Mao as the most outstanding leader and the greatest
teacher of the proletariat of the present era and a Lenin of the
present era; emphasis on expounding Mao Zedong thought as the
pinnacle of Marxism-Leninism of the present era and the banner
of our era; emphasis on expounding China under Chairman
Mao's leadership as the center of the storm of world revolution
of the present era; emphasis on expounding the fact that the
Great Proletarian Cultural Revolution in China initiated and led
by Chairman Mao has opened a new era of the international
communist movement. We constantly grasped the problem of
attitude toward Chairman Mao and Mao Zedong thought.

On the eve of the teaching of this lesson, the classmate responsible for teaching this lesson made an experiment of teaching in the group, widely solicited opinions from among other
classmates, and made further amendments and revisions.

On November 17, the young fighter of Red Guards ascended
the platform to teach the first lesson after class had been resumed to make revolution. Revolutionary teachers and comrades-in-arms of other classes heard our lesson. In the classroom, the classmates fully confirmed, on the spot, the correct
orientation of this lesson, pointed out the shortcomings and put
forth opinions on improving the lesson. A scene of keenness
and activity was seen in the classroom.

After the lesson, all classmates further studied the works by
Chairman Mao and Vice Chairman Lin Biao and made a profound discussion centering on the questions explained in the
lesson. The revolutionary teachers and students unanimously
praised that the teaching of lesson by the revolutionary young
fighters had basically changed the aspects of the course of political theory.

The teaching of lessons by students is also a tremendous push
for the revolutionary teachers. Now, the revolutionary teachers
and students of our class get together to study Chairman Mao's
works, criticize and repudiate the bourgeois and carry out educational revolution. A new type of relationship of mutual teaching and mutual learning between the teachers and the students
is being established.

Appendix / II:b:v

Letter and Excerpts from the Diary
of a Primary School Pupil*

Renmin Ribao

Renmin Ribao Editor's Note

The Beijing ribao [Beijing Daily] of December 12 published the letter and
excerpts from the diary of Huang Shuai, a little red soldier, with a note added.
These are reprinted below for comrades to study and examine.

The fact that Huang Shuai has dared to open fire at the pernicious influence
of the revisionist line in education graphically shows the revolutionary spirit
of the younger generation nurtured by Mao Zedong thought. There are many
such young people and children in our country today, numbered not in the thousands but tens of thousands.

In this movement to criticize Lin Biao and rectify the style of work, we
should pay attention to grasping the actual struggle between the two classes,
the two lines and the two ideologies, deepen education in the ideological and
political lines among leading cadres working in the field of education, revolutionary teachers and students and among parents, oppose revisionism and persist in a proletarian political orientation. Meanwhile, we should seriously sum
up experience in the revolution and education, rely on activists who are determined to carry the proletarian revolution in education through to the end, unite
all forces that can be united, unswervingly put Chairman Mao's thinking on education and the various related policies into practice, and ensure that our young
people grow up with even greater vigor and vitality.

Beijing Ribao Editor's Note

We wish to arouse discussions by warmly recommending to our readers the
letter and excerpts from the diary of Huang Shuai (female), a little red soldier

*People's Daily, December 28, 1973. Translated in SCMP, No. 5539 (Janu-
ary 22, 1974), pp. 29-31.

191

and fifth-grade pupil at the Zhongguan Village No. 1 Primary School in Heitian District. In the revolutionary spirit of going against the tide, this twelve-year-old primary school pupil pinpointed a key question in the revolution in education, that is, the poisonous influence of the revisionist line is far from being eliminated in education, and the traditional ideas hold on tenaciously.

Under the excellent situation of the thoroughgoing development of the revolution in education, we must never forget the protracted and complex nature of the struggle between the two lines and the two ways of thinking on the educational front. Although the question raised by Huang Shuai touched directly on only "the schoolmaster's authority," the poisonous influence of the revisionist line on the educational front goes far beyond that. Acute struggles also exist in such questions as the relation between politics and work, going to the mountains and the countryside, sending workers, peasants and soldiers to universities, the "May 7" road, running schools with open doors, the examination system, the ideological remolding of teachers and schools under the leadership of the working class, and we must continue to fight hard. In this struggle, the revolutionary teachers and pupils are comrades-in-arms fighting in the same trench. They should learn from each other, support each other and unite to open fire on the revisionist line in education. It is hoped that we can all become promoters of progress in the revolution in education and oppose those promoters of retrogression. We must become the motivating force and not the obstructing force, and must not by any means stand opposite to the movement.

Chairman Mao teaches us, "The proletarian revolution in education should be carried out by relying on the masses of the revolutionary students, teachers and workers in the schools, by relying on the activists among them, namely those proletarian revolutionaries who are determined to carry the Great Proletarian Revolution through to the end." As long as there are many activists like Huang Shuai, there is great hope for carrying out the revolution in education through to the end. The leading cadres and revolutionary teachers in the schools, including comrades who have shortcomings in the revolution in education or who have blundered but are willing to rectify their mistakes, must energetically throw themselves into this struggle, resolutely support the revolutionary newborn things emerging from the revolution in education, enthusiastically welcome and support these adorable revolutionary young fighters, and help them forever advance along Chairman Mao's revolutionary line. We must conscientiously study the documents of the Tenth Party Congress and implement the spirit of the Tenth Party Congress. We must arm our brains with the Party's basic line, thoroughly criticize Lin Biao, rectify the style of work and criticize revisionism and the bourgeois world outlook. Under the centralized leadership of the Party and on the foundation of raising our awareness of the two-line struggle, we must sum up our work, do a good job in struggle-criticism-transformation on the educational front and heighten our vigilance against the backwash of revisionism. In the struggle, we must seriously implement the Party's policies, strictly distinguish between the two types of contradictions which differ in nature, distinguish the correct from the erroneous and integrate the revolutionary spirit with the scientific atti-

tude. In the revolution in education, we must also pay attention to supporting
the proletarian teaching system, discipline and order set up in accordance with
Chairman Mao's revolutionary line in education. We hope that the cadres,
teachers and students of the universities, middle and primary schools will submit articles to us on their experiences and insights obtained in this struggle,
and even essays criticizing the various erroneous viewpoints and tendencies,
so that wide and thorough discussions can be unfolded in the newspaper, thus
giving impetus to the development of the revolution in education.

*   *   *

The Letter

I am a pupil in Class No. 2 of the 5th Grade at the Zhongguan
Village No. 1 Primary School. In September, I was inspired
after listening to the Red Guard Program which reported the
accomplishments of the Red Guards in helping their teachers
at the Lanzhou No. 14 Middle School. I then wrote three essays
in my diary to give suggestions to my teacher. Instantly, the
relation between the teacher and myself became strained. The
teacher criticized me for "pulling down the stage of the teacher,"
"harming the prestige of the teacher" and "maliciously attacking the teacher." I thought that the teacher was "suppressing
democracy" and "hitting back in retaliation." The class was
this week full of hustle and bustle. The teacher's main task
during lessons was to incite my classmates to repudiate me,
and whenever I attended class, I was bound to face a rectification. With an angry stare, the teacher pounded on the desk and
said, "Up to now, I still openly call upon our fellow pupils to
alienate themselves from Huang Shuai." "People who run together with Huang Shuai take the wrong stand." A wall-paper
was also posted in class and a roll call made to criticize my
diary. Normally the wall-paper is changed every day, but the
teacher announced that this wall-paper would be posted for a
week. He also expressed his "gratitude" to the wall-paper
group. Under the leadership of the teacher, my classmates have
recently constantly jeered and mocked at me, and vociferously
attacked me on all sides. There were even individual classmates voicing the slogan for "toppling and discrediting me by
criticism."

I am a little red soldier and I love the Party and Chairman Mao. In the diary, I have only articulated what I feel at heart and I admit that there are shortcomings in the diary, such as the inappropriate use of individual words which have challenged the authority of the teacher. But in the past two months, the teacher has clung to this and refused to let go. For many days, I have lost my appetite for food and cried aloud in my sleep at night. However, I have not been subjugated and have repeatedly raised suggestions.

What wrong have I done? Are we children of the Mao Zedong era to be made to act like slaves under the "schoolmaster's absolute authority" created by the old educational system?

> Huang Shuai, pupil in Class No. 2 of the 5th
> Grade at the Zhongguan Village No. 1
> Primary School, Heitian District
> October 21, 1973

Understand Clearly the Reactionary Essence of
the "Dignity of the Teaching Profession"*

Wang Qian

The Great Proletarian Cultural Revolution has dealt a blow
to the ancient ideas which for the past several thousand years
have occupied the battlefront of education and also dealt a blow
to "dignity of the teaching profession." Tempered in the Great
Cultural Revolution, many of the teachers have diligently transformed their world outlook, established a new teacher-student
relationship and brought into play their enthusiasm for both
teaching and study, thus enabling the students to take the initiative in vigorously developing themselves morally, intellectually
and physically. However, the struggle between the two classes,
the two roads and the two ideologies has always been violent.
Some people have under the name of "improving the quality of
teaching" again used the "dignity of the teaching profession" to
push the "practice of intellectual culture behind closed doors
above all else" which is one of the manifestations of this kind
of struggle.

The "dignity of the teaching profession" was advocated by
Confucius for serving "subduing one's self and returning to propriety" as well as the practice of restoration and the training
of docile slaves. The period in which Confucius lived happened

*Guangming ribao [Guangming Daily], April 24, 1974. Translated in SCMP,
No. 5621 (May 24, 1974), pp. 200-202.

to be an era of great social upheaval which witnessed the transformation of the system of slavery into the feudal system.
Stubbornly taking the stand of the slave-owner class, Confucius
frenziedly tried to restore the system of slavery. His object
of taking up education was for bringing up successors to the
slave-owner class. Therefore he invariably placed "returning
to propriety" above all else and required his students to "study
extensively all learning and keep themselves under the restraint
of the rules of propriety." For the sake of using the doctrine
of "subduing one's self and returning to propriety" to arm the
students, Confucius actively propagated the precept that "if the
teacher is not strict, his teaching will not be respected and the
learning will not be solid." The purpose of Confucius in pro-
posing the honoring of the teacher was for the sake of honoring
the doctrine of "returning to propriety." When he discovered
that his student Zhan Qiu was helping the newly emerging landlord class to carry out reform and contravening his counterrevolutionary doctrine, he immediately exercised his "teacher's
authority" and proclaimed to one and all: "He is no disciple of
mine. My little children, beat the drum and assail him!" He
was not satisfied with merely stripping Zhan Qiu of his status,
but also mobilized the other students to attack him. From this
we can see that the reactionary essence of his "dignity of the
teaching profession" was for serving his "subduing one's self
and returning to propriety" or training people for restoring the
system of slavery.

   Lin Biao wrote the "gospel" of Confucius for carrying out
restoration into a scroll for hanging in his bedroom, and used
"of all things this is the most important; to subdue one's self
and return to propriety" to remind himself that he must never
forget the doctrine of restoration taught by his teacher. Lin
Biao could indeed be said to be a "model" of honoring the
teacher of the age. From Confucius to Lin Biao, the "dignity of
the teaching profession" they advocated was all for the sake of
restoration. In criticizing the "dignity of the teaching profession" it is necessary to grasp this reactionary program of "subduing one's self and returning to propriety" which Lin Biao

copied from Confucius before criticism could hit home.

The "dignity of the teaching profession" was a product of the caste system. All his life, Confucius looked upon "returning to propriety" as his duty, and faced with the situation of "propriety ruined and music lost" and "when the prince is not a prince, and the minister is not a minister, when the father is not a father and the son is not a son" in the latter part of the period of Spring and Autumn Annals, he thought of using "the rectification of titles" to restore the order of the slave-owning society and listed the heaven, the earth, the prince, the parents and the teacher among the sacred and inviolable principles of human relationships. It was said that "once a student always a student," and that the "relationship" between the teacher and his student was binding for life. The teacher could thus dominate the student with the correct title and language in accordance with the truth of things. He required the student not only to "bring his bundle of dried meat" while receiving instruction at his school, but also to adhere at ordinary times to the following practice: "If, when their elders have any troublesome affairs, the young take on their toil, and if, when the young have wine and food, they set them before their elders." Although this was the answer given by Confucius to Zi Xia on the way of filial piety, yet it was also meant to cover the way one should behave toward his teacher. The teacher should be one grade higher than the student, and the student was required to show absolute obedience to the teacher. The slightest sign of disrespect would be considered a "transgression." The relationship between the teacher and the student was the relationship between the ruler and the ruled.

Today, the teacher-student relationship under the socialist system in China is neither the parent-son relationship, nor the brotherly relationship, nor the relationship between the ruler and the ruled, but a revolutionary relationship of teaching and learning from each other. The Great Cultural Revolution has violently buffeted the "dignity of the teaching profession" of the past several thousand years and scored great achievements. Today, whether one voices approval of or discomfit toward the students' revolutionary spirit of going against the tide is a test for the teacher. If we still rely on the "teacher's authority" to instruct the students, teaching will not be easy. If we vigorously shatter the "dignity of the teaching profession" and persist in placing politics in command and positive education, then the students are easy to instruct. In the past few years, by using Mao Zedong thought to educate the students, we have successfully transformed the thinking of more than a score of students, and their improvement from the backward to the advanced is a very good testimony.

The "dignity of the teaching profession" is based on the "theory of innate genius" which claims that "there are only the wise of the highest class and the stupid of the lowest class who cannot be changed." Because Confucius wanted to restore the system of slavery, he glorified the slave-owners as the "wise of the highest class" who were "born with knowledge," and vilified the slaves as "the stupid of the lowest class" who "are dull and stupid and yet do not learn." His counterrevolutionary object was to prove that slaves were born to be ruled by slave-owners. For the sake of making his students firmly believe in his doctrine of restoration, Confucius even described himself as a "sage" with "foresight and vision" and said, "Heaven produced the virtue that is in me!" From history, we can see that all those who wanted to carry out counterrevolutionary restoration would invariably try to describe themselves as "genius" "born to be different from other people." Didn't Lin Biao, who dreamt of restoration, claim: 'I've got a good head, different from others. It's especially clever." Actually Lin Biao was a big Party tyrant and warlord who neither read books nor the daily press nor documents and had no learning whatsoever. He wildly thought that by means of propagating the "theory of innate genius" he could become the Chairman of the state and attain the object of usurping leadership in the Party and seizing power. Lin Biao's imitation of Confucius' transcendentalist theory that "there are only the wise of the highest class and the stupid of the lowest class who cannot be changed" is reflected in the teaching profession through the "theory of self-glorification."

He regarded the teachers as "Zhuge Liangs" [wise men] and the students as "fools" and wanted the students to believe blindly in everything the teachers said. Since the Great Proletarian Cultural Revolution, there have been more and more of such newborn things as young fighters spurring on the old fighters. Educators "should learn from the students, and learn from their own object of education." This is an absolute truth.

The "dignity of the teaching profession" is reactionary no matter whether we look at it politically or epistemologically. It is for the training of "full-mark lambs" and for serving the restoration of capitalism. At present, the struggle on the educational front is focused on one point, and that is the question of which class we are training successors for. We must deeply criticize the "dignity of the teaching profession." To be sure, after smashing the "dignity of the teaching profession" we must still impose strict demands on the students. The adoption of an irresponsible attitude toward the good or bad grade made by the student is also a variety of the "dignity of the teaching profession." We must clearly see the reactionary nature of the "dignity of the teaching profession" from the wide publicity given it by Confucius and Lin Biao for training successors for counterrevolutionary restoration. We must hit back by giving tit for at, and carry this great struggle for criticizing Lin Biao and Confucius through to the end.

Disrupting the Relationship between Teachers and Students*

Peking Review

In the winter of 1973, a fifth-grade pupil in a primary school in Beijing had an argument with her form master. Disgruntled, she made some entries in her diary giving vent to her complaints. This was later criticized by the teacher. The relationship between the teacher and the pupil thus became somewhat strained.

It is not unusual that such things should happen in a school. But the "Gang of Four" chose to blow up this incident and make a big fuss of it.

After some careful retouching, two trusted followers of the "Gang of Four" dished out a sensational piece of legerdemain in the form of "A Letter From a Primary School Pupil and Excerpts From Her Diary" and published it in a newspaper together with an editor's note instigating the students to rise and criticize the so-called "absolute authority of a teacher." They claimed that this was "a big issue on the educational front at present," "a major issue in the struggle between the two classes and the two roads," "a question of orientation of whether to persist in restoring the old order or adhere to Chairman Mao's revolutionary line" and "a typical problem in the country today."

Marxists hold that the proletarian relationship between the teachers and students is one between comrades. The duty of

---

*Peking Review, No. 27 (July 1, 1977), pp. 15-17.

the teachers is to educate the students in Marxism-Leninism-Mao Zedong Thought and help them acquire knowledge. Teachers should care for and cherish their students and should, like comrades in the revolutionary ranks, educate and help those who have shortcomings in their ideology or study. Students, in turn, should respect their teachers and, under the latter's guidance, raise their level of ideological consciousness, study hard and master socialist cultural subjects. Should there be any defects in the teachers' work, they ought to give their criticisms in a comradely way and help the teachers do a good job.

The "absolute authority of a teacher" reflects the feudal relationship between the teachers and students. It has nothing in common with the revolutionary, comradely relationship between them. It hampers the revolution in education and impairs the unity between the teachers and students. Though it has been criticized during the Cultural Revolution, the influence of this traditional concept still lingers among certain teachers and sometimes manifests itself in their teaching. This, of course, is a matter of thinking and the style of work, which falls under the category of contradictions among the people themselves. It is therefore a question which should be solved by the method of criticism and self-criticism and through persuasion and education, and we must never resort to the method we adopt toward enemies.

In order to undermine the revolution in education, the "Gang of Four," in the name of criticizing the "absolute authority of a teacher," deliberately confused the two types of contradictions which are different in nature and exaggerated the shortcomings of the teachers to the maximum. The gang's aim was to realize its scheme of throwing the educational front and the whole country into disorder so as to usurp Party and state leadership. They attacked the teachers as a "restorationist force" and even slandered the correct education given by the teachers and the necessary discipline required of the students as the "absolute authority of a teacher." At the same time, they lauded some extremely erroneous acts by the students against the teachers as "revolutionary actions." As a result, disorder ensued in some schools and anarchism was rampant. Necessary rules and regulations were brushed aside, desks and chairs and other public property were damaged, and the teachers could not teach, nor could the students study. Thus serious antagonism emerged between the teachers and students, and class enemies took the opportunity to instigate the youngsters to do evil things.

The "Gang of Four" gleefully praised all this. A woman follower of the gang babbled that the students' damaging of school property was a manifestation of their "resistance against the bourgeois intellectuals" and amounted to a kind of "punishment for the 'absolute authority of a teacher'" and a "revolutionary action" comparable to the damaging of machines in the eighteenth century by workers who feared unemployment.

The "Gang of Four's" perverse action evoked strong resentment from the workers, peasants and soldiers, the parents of the students and, in particular, the teachers and students at large. Out of concern for the proletarian revolution in education, three young cadres of the Inner Mongolian Production and Reclamation Units wrote a letter to that primary school pupil, pointing out that in her diary and letter she had "directed her attack against the wrong target." They said she should direct her attack at the revisionist line and not the teacher, that her argument with her form master was not a question of principle and could be solved through criticism and self-criticism. They also said that teachers and students should unite and work together to make the revolution in education a success. After receiving the letter, that pupil wrote a reply to the three young cadres, saying that she was still young and immature in thought and that she needed further help from them.

The three young cadres' letter, however, infuriated the "Gang of Four" and its close followers. They slandered the letter as "couched entirely in the words of counterrevolutionary restorationist forces." They cooked up an "open letter" to the three cadres in the name of that primary school pupil together with an editor's note which, approved and revised by Wang Hongwen, Zhang Chunqiao, Jiang Qing and Yao Wenyuan, were published in a newspaper. The "open letter" labeled the three cadres as "bourgeois restorationist forces" and "disciples of Confucius."

The publication of the "open letter" gave rise to great confusion among the teachers and students and caused very bad consequences. Because truth was not in their hands, the "Gang of Four" dared not publish the three young cadres' letter. Refusing to be cowed by the "open letter," the three youths held their ground and demanded that a debate on this question be carried on. Many workers, peasants and soldiers as well as teachers and students sent them letters supporting their revolutionary action and praising them as "genuine fighters going against the tide."

After the smashing of the "Gang of Four," the people's minds were emancipated. Under the leadership of the Party Central Committee headed by Chairman Hua, the educational front is now full of vitality. The new-type relationship between the teachers and students has been restored. Bursting with socialist enthusiasm which was once suppressed, the teachers are now doing their best to train successors to the proletarian revolutionary cause. Revolutionary discipline has been strengthened among the students who are now studying hard for the cause of the revolution.

Appendix / III:i

A Talk with Teachers on Wage Reform*

Feng Suhai, Secretary-General, National Committee
of the China Educational Workers' Union

The State Council has decided that this year there shall be
a nationwide comprehensive reform of the wage system on the
basis of a wage increase. It has also been decided that the
newly stipulated wage guidelines shall be enforced from the
month of April. This resolution has received immediate and
enthusiastic support from the nation's wage earners. Here we
would like to talk with teachers about the problems of reforming the wage system.

In the past few years, along with the recovery and development of the national economy, schools at various levels have
carried out wage reform and adjustment one by one. In 1952,
when the Ministry of Education of the former Central People's
Government set wage guidelines for the nation's teachers,
administrative personnel, and workers in schools at various
levels, a general wage reform was carried out in all parts of the
country. In 1954, when the Ministry of Higher Education and
the Ministry of Education separately set new wage guidelines
for the nation's teachers, administrative personnel, and workers in schools at various levels, the nation's schools carried
out adjustments according to these new guidelines and on the
basis of the original wage levels. After several wage adjustments, the wage standards and standard of living of teachers,

---

*Jiaoshi bao [Teachers' News] (Beijing), July 3, 1956. Translated in CED
XII:4 (Winter 1979-80), pp. 98-103.

administrative personnel, and workers have been raised step
by step. Their average wages in higher educational institutions
in 1952 was 18.6 percent higher than that in 1951; for secondary
educational levels, the increase was 15.5 percent; for primary
schools, the increase was 37.4 percent. When we compare 1954
with 1953, the rate of increase of total wages paid was 5.8 percent. The rate of wage increase described above amply indicates that our nation's wage system is a socialist wage system,
i.e., pay according to work. The uniqueness of this system is
that workers' wages are raised step by step along with the development of production, so that not only is there a guarantee
of the continuous development of the nation's construction, but
also of the continuous improvement of people's livelihood.
This reflects the unity of national interest and the interests of
the individual. However, in carrying out the Party's and the
state's wage policy in the past two years, some teachers have
greatly raised their teaching ability and shown good accomplishments in teaching; but their wages have not yet been adjusted. For instance, a primary school teacher in Wuyi County
in Zhejiang Province was transferred to teach in a secondary
school. His original wage scale was 195 points. After two
years' work, with good teaching accomplishments, his wage
scale has remained at 195 points, when most of his fellow
teachers' wage scale is 210 points. There is still a segment of
teachers who, long after their periods of probation, have not
yet had their salaries adjusted. According to the statistics of
Heilongjiang Province for July 1954, there were 356 secondary
school teachers and 4,275 primary school teachers who had all
gone through the probationary period but whose salaries had
not yet had their deserved adjustment. These cases were all
contrary to the principle of pay according to work. Furthermore, in the original wage system, there existed a tendency
toward egalitarianism. For instance, in a county in Liaoning
at the time of wage adjustment in 1953, each of the principals of the six priority [secondary] schools was awarded
200 points, deans of students, 190 points, and the principals of primary schools, 180 points. In a certain pri-

mary school in Hunan Province, the average salary of all
the teachers has become the actual salary of each teacher.
Furthermore, there is this unreasonable phenomenon of unequal pay for equal work. For instance, there are 1,332 teachers in Tongxian in Hebei Province, of which 230 are female,
occupying only 17.26 percent of the total number of educational
workers there. The average female teacher's cultural level in
general is higher than that of the male teachers. However,
according to their salary scales, the pay of female teachers
is considerably lower than that of male teachers. Of the 1,332
teachers, there are only 39 teachers who are in ranks 9 to 11,
and none of the 39 is female; there are 47 teachers in rank 12,
of whom only 7 are female, but all these 7 are doing administrative work, not teaching. Among female teachers, not a single
one has attained rank 13. Below rank 13, the ratio of wage and
rank of the female teachers increases as their ranks decline.
Isn't this unequal pay for equal work? These unreasonable
phenomena are contradictory to the spirit of the nation's wage
policy. They are greatly hindering the professional initiative
of educational workers, and they greatly affect the improvement of the quality of educational work.

This time, the wage reform is aimed at the unreasonable
phenomena described above. On the basis of raising the wage
scale in general, it goes a step farther in the reform of the
wage system. This so-called "on the basis of raising the wage
scale in general" means that this wage reform does not involve
lowering existing wages, but rather raising pay in general.
According to the stipulations, the average monthly pay of
teachers, administrative personnel, and workers of the organizations under the Ministry of Education after the adjustment
should show an increase of 28.72 percent over that before the
adjustment. That is, average pay should be raised from RMB
$33.93 to $43.67. Among educational workers, the increase of
the average wage of primary school teachers will be more;
their monthly average wage after adjustment should show an
increase of 32.88 percent, i.e., an increase from RMB$30.20
to $40.13. The so-called "wage reform on the basis of raising

pay" means not only that there is a pay increase and a further step toward the improvement of the teachers' livelihood, but also that the increases should be rational. In concrete cases, there are possibly larger increases and smaller increases, and perhaps cases where there would be no increase. When things are put on a rational basis, the nation will be able, through the wage system, to bring into alignment the social benefits of the educational workers with the personal material interests that result from their labor. In this way, educational workers will be stimulated to improve their professional ability and actively raise educational quality to realize the nation's educational plans.

How can we make this wage reform proceed even more rationally? First, we must carry out the principle of "pay according to work." The wage guidelines set by the state are based on this principle. This is to say, compensation for work is in accordance with the quality and quantity of each teacher's work. Next, the organization of wages must be based on the principle of more work more pay. That is to say, when a secondary school teacher's weekly teaching load exceeds the stipulated hours, overtime should be paid in accordance with the original pay rate. Teachers of special subjects in secondary schools (when their weekly teaching load has reached the minimal requirement), who are concurrently in charge of a grade of pupils, should be given suitable subsidies each month. Furthermore, the organization of wages must be based on the principle of equal pay for equal work. This means that in schools of the same level, geographical location, and working conditions, when the teachers' educational levels, levels of instruction, teaching loads, and teaching results are similar, they should be compensated equally for their work, whether they are male or female.

In wage reform we must follow the above mentioned principles to make our wage system more rational. The organizations at different levels of our educational workers' union (especially unions of the basic level), must, under the joint leadership of the Party secretaries (at different levels) and the

local unions, assist the administration in performing the following tasks well: First, we must organize the masses of educational workers to seriously study the nation's wage policy
and the measures for wage reform, to make each teacher, administrative personnel, and worker understand the meaning of
this wage reform and understand that the interests of the individual and the nation's interests coincide. At the same time,
we must recognize that in order to have a unified and rational
wage system, we must correctly carry out the principle of
"pay according to work." Through studies each educational
worker will increase his understanding, raise his socialist
consciousness, and develop his ability to distinguish what is
rational and what is irrational. Only in this way can we guarantee the correct implementation of the nation's wage policy
and wage system. Second, the unions at the basic level should
organize and mobilize each and every educational worker to
actively participate in the work for wage reform in schools and
to seriously carry out discussions on the wage reform measures announced by the school administration in accordance
with the nation's policy and the school's concrete situation.
During discussions, everybody must be allowed to speak openly
and exhaustively. Especially in the criticism of incorrect
thoughts, we must develop criticism and self-criticism to make
our evaluation work not only correct but also rational. Third,
union organizations have to exercise their supervisory function over the masses of the educational workers to carry out
struggles against those phenomena that are contrary to the
various stipulations in wage policy and wage reform of the nation. Fourth, we hope that, through this wage reform work,
we'll establish wage labor and the wage mechanism as a function of the various levels of the organizations of the educational
workers' union.

Right now, our nation is in the midst of the high tide of socialist construction. This important measure of wage reform
will stimulate the worker masses to higher enthusiasm for
work; this has a very positive meaning for the promotion
of our nation's enterprise of socialist construction. We

believe, through this wage reform, that all teachers, administrative personnel, and workers will definitely demonstrate further a positive attitude toward working more and
faster on the foundation of quality and economy, and toward
working incessantly for the promotion of educational quality.

My Opinions Concerning the
Calculation of Teachers' Salaries*

Shi Tianhe

The directive concerning work in 1956 to reform the wages
of teachers, administrative personnel, and workers in secondary schools, primary schools, and normal schools was issued
on July 9 by the Ministry of Education to the various educational departments and bureaus of the provinces, autonomous
regions, and special municipalities. This wage reform work,
involving nearly two million teachers, administrative personnel, and workers, will begin on a nationwide scale. In this wage
reform, administrative personnel, workers, and secondary
and primary school teachers (especially the latter) will not only
have their pay levels raised considerably, but also, in accordance with present conditions and the needs of the development
of our undertaking, the wage system will be improved, new
wage guidelines established, and the existing wage-grade system altered. For this reason, the directive of the Ministry of
Education has emphasized the following: "This year's wage reform in the educational field will guarantee a rational calculation of ranks to realize the principle of pay according to work.
This is central to wage reform work." Therefore, we must pay
great attention to this issue to guarantee the smooth completion
of the wage reforms. Now, I would like to give some of my opinions
on the work establishing [wage] grades according to my own

---

*Jiaoshi bao [Teachers' News] (Beijing), July 20, 1956. Translated in CED
XII:4 (Winter 1979-80), pp. 104-108.

understanding, for your reference.

First, why should there be new calculation and establishment of grades? Can't we carry out reform on the basis of the old ranking system? The tasks and aims of the present wage reform are to carry reform of the socialist wage system a step further on the basis of a wage increase, according to the principle of pay according to work and to eliminate defects in the wage guidelines of the past, such as too many grades and too little differentiation between grades. The wage system in the past was characterized by egalitarianism, whereby the guidelines for the highest and lowest wages were not suited to the people of the departments concerned, and primary school teachers in particular had a fairly low wage level. Therefore, in order to more rationally apply the wage increase guidelines given to us by the state, to better carry out the new wage system, and to further demonstrate the function of material motivation, we must — in this wage reform — follow the principle of calculation suggested by the Ministry of Education, to coordinate with conditions in the localities, to stipulate concrete measures for calculation according to the conditions in different areas. and to give every teacher a newly calculated wage level according to the new wage guidelines.

Looking at the state of preparatory work for wage reform in the various areas at the present time, [we have found] that in some places preparations have already been made to carry out reform according to the old systems of ranks and grades. Moreover, there are individual schools that have already announced to their teachers schemes for the adjustment of wages based on transferring the ranks of the old system to a new ranking system, before the notices of the provincial educational departments could reach them. This merits our attention. Of course, this time, when we have wage reform, we should refer to the teachers' original pay and treatment, because the present wage reform is being carried out on the basis of increasing pay. After the reform, salaries and wages will be generally higher than before the reform. But we have to carry out the reform in accordance with the guidelines for wage increases

stipulated by the state, to make the increase in wages totally
rational. If we use the method of transferring old ranks to a
new ranking system, and raise pay equally across the board,
we will be retaining the irrational characteristics of the old
wage-grade system, and will be enhancing the irrational phenomena of the past. This will create even greater passivity
in our future work and cause more losses for our undertaking.
At the same time, because the quality of personnel and the
wage levels are different, the problems that exist in each
county or school, in every province (district, municipality),
are different, and the guidelines for wage increase cannot be
the same. Therefore the measure to transfer ranks uniformly
will be unlikely to suit the concrete situations of the counties
and schools. We cannot, then, adopt this simple measure of
mechanically transferring ranks and increasing wages equally
across the board. Only by evaluating and grading anew can
we eliminate internal defects and irrational phenomena, enabling every teacher to be concerned with the fruits of his labor from the angle of material benefit, his own cultural level,
the raising of his own professional level, and the improvement of teaching.

Second, to carry out the tasks of calculation, we need to consider both the actual conditions of the teachers' pay and their
problems. We must correctly understand and handle the principles of calculation. The principles for calculating the ranks
of teachers have been clearly described in the July 10 editorial in Jiaoshi bao — to take into consideration differences
in educational achievement, seniority in teaching, work capacity, and quality of work. Generally, teachers who have
higher educational achievement, with richer scientific knowledge, who have been teaching for a long time and have a great
deal of teaching experience, are also teachers who get good
results. Therefore, in this reform, we have to make distinctions in pay among teachers who have different levels of cultural attainment and also among those who have been teaching
for different lengths of time. Especially with regard to those
older teachers who possess scientific knowledge, who are rich

in teaching experience, and whose teaching quality is high, we
must correctly recognize their role in the improvement of
teaching and raising the quality of our educational work, and
give them higher pay so they will step forward to further demonstrate their positive attitude and transmit their scientific
knowledge and teaching experience to our younger teachers.
On the other hand, however, we cannot unilaterally emphasize
academic attainment and neglect a large segment of younger
teachers who have raised their own cultural level and have had
good results in concentrated study, improving the quality of
their teaching skills. They are the new reinforcements for our
educational undertaking. If we neglect this point, we'll hinder
the growth of these new reinforcements and bring bad consequences for our work. Therefore, when we evaluate their wage
grades, we must look after them and should not be restricted
by general conditions. In addition, when we evaluate those
comrades who have been transferred from various organs of
the Party, government, and army to work in the schools, we
should consider their experience in revolutionary struggle,
their work experience, and their present actual cultural levels
in assigning them suitable wage ranks. We should not simply
and mechanically emphasize teaching experience and teaching
results; we should help them raise their professional levels in
their actual work, to gradually meet the demands of teaching.
If we can correctly understand and handle these principles, we
can make our efforts of calculation achieve the aims of encouraging progress, motivating the backward to move forward,
and strengthening unity.

   Third, aside from paying attention to the two items stated
above, in the work of calculation we must also pay attention to
the work of obtaining a general balance; that is, in the process
of calculating grades, we must try our best to make the wages
of teachers of comparable qualifications, but different schools
and regions, basically balanced and rational. This so-called
balance and rationality means the use of unified principles and
qualifications to investigate and assess the work of evaluating
teachers in various units to see that there is no partiality or

neglect, and that there is no situation such as one in which teachers are evaluated higher or lower than they should be evaluated. We cannot simply think that because different teachers have the same tasks (such as the task of principal or dean of students) or because they have taught for the same number of years, giving them the same levels of pay is being balanced and rational. If we look at the actual present situation, we find that although there are principals and deans of students, or teachers of a certain grade, their concrete qualifications and quality and quantity of work are different. Therefore there should be some reasonable differentiation in their pay; otherwise we cannot eliminate the existing phenomenon of egalitarianism. When we calculate grades, we must listen to the opinions of the broad masses of educational workers, and accept their supervision. The method of decision by a small number of people after mutual consultation is not correct. At the same time, we must also notice and prevent, in time, certain other mistaken methods such as not following the principles of evaluation; starting only from the interest of one's own units; mutually elevating each other's evaluated levels; or overemphasizing material livelihood, work style, and mutual attacks. We must make the implementation of the guidelines for wage increase practical and rational in order to carry out wage reform work to everybody's satisfaction.

Guangming Daily Appeals for Better
Conditions for Teachers*

New China News Agency

(Beijing, September 19 [Xinhua]) Today's Guangming Daily
carries investigations on teachers' living and working conditions.

An editor's note points out that the material is intended to
draw attention to teachers' living conditions and their work. If
educational work is to be done well it is necessary to be concerned about improving teachers' conditions, the note says.

An investigation by the educational workers' trade union of
China in seven primary and middle schools in Beijing shows
that the wages and material benefits for teachers are lower than
in other fields. Improvements are especially needed in housing
and childcare facilities, it says.

Another investigation by the Chongqing Education Bureau
points out that the problem of teachers' wage is mainly caused
by an inadequate system of wage increases, and that reforms
in the system are essential.

A research team from Shanghai's Fudan University has found
that the major problem is that wages for middle-aged teachers
in schools of high education are unrealistic, and gives the example of the wages of workers who entered factories in 1953
after graduating from middle school. These people earn 20 yuan
more than those who graduated from middle school the same

---

*NCNA (English), Beijing, September 19, 1979.

year, went through senior middle schools and universities and
became teachers. Among the 1965 graduates, those who work
in factories get 20 yuan more than teachers as net income every month.

The national committee of the educational workers' trade
union of China says in a letter to the editorial board of the
Guangming Daily that teaching is not an easy job. Attention
should be paid to teachers' problems. The great majority of
teachers realize that there are many problems that cannot be
solved all at once, but there are problems that would not be too
difficult to solve were the relevant leaders to pay sufficient
attention to them.

IV. THE POLITICAL STATUS OF TEACHERS

(a) Political Attitudes and Ideological Training

Appendix / IV:a:i

Use the Spirit of the General Line to Criticize Further Bourgeois Ideas Existing among Teachers*

Xiaoxue Jiaoshi

Xiaoxue Jiaoshi Editor's Note

Since the establishment, long ago, of revolutionary base areas, primary school teachers in our country have fostered a work style of arduous struggle and serving the people. At the same time, however, owing to the influence of society, most teachers are affected by bourgeois ideas to varying degrees. This is inevitable. It is hoped that teachers will criticize their own bourgeois ideas in the spirit of the general line so they can better educate their pupils in socialist ideology.

* * *

As a result of their study of the nation's general line during the period of transition and participation in a primary school teachers' congress by teachers from various regions, primary school teachers in different parts of the country have shown a remarkable improvement in their socialist awareness. They have perceived the vista of socialist society in our country and their own bright future, and have realized both the honor of being a people's teacher and the gravity of their responsibility. Consequently, most of the teachers have criticized, of their own free will, bourgeois individualist actions such as belittling primary school education, being irresponsible in teaching, making selfish calculations, feeling discontentment about their

---

*Xiaoxue jiaoshi [Primary School Teacher], 1954, No. 8, p. 7. Translated in CED XII:4 (Winter 1979-80), pp. 39-43.

jobs, etc., which had affected them in the past. At the same
time, some preliminary criticisms have been made of bourgeois
educational ideas and concepts manifested in teaching. In order
to make all of us aware of the bourgeois ideas in primary schools
which run counter to the spirit of the general line and jeopardize the
cause of the people's education, we shall now give a summarized
account of part of this situation, so that schools in different localities can use it as a reference for further criticism and ex-
posure of these bourgeois ideas.

Bourgeois Ideas and Viewpoints Manifested in Teaching

1. Some teachers divide students into different categories.
One category of students is called "naturally gifted" (mostly
children of the landlord and capitalist class); teachers spare
no efforts in guiding and cultivating them. Another category
is called "born stupid" (mostly children of the laboring people); teachers adopt an attitude of abhorrence and disdain toward them. For example, a certain public school in Nanjing
refused to accept the child of a worker in the school. Rather
than giving preferential treatment to the offspring of peasants
and workers, the school's enrollment principle is based on the
criterion of being "clean and pretty," "clever and cute,"...
It was not until the municipal education bureau criticized the
school leadership that the pupil was accepted. There are also
some teachers who are partial to students with good grades.
They lend little help to students who have difficulty in their
studies and do not have good school records, even to the point
of discriminating against them (especially those who are held
back in the same grade). A certain primary school in Nanjing,
for example, asked "good pupils" to supervise "bad pupils."
Obviously this was very wrong.
2. Some teachers only impart knowledge; their teaching is
divorced from politics and lacks ideological content.
A small number of teachers disseminate, in their classes,
the concept of putting technique above everything else and the
bourgeois ideas of seeking fame, gain, and status. In a certain

primary school in Xuzhou Municipality, the teacher told the
pupils: "You'll do well if you have skill. Primary school
teachers who have been promoted to be deans and headmasters
are all the skilled ones." Another teacher of fine arts said to
his pupils: "Do your best to paint. Once you can paint well,
it will become a skill. With one painting some people can earn
as much as several tens of thousands of dollars!"

3. Belittling labor, an idea of the exploiting class, seriously
affects quite a few of our teachers. A certain teacher of
Yongqing County in Hebei, for example, said to his pupils: "If
you do not study hard, you will not find jobs in the future, and
you'll have to till the fields at home. How awful it would be to
toil all the year round!" A teacher of Tangshan Municipality
took his pupils on a trip. When passing the fields, he pointed
at the peasants and said to the pupils: "If you do not study
hard, you'll have to swing hoes even in dog days." In isolated
cases some teachers are involved in serious exploitation. A
teacher of Weixian County in Hebei made usurious loans of
over 2,400 catties of millet. The headmaster of a certain primary school in Shuangcheng County of Songjiang Province
used school workmen to help collect his wheat, charged the
school for train tickets on trips for personal matters, and sold
the school wheat stalks at a high price. In short, he tried to
take advantage of the school whenever possible. Influenced by
such ideas, children will certainly "indulge in pleasure and
abhor work"; they will look down upon the laboring people and
the consequences will be very grave.

Bourgeois Ideas Manifested in Attitudes toward Work
and in the Sphere of Ideology

1. Some teachers are irresponsible toward their jobs and
work with a hired-hand mentality. A headmaster of a certain
primary school in Lixian County of Hebei Province said openly
to the teachers: "We do not want to be in the limelight; nor do
we want to become model teachers. It's all right if we can
hold on to our jobs." Some teachers of Jingan District in

Shanghai Municipality only jotted down a few dozen words as notes for their lectures. Some just copied other teachers' lecture notes. Some didn't even bother to copy; they simply borrowed the notes from others and had the pupils of senior grades do the copying. One teacher of a certain primary school of the same district held onto the pupil's exercise books for over half a year without correcting them, causing a serious backlog. One teacher said: "I teach in order to make a living." Some teachers are very particular about their pay but are unwilling to do some additional work. A teacher in a central primary school in No. 9 District of Daye in Hubei, for example, fooled around and played the huqin* all day, teaching only a few classes. He went home eighteen times in less than one month since starting to work in the school. Such irresponsible attitudes toward one's work inevitably lower the quality of teaching and result in the pupils' poor performance in their studies, falling short of the requirements for the cause of people's education.

2. Some teachers constantly cause trouble over their status and payment; they are discontent with their teaching jobs. For example, a teacher in the primary school affiliated with Xuzhou Municipal Normal School said: "Some of my classmates who graduated with me have already become teachers in the normal school. I still teach third grade pupils. This is really disappointing." In Zhangjiakou Prefecture of Hebei Province some teachers haggle over their positions and payment all the time. They are slack in their work, and there is a serious problem of absenteeism without leave. Some teachers work only to earn more money. For example, a teacher in a certain school in Jingan District of Shanghai Muncipality said: "I teach twenty class periods a week, two periods more than others, but I'm paid the same." He thought it wasn't fair. Another teacher said: "You should work no more than you are paid for. It doesn't matter if your job rank is fixed one grade lower; write a few articles and you will make more money than the others."

---

*Huqin: a two-stringed instrument. — G.W.

3. A spirit of collectivism is lacking. Quite a few teachers only take their own interests into account and care nothing about the collective; they show no concern for each other and do not communicate with each other. They are even jealous of each other and are often at odds. For example, a teacher in Peiming Primary School of Jingan District in Shanghai, on hearing that some pupils had had a quarrel, first inquired to which class the pupils belonged. He would not get himself involved if they were not pupils of his own class. Another teacher said openly: "It will be fine if I do not make mistakes in my work. I do not interfere in other's affairs. The less involvement, the better." Some teachers contend against each other; [as already described] they are jealous of each other and are at odds. Some teachers of Jingan District in Shanghai, for example, prepare their lessons each in his own way, unwilling to study the materials together or exchange experiences. The primary school affiliated to the No. 1 Normal School has a teaching and research group comprised of four people. When the group is in session, few people speak, and everyone tries to hold something back for fear that others might surpass him. They make sarcastic remarks about the key class. Instead of helping to do a good job with this class, which they should regard as a joint responsibility of the whole school, they are jealous of the teacher in charge and pour cold water on his efforts.

Manifestations of the bourgeois ideas mentioned above are only part of the materials we have collected. We must make it clear that bourgeois ideas have extensive influence and their manifestations are varied. Therefore it is hoped that the school leadership and teacher comrades in various localities will not rest content with the achievements and progress they have already made, but will continue to deepen their study of the general line of their own free accord, and in close conjunction with their ideology and actual work, gradually and thoroughly liquidate bourgeois ideas so that they can become people's teachers armed with Marxism-Leninism.

Professions and Politics [Excerpts] *

Renmin Jiaoyu

The Hu Feng counterrevolutionary clique put forth a program under the guise of literary theory. Furthermore, this counterrevolutionary program has as its central idea the proposals that writers should not concern themselves with politics, and literature should not serve politics. . . .

They directly address our writers. They want writers not to concern themselves with politics, and art and literature not to serve politics. As a matter of fact, they are addressing all revolutionary working personnel, all revolutionary intellectuals, that is, the people of the entire nation. Why does the counterrevolutionary clique want to grasp this point? This is what they call hitting home — the so-called strategy of psychological attack. Just imagine, what would be the consequence if all the writers, revolutionary working personnel, and revolutionary intellectuals actually showed no concern for politics? There would result a disintegration of socialist ideology, and there would be no place for socialist construction and for a great socialist fatherland. That would mean a counterrevolutionary restoration.

Of course, it is impossible today to openly advocate such a counterrevolutionary proposition. This is just part of their "private talk." They are compelled to disguise themselves by

*People's Education, 1955, No. 8, pp. 6-7. Translated in CED XII:4 (Winter 1979-80), pp. 44-50.

pretending they are merely discussing their thoughts. Moreover, they use ambiguous language and restrict their discussion to matters of art and literature. Stealthily, they have
made an issue of the relationship between profession and politics, drawing a hard and fast line between the two. According
to their kind of reasoning, professional work is professional
work, and politics is politics; the two are not related to each
other. They pretend that they are not opposed to politics, but
are opposed to those specialists, or to people who are engaged
in a special line, who concern themselves too much with politics. Are we not now in great need of specialists in different
trades and professions? Are we not expecting many cadres to
exert themselves to acquire a command of professional knowledge and become specialists in their own vocation? They have
made use of those intellectuals who are relatively deeply affected by bourgeois thinking and entertain suprapolitical ideas.
They have made use of people who work in specialized departments, who, limited by the work in their own departments,
are prone to neglect politics. They have exploited the current
urgent need for specialized personnel, and taken advantage of
the failings of leaders of certain departments, who are caught
off guard, and unable to provide strong political leadership, or
have slackened their political vigilance, etc. Only under such
circumstances can these absurd arguments of theirs exert influence over unhealthy places and people, causing ideological
confusion and encouraging the tendency to neglect politics.
This is exactly their hidden revolutionary purpose in severing
the ties between profession and politics. . . .
    As far as educational departments are concerned, the re-
lationship between vocational work and politics is the relationship between education and politics. This is the most
fundamental issue of pedagogy, and also the problem that all
those engaged in educational work must resolve first. The
answer to this question depends on the answer to the question,
"Who does education serve?" There can be two answers. The
bourgeoisie holds that education is above politics. In order to
cover up its class objective, the bourgeoisie dare not speak up

on the class nature of education; rather, it has created the
theory that education serves the whole society, asserting that
education is above politics and thus has nothing to do with politics. Marxists have another answer to this. Contrary to what
the bourgeoisie holds, the Marxists believe that education is
subordinate to politics and serves politics. As Stalin said:
"We must realize that education is a weapon. Its effect is determined by who is holding it and whom is struck by it." And
Kalov had this to say: "Education is a social and historical
process. . . . Education has always been related to politics.
The socialist revolution of the proletariat is bound to eliminate
the class education of the bourgeoisie — which is impeding the
progress of society — and replace it with Communist education." We are supporters of the second solution.

A correct solution to the issue of how education is related
to politics must be arrived at; otherwise, no theoretical or
practical educational problems can be resolved correctly.
Similarly, an educational worker, in order to do his work well,
must first make clear whom he serves. During the rectification campaign conducted in Yanan from 1942 to 1944, cadres
doing educational work there engaged in concentrated discussion of this problem. As a result, the cadres were able,
at that time, to draw a clear line of distinction between the
ideology of the working class and that of the bourgeoisie,
clarifying the stand of a revolutionary educational worker, and
finding, in connection with the question of "how to serve," a
method of rendering service suitable to the war conditions and
rural environment of that time. This helped educational undertakings in the Shaanxi-Gansu-Ningxia Border Area achieve
new development after 1944. Out of the same consideration,
we have laid special emphasis since Liberation on conducting
political education among educational workers, enabling them
to remold themselves ideologically. Our first purpose is to
resolve this problem; this is the starting point of our work.
Over the last few years we have achieved progress in our educational endeavors. The achievements are inseparable from
the work we have done in this respect; the broad masses of our

teachers have resolved the problem of their stand and have stressed politics.

However, this does not mean to say that all educational workers have correctly resolved the question of the relationship between education, vocational work, and politics, or that the tendency to focus attention only on vocational work to the neglect of politics no longer exists among them. On the contrary, this tendency is fairly widespread among educational workers, though it is manifested in varying degrees. There are still some who entertain a suprapolitical point of view, showing no interest in and no enthusiasm for politics, but merely confining their efforts to "teaching." There are also some who deny the existence of class struggle in schools and hold that only be engaging in professional work can one have a future; doing political work will earn one nothing. There are still others who even divide sciences into different grades and regard natural science as grade A, asserting that once one has mastered it, "one is not afraid to travel the length and breadth of the whole world." As for the social sciences, they believe that it makes no difference whether one studies them or not. Affected by erroneous ideas such as those outlined above, often some educational workers pay no attention to current events either at home or abroad and do not study the major issues of international and domestic affairs. Without studying the state's fundamental policies and its policies on culture and education, and without digging into syllabi and materials for teaching, these people lose their sensitivity to the colorful and varied new phenomena emerging in our great fatherland over the last few years. They grow increasingly ignorant, ill informed, and shortsighted day after day and are confined to the small amount of shallow knowledge in their possession. This has its concentrated expression in the poor quality of teaching in schools at various levels. This teaching lacks ideological content, has little association with reality, and is unable to give expression to many vivid occurrences in the new China. This development is completely understandable; once a teacher is divorced from politics and reality, he will be cut off from the

source of teaching. When reflected in the practice of education, this results in ideological and political education becoming disjointed from the teaching of various courses; at the
same time, classroom work becomes transformed into the simple process of imparting knowledge. As [complete] education
by the school is out of line with the work of teaching, it happens that many teachers show no concern for the students'
ideology. Organizationally it has become a common practice
to have some people engaged in teaching work and others in
ideological work. It happens in some colleges and universities that department heads and chiefs of teaching and research
groups do not bother about ideological and political work for
students. Instead, they have simply relegated this important
educational task to the care of a few young people of the student affairs' section in the school. The idea of "holding oneself responsible only for the teaching of information and not
moral education" is widely circulated in primary and secondary
schools.

Some educational workers are extremely vague on their class
viewpoint and even go so far as to deny the existence of class
struggle in the schools. They adopt an attitude of liberalism
toward their teaching work, an attitude of peaceful coexistence
and noninterference toward bourgeois ideas and even toward
extremely reactionary arguments. The teaching and research
groups in certain colleges and universities fail to put the criticism of bourgeois ideas in its rightful place, thereby touching
off debates over major ideological issues. School authorities
seldom seriously check up on teaching work. Among teachers
and school leaders are people who often fail to proceed from a
political point of view when handling personnel matters or implementing the policy on cadres. They take only the candidates'
seniority and "learning" into consideration or relate the issue
to whether they are their friends or schoolmates. A widely
prevailing opinion at the moment is the incorrect idea that a
good teacher is one who possesses adequate professional
knowledge no matter whether or not he is inadequate ideologically or politically. They have split professional work from

ideology and politics, without knowing that these cannot be
separated. One who is politically weak and ideologically impoverished is unable to do a good job of vocational work. A
fellow with a reactionary political background or reactionary
ideas will pose a greater danger as a teacher if he is well
equipped with professional knowledge; he may spread more
venom in a more clever way. If we do not look at people and
events from a working class point of view, we will be providing
a place in our schools for the remnants of past factionalism
to live a parasitic life. This will provide counterrevolutionaries such as the Hu Feng Clique with a chance to break in and
increase unprincipled disputes in schools; consequently no
clear distinction between right and wrong will be made over
major issues. Inevitably, the political atmosphere in such
schools will be thin, and progressive forces will, in no way,
be brought into play. If the schools abandon class struggle,
the enemy will naturally step up their counterrevolutionary
activities.

We have cited only a few examples above. In order to overcome the tendency to focus attention only on profession to the
neglect of politics in the field of educational work, it is necessary to use the Hu Feng affair as an example in conducting
political education among the large numbers of educational
workers and elevate their political awareness. Analysis must
be made and ideological struggle conducted in connection with
concrete incidents of neglecting politics that involve schools
and individuals to varying degrees. The schools should
strengthen their political leadership and ideological work.
School authorities must rely on the leadership provided by
Party committees at various levels and get concrete assistance
from the Party committees. Today there are a large number
of educational workers who still need to work continuously on
solving the problem of their stand, that is to say, they have to
shift their stand to that of the working class. This is no easy
matter and can only be achieved through a long period of tempering. In light of this, it is necessary to help educational workers
strengthen their study of Marxist-Leninist theory, policies,

politics, and current events, and, through practical experience,
guide them in getting involved with politics. They must take
an active part in the political life of the nation, primarily the
political life at school, and gradually rectify their apathetic
attitude toward politics. It will be a long-term struggle for us
to constantly rectify and prevent the tendency to neglect politics. Only on the premise that we are filled with political vigor
which assiduously drives us to study professional knowledge
can each one of us be led to the correct path of development.
Only in this way can our great contingent of people's teachers
be well versed in their own professions and serve, at the same
time, as propagandists of Marxism-Leninism and state policies. Only thus can they become worthy of the title "engineers
of the soul."

Is It the Case That Primary School Teachers Have Complicated Class Status, Are Backward in Thinking, and Have Unimportant Jobs? [Excerpts] *

Investigative Report on
Taigu County, Shanxi Province

Jing Shihua, *Jiaoshi Bao* Reporter

One often meets people who, when the issue of primary school teachers is raised, always consider them backward in their thinking and as having a complicated class status, or assert that their work "has no future" but is just taking care of the kids, that's all. It is said that some people use this argument as a basis for discriminating against teachers. Are such assertions correct? In other words, do they reflect objective reality? The situation in Taigu County can probably serve as an answer to this question.

Complicated or Not Complicated?

On October 11, before I went to Taigu County in Shanxi, I paid a visit to Hucun Township by the side of the Wuma River and to the east of the county seat on a fact-finding trip. This township, I found, has 10 lower primary schools and 3 complete primary schools staffed by 80 teachers. In terms of the political composition, 2 out of these 80 are Party members and 26 are Youth League members, which means that teachers with Party and League membership account for 35 percent of the total. As for age bracket, there are 60 young teachers — under thirty — and 20 above thirty, i.e., young teachers make up 75

---

*Jiaoshi bao [Teachers' News], November 2, 1956. Translated in CED XII:4 (Winter 1979-80), pp. 51-54.

percent of the total. Furthermore, all these young people were
trained after Liberation. Looking at class status, there are 71
with a middle or poor peasant background accounting for 88.8
percent of the total number of teachers. What is more, 95 percent of all the teachers are members of the Educational Workers' Union.

Judging from the teachers in this township, there is proof
that nowadays primary school teachers cannot be regarded as
complicated [in terms of their class status].

However, does this represent the political situation in regard to the primary school teachers of the entire county? I
was a bit doubtful. Therefore I went to the Taigu County Education Bureau and visited the bureau head, Comrade Cao Yong-
tai. He told me that Taigu County has a total of 566 teachers.
Of this total, 88.3 percent have family backgrounds of the laboring people; teachers with a League membership account for
53.1 percent of the total, and teachers who are Party members
comprise 6 percent of the total. Ninety-three percent of the total
number of teachers in the county are members of the union.

Judging from my investigation of a township and the county
education bureau's briefing on the political makeup of teachers
in the entire county, we can definitely arrive at the verdict:
"Not complicated." Then why is it that people often maintain
that the ranks of primary school teachers are complicated?
During my visit to the head of the county education bureau, he
said categorically that all those who still allege that the ranks
of primary school teachers are complicated are subjectivists.
They have not conducted any investigation or studies among primary school teachers, and like "a blind man touching an elephant,"
they seize on a trifle and insist that it represents the whole.

Backward or Not Backward?

In his report on the question of intellectuals, Premier Zhou
had this to say:

As regards the present political situation of intellectuals, progressives who

actively back the Communist Party and the people's government and enthusiastically support socialism and serve the people account for approximately
40 percent of the total number of intellectuals. Intermediate elements who
support the Communist Party and the people's government, and are generally
able to fulfill the tasks assigned them, but are not politically enthusiastic, account for approximately 40 percent. These two sections make up some 80
percent of the total.

Can the above analysis answer the questions raised by some
people ? Is it possible that the political and ideological situation among the ranks of primary school teachers is an exception ? Now let us take the 566 teachers of Taigu County as an
example and see how they behave themselves politically and
ideologically. Altogether there are 244 teachers who have always been energetic and responsible, quietly immersing themselves in hard work without ever asking the price, who have
made achievements in their work and are eager to make ideological progress and draw close to the Party, always advancing
in the forefront in all political movements. They account
for 42.8 percent of the total number of primary school teachers in the county. Those in the category of generally being
able to fulfill their tasks, able to bear hardship and stand hard
work, but not eager to make progress ideologically (even
though they could lead the pupils in directing propaganda at
the broad masses in various social movements) are 313 in
number and account for 55.3 percent of the total number of
teachers. Of all the teachers in the county only 9 are not
steadfast in their work, not honest and upright in their behavior, and exert an extremely bad influence among the masses.
They make up 1.9 percent of the total.
   Furthermore, we can cite the work of teachers in one township as an example to show how they conduct themselves
toward the Party's educational cause. In Hucun Township of
Taigu County there are 80 primary school teachers. Thirty of
them have to teach 24 class periods a week, averaging 4 class
periods a day. Aside from teaching, they either serve as class
masters and counselors for the Young Pioneers or as leaders
of the teaching and research groups and as cadres for the union.

Every day they have to fulfill all these daily chores and handle
the preparation of three meals. It is just as the saying goes:
"Even the Wangmu Goddess has to go to the kitchen and prepare the meal herself." However, none of them has ever complained of a heavy work load or a hard life. They always get
up at five o'clock in the morning and go to bed at eleven
o'clock at night in a tenacious effort to educate the children.
Let us ask: can this be seen as being backward in thinking?

To Be a Teacher Is to Make Revolution*

Editorial, *Wenhui Bao*

What does a teacher do? It seems that all teachers can answer this question, but their answers are many and varied.

It is said that teachers teach, of course; but then what is teaching for? Some say it is to have, for the future, "peaches and plums [students or disciples] all over the world" [tao li man tianxia]. Some say that the work of a teacher is no more than going to class and leaving class; it is merely an occupation, and so forth. Comrade Yao Peikuan [a model teacher] has been a teacher for ten years; she thinks that this issue is extremely difficult to solve.

Reality is just like that. Most teachers have good intentions of doing their job well. But some have not yet found a correct solution for what Comrade Yao Peikuan considers to be the most difficult problem. Consequently, things go contrary to their wishes. So, let us now consider for a while how Comrade Yao Peikuan solved this difficult problem. This has great significance for our present educational work.

The Party and Chairman Mao have repeatedly taught us that one of the basic tasks of the Party in this entire transitional period involves the struggle with the capitalist class for the allegiance of the younger generation, and the struggle to prevent and to resolutely oppose revisionism. Do we educate the younger generation with proletarian ideology to embark on the

---

*Wenhui bao (Shanghai), May 25, 1965. Translated in CED XII:4 (Winter 1979-80), pp. 55-59.

great road of socialism, or do we use bourgeois ideology to
attract youth in the opposite direction? This is the first problem the teacher has to consider. Behind the scenes of going
to class and leaving class and reciting from books exists the
struggle of "who educates whom," and "who influences whom."
If one does not look at the problem from the proletarian standpoint or viewpoint, one will definitely be unable to complete the
task given to one by the Party, and will be unable to fulfill the
obligation of a people's teacher. Comrade Yao Peikuan has
started precisely from this standpoint to resolve the issue of
the aim and responsibility of the teacher's task.

If we start from the standpoint and viewpoint of class struggle, we'll raise our own sense of political responsibility:
"When our hearts are in the classroom, our thoughts are round
the world." We'll start from a concern for the benefit of the
socialist collective. Not only should we energetically train
children of workers and peasants, and struggle against the phenomena of despising their children but we should also actively
win over and reform children from nonworker and nonpeasant
family backgrounds, enabling them to shake off the family influence of the exploiting class and become, step by step, workers with a socialist consciousness and culture. It is always
better to have more people participate in socialist construction. Our younger generation has spent most of their lives in
the great era of Mao Zedong. With continuous education, it is
possible for the youth of nonworker and nonpeasant family
backgrounds to become revolutionary successors. In order to
make the socialist enterprise more prosperous and exuberant,
we the teachers should try our best to educate every youth,
enabling him to come and stand in the ranks of the working
class.

If you maintain the standpoint and viewpoint of class
struggle, you will always be very concerned about events
occurring around you. You will actively support things
that are beneficial to carrying out the Party's educational
policy; you will resolutely oppose anything that is harmful to
the Party's educational policy.

The standpoint and viewpoint of class struggle will be helpful in facilitating your thought reform and in raising your work
efficiency. That is, in the practical struggle, to educate children of workers and peasants as well as children of nonworker
and nonpeasant family backgrounds, you are bound to meet up
with this or that problem, and they touch upon your own thought.
We can constantly compare the words and deeds of the children
of workers and peasants with those of children of nonworker and
and nonpeasant families, and of their respective parents, by
means of class analysis. We can learn, and we can criticize.
This way we can not only accumulate experience and raise our
work efficiency through constant practice, but we can also facilitate the revolutionizing of our own thought.

Comrade Yao Peikuan's experience tells us that the standpoint and viewpoint of class struggle is the revolutionary
standpoint and viewpoint. What does one do as a teacher? One
is waging class struggle and joining the revolution. We should
learn from her the concept that being a teacher is joining the
revolution. We should learn from her the concept that in our
brains there is always the idea of "struggle." In the current
excellent situation of educational revolution, the great majority of teachers demand to be revolutionized and to be engaged in labor. The progressive example of Comrade Yao
Peikuan is a revelation to all of us teachers.

Some people say, "I am not from a worker or peasant family
background, and I don't have such deep class sentiment. So I
can't learn." This kind of statement is too one-sided. If one
is from a worker or peasant family, has been educated in the
revolutionary tradition of the older generation, and harbors
deep class sentiments, it is easier to walk on the great road
of revolution. On the other hand, though one has a nonworker
or nonpeasant background, if one can clearly understand that
one's own standpoint, viewpoint, and world view are nonproletarian, if one can resolutely learn from the writings of Chairman Mao, study and apply them creatively, unite with the
masses of workers and peasants, steel oneself in labor in a
down-to-earth way, learn through work and incessantly reform

one's own thought, then one can also walk on the road of revolution and labor. One cannot choose one's birth, but one can
choose what road to take.

Some say, "I am a subject teacher [keren jiaoshi]. I'm in
the second line. I'm not like Comrade Yao Peikuan, who is
both form mistress [ban zhuren] and politics teacher. She
should stand in the front line." Teachers may be assigned different jobs and their tasks are not entirely the same. But the
training of revolutionary successors is the common responsibility of each one of us teachers. It is the job of all teachers
to give political education to our students. Politics takes command, and politics has a unique place. The schools are definitely no exception. There cannot be the division of front line
and second line. The purpose of such a division is to separate
teaching from politics, and it is a reflection of the thought
which emphasizes "teaching the subject, not the person [jiao
shu bujiao ren]. Comrade Yao Peikuan maintains the standpoint and viewpoint of class struggle. She has resolution. She
has action. Everywhere she goes she pays attention to see that
what she does is beneficial to the training of revolutionary successors. In this way, she has results to show. Every teacher
should do likewise; with effort, everyone can learn this.

Some say: "It is indeed important for Comrade Yao Peikuan
to establish a revolutionary standpoint and viewpoint. But it
would be better if we could have more teaching methods."
Teaching methods are indeed important. To carry out the people's educational policy we must have correct teaching methods. But where can we get correct teaching methods? First
we must have correct ideology. Comrade Yao Peikuan has this
experience. She says that with deep class sentiment and the
viewpoint of class struggle, one can become clever, and can
think of more methods. This experience is very important.
Methods can be learned. But they cannot be mechanically
copied. The concrete situation of Comrade Yao Peikuan's students and the situations of students in other schools may be
similar or different. Concrete situations have to be analyzed
concretely. One can borrow others' advanced methods in order

to learn, but the most important is in one's own practical experience. Methods are derived from the continuous summation of experiences and lessons, resulting from someone's having "dared" to try. In the course of practice, some are correct and some are wrong. The correct ones can be summarized as experiences; the mistakes can be lessons. Having had correct experiences and lessons from mistakes, one will have a comprehensive understanding of things and will gradually find a series of methods. We should not be afraid of failure. If we fail, we will summarize the lessons learned and try again. We'll not be afraid of upsets. If we have noticed that some students' thinking has changed, we'll concretely analyze the changed situation to find a correct way to educate them. As long as we persist in our endeavor, we'll eventually reap a harvest.

The teacher's work is difficult, but glorious. Comrade Yao Peikuan follows the ideology of joining the revolution and carrying out class struggle. This is not only beneficial to educational work, but is also beneficial to the struggle [for control] of the younger generation. Furthermore, she is struggling continuously against her own thought. In fact, the process of establishing revolutionary ideology is also a process of self-education. Correct things always emerge out of the process of struggle with incorrect things. The elimination of the nonproletarian thoughts in our own minds also needs to pass through incessant struggles. There is the problem of "struggle," the problem of "who's vanquished whom." In the process of "struggle," if proletarian ideology gets the upper hand, then the struggle [for the control] of the younger generation will be carried out even more thoroughly. In the struggle, the process will also work in the opposite direction to facilitate the raising of our own consciousness. Therefore, this concept of "struggle," and the thought of joining the revolution, are worth studying seriously.

Revolutionary Committee of First Middle
School, Shunchang, Fujian, Promotes
Revolutionization of Teachers' Thinking
and Exploits Their Revolutionary Enthusiasm*

Guangming Ribao

Obeying great leader Chairman Mao's teaching, "The problem
of educational reform is principally a problem of teachers,"
and helped by the worker-PLA Mao Zedong thought propaganda
team stationed in the school, the revolutionary committee of
First Middle School, Shunchang, Fujian Province, conscientiously carries out the Party's policy toward intellectuals,
tightly grasps the remolding of the teachers' thinking and, in
the course of educating the teachers, boldly uses them and
fully exploits their revolutionary enthusiasm.

In the past, some teachers of this school were influenced by
the "theory that it is unfortunate to be a teacher" and the "theory that cultural work is dangerous," so that they felt that "it
was difficult to be a teacher and to teach students" and they
were afraid that they might make more mistakes if they did
more work. In view of this living idea, the school's revolutionary committee and the propaganda team stationed in the school
organized the teachers to profoundly study Chairman Mao's
brilliant ideas of revolutionizing education and the "three constantly read articles" and to sharply criticize big renegade
Liu Shaoqi's counterrevolutionary revisionist line of educa-

---

*Guangming Daily, April 28, 1970. Translated in SCMP, No. 4651 (May 7,
1970), pp. 146-148.

tion, and induced them to consciously fight self and criticize revisionism and eliminate "Liu's poison."

Through study and criticism, the broad masses of teachers heightened their consciousness of the struggle between the two lines and promoted revolutionization of their thinking. While helping the teachers heighten their ideological consciousness, the school's revolutionary committee boldly gave them free rein in their work and exploited their revolutionary enthusiasm. The broad masses of teachers replaced "fear" with "courage" and actively and enthusiastically took the heavy load of bringing up successors to the revolutionary cause of the proletariat. The methods of work they adopted were:

1. They Take the Lead in Sharply Criticizing the "Deference to Teachers" and Establish the Proletarian Relationship of a New Type between Teachers and Students

Obeying Chairman Mao's great teaching that "To be a good teacher, one must first be a good pupil," the teachers apply Mao Zedong thought in educating the teenagers. Together with the students, they take the lead in sharply criticizing the "deference to teachers" and vigorously fighting their ideas of "teacher's rights," further eliminate the pernicious influence of the "theory that students are backward," shed their airs of loftiness on their own initiative, and humbly learn things from those whom they teach. In doing their work, they are fully confident that the students will be able to teach themselves, and perseveringly apply Mao Zedong thought in patiently and meticulously doing their work. Because their ideological feeling and their attitude have changed, the teachers can quickly establish a relationship with their students in which the teachers and the students push each other forward politically, help each other ideologically, learn from each other in teaching and learning, and show concern for each other in everyday life. Subsequently, a new atmosphere of teaching and learning for the revolutionary cause prevails.

2. They Attach Greater Importance to Personal Demonstration Than to Verbal Instruction and Use Revolutionization of Their Thinking to Lead the Revolutionization of the Students' Thinking

In the course of studying Mao Zedong thought, revolutionizing education and conducting training in labor, the teachers go in the fore to learn and to work.

One of the teachers once led the students to go to the countryside and learn to grow potatoes. Despite the fatigue resulting from the day's labor, he persevered in studying Chairman Mao's works. He and the students together carried out study on the one hand and examined and summed up their gains from the day's labor on the other hand. They scored relatively good results.

3. They Extensively Carry Out Activities of Friendly Chats and Meticulously Conduct Ideological and Political Work

Obeying Chairman Mao's teaching, "Ideological remolding involves long-term, patient, and painstaking work, and they must not attempt to change people's ideology, which has been shaped over decades of life, merely by giving a few lectures or by holding a few meetings," the teachers change their former methods of teaching, go deep among the students to find problems and have chats with them.

A certain student was once critical about his teacher. This teacher first examined himself and then sincerely had chats with the student many times and exchanged opinions with him. They quickly removed the barrier and strengthened unity between themselves by applying Mao Zedong thought.

A teacher discovered that a few students smoked in the dormitory at night. He immediately organized them to set up a study class and patiently led them to conscientiously study Chairman Mao's teachings concerned and helped them concentrate their energies on their studies.

4. They Form a Three-in-One Combination of School Education, Social Education and Family Education

The teachers of this school persevere in visiting the students' homes once a week or every two weeks and calling meetings of revolutionary parents of students three times in a term, so as to promptly report the students' conditions to their parents, to hear the parents' opinions, to inform each other of the students' conditions and to do well ideological and political work on the students.

Last year, a student who had just entered the school was absent without sufficient reason. Upon discovering this, the teacher immediately contacted the student's parent and told him about the matter. The student's parent held a family Mao Zedong thought study class that night. The whole family sat together to recall past bitterness and think about the happiness in which they now lived. The student learned an impressive lesson and very quickly went through a change in thought and practice.

Thoroughly Transform the
Original Ranks of Teachers*

Zhongshan Medical College
Revolutionary Committee

(Guangzhou, Guangzhou hongdaihui, June 17, 1970).   The
great leader Chairman Mao teaches us: "In the problem
of teaching reform it is the teachers who are the main
problem." To a great extent the thorough implementation
of the proletarian educational line, principles, policies and
methods depends on the teachers. Whether teachers should
foster successors to the proletarian revolutionary cause
or bring up members of the bourgeois "spiritual nobility"
is an important question which has a bearing on whether
or not the proletariat is able to hold a good grip on its cultural
power and consolidate its political power.
 The teachers of our college were all trained in old schools.
Their world outlook is, or basically is, bourgeois. This falls
far short of meeting the requirement for the revolutionary development of proletarian education. Only by remolding them
with Mao Zedong thought and by fostering and building up a proletarian teaching force is it possible to thoroughly change the
present condition of schools being controlled by bourgeois intellectuals and to run the Zhongshan Medical College as a socialist university of medicine really in the service of proletarian politics.

---

*Guangzhou hongdaihui [Guangzhou Red Guard Congress], June 17, 1970.
Translated in SCMP-Supplement, No. 276 (August 10, 1970), pp. 19-26.

With the assistance of the PLA propaganda team, through the purification of class ranks and by going down to the countryside for labor tempering, the workers of our college have during the past year or more waged a revolution in education, earnestly implemented the Party policy on intellectuals and united and educated the vast majority of the teachers. On the basis of their varying conditions these teachers were arranged to take up various fighting posts in a planned manner and with definite objects in view, so that in the course of being so used they were gradually remolded into teachers of a new type.

To Transform Original Ranks of Teachers Calls for Implementation of Party Policy

If the Party policy on intellectuals is to be implemented, it is necessary to treat teachers with the viewpoint of "one dividing into two" and to continuously overcome the erroneous deviation toward either the right or the "left."

When the revolution in education first began, there were two attitudes toward the teachers. One was: "To learn technical knowledge we still have to depend on teachers who, though leaving much to be desired politically, still have professional merits." Those holding this attitude did not realize that the academic ideas of these teachers were, or basically were, feudalist, bourgeois and revisionist. They were in favor of adopting their academic ideas intact.

The other attitude was that there were "four many's" among the old teachers, (namely, many old teachers were not of laboring-people-family origin; many had a complexity of political history and social relationships; many were feudalist, bourgeois and revisionist in their work; and many had not transformed their bourgeois world outlook). As to the middle-aged teachers, many had suffered deeply from the pernicious influence of revisionism. And many young teachers had committed mistakes during the Great Cultural Revolution. Those holding this attitude were in favor of "changing the whole lot" indiscriminately.

The old teachers, in particular, were understood to be "polit-

ically reactionary, ideologically decadent and academically incapable. They should be swept outright into the dustbin of history."

How should these teachers be treated? We studied again and
again Chairman Mao's "Speech at the CCP conference on nationwide propaganda work" and his instruction, "The majority
or the vast majority of the students trained in the old schools
and colleges can integrate themselves with the workers, peasants and soldiers, and some have made inventions or innovations; they must, however, be reeducated by the workers, peasants and soldiers under the guidance of the correct line and
thoroughly change their old ideology. Such intellectuals will
be welcomed by the workers, peasants and soldiers."

We made a class analysis of the teachers who, in general,
might be divided into two types: one consisted of the old intellectuals fostered by the bourgeoisie and the other, of the bourgeois intellectuals brought up after the liberation.

In regard to the former type, apart from some isolated cases
of hidden class enemies and from a small minority of bourgeois
diehards, it should be seen, on the one hand, that many of these
teachers were unsatisfactory in origin and complex in history
and, on the other, that the majority of them generally came
under the question of political history. So long as they could
make a clear explanation of themselves, they should be treated
from a historical viewpoint.

It should be seen also that, on the one hand, their world outlook was bourgeois and that, on the other, after being tempered
by the Great Proletarian Cultural Revolution, they were willing
to remold themselves. So long as they were prepared to "fight
selfishness and criticize revisionism," they could be gradually
remolded under the leadership of the correct line.

Moreover, it should be seen, on the one hand, that their academic ideas belonged to the feudal, bourgeois and revisionist
system and, on the other, that after the revolutionary mass
criticism movement had broken up the old system, their special
abilities could be used to advantage and, so long as they could
integrate themselves with the workers, peasants and soldiers,

continuously receive reeducation from them, and thoroughly change their old ideas, they could still contribute their energies to socialism.

In regard to intellectuals of the latter type, it should be seen that, on the one hand, in their old schools they had been poisoned by the feudal, bourgeois and revisionist influence and for a long time they had "separated themselves from three" things. In varying degrees, under the corrosive influence of old ideas, they had neglected politics, looked down upon the workers and peasants and despised labor. On the other hand, it should also be seen that the majority of them came from families of the laboring people and that for many years, nursed in Mao Zedong thought, had developed an ardent love for Chairman Mao, for the Communist Party and for socialism.

For these reasons, it would be a mistake to make a wholesale use of the original ranks of teachers without transforming them or to change the whole lot without a class analysis. It would run counter to the Party policy of uniting, educating and re-molding the intellectuals. Also, it would not conform to the fundamental interests of the proletariat or the laboring people.

In order to turn the Party policy into an action of the masses, we organized the revolutionary teachers and students of the whole college to study Chairman Mao's teaching, "All Party comrades must understand that a correct policy toward the intellectuals is one of the important conditions of revolutionary victory."

As an example we cited the case of a certain professor of the former parasitological teaching and research group and let everybody arrive at a uniform understanding of "dissecting a sparrow." This professor was originally doing research work on the prevention and treatment of schistosomiasis. In 1956, the great leader Chairman Mao received him and directed him to make a contribution to the extermination of schistosomes.

However, acting on the instruction of the capitalist-roaders of the "bureaucratic medical and health department," he turned his attention to chasing after fame and profit and steered the parasitological teaching and research group toward research into pulmonary schistosomes, a so-called "world blank."

During the Great Proletarian Cultural Revolution the masses criticized his mistake. Unwilling to accept this criticism he told the people at the time, "I'd rather sell bean-curd than engage in scientific research." Then some people said, "This person is really exasperating us. He doesn't listen to Chairman Mao's words but vigorously pushes Liu's revisionist line in medical research. Up to now he hasn't awakened. What's the use of keeping a man like him!" But the majority held this view: "The matter with him mainly concerns the question of world outlook. He has no feelings of hostility toward socialism. He still can be remolded."

Having unified our understanding, we let him go to take part in scientific research work in an area infected with schistosomiasis. Reeducation by the poor and lower-middle peasants enabled him to realize further that, in the past by showing his interest in parasites and not in man and by filling his mind with ideas about fame and profit, he really could not face Chairman Mao or the poor and lower-middle peasants.

We made up his mind to "contribute the remaining years of his life to the eradication of schistosomes." While conducting research in the prevention of schistosomiasis he was afraid of neither infection nor danger. Fighting side by side with the young teachers, he obtained comparatively good results.

During the past year or more, while implementing the Party policy on intellectuals, we had to struggle repeatedly with the interference either from the right or from the "left" in every forward step we took. We persisted in remolding the intellectuals while using them and in using them while remolding them. We united the broad masses of teachers and mobilized their revolutionary activism.

Some old teachers, who in the past believed that "politically they stank, their old methods no longer worked, they waited for the masses to finish digging them out and struggling against them and then they would retire to their villages and end their lives there," now expressed this view: "Politically there are great prospects. Academically much remains to be done.

There is no limit to the way we can serve the people. We should follow Chairman Mao closely and should never turn back."

Some of those who were unwilling to be teachers expressed the view that "One must be faithful to the Party's educational cause." They said with great emotion, "It is Chairman Mao's brilliant thought that illuminates our road to continuing the revolution."

Solution of Fundamental Question "For Whom We Teach" Is Necessary to Teacher Remolding

After taking part in the educational revolution for a time, the teachers again developed many living ideas. Some were worried about "the lack of technical advancement if they taught in rural areas for long." They said that "they were placed at a disadvantage when sent down to the countryside." Others had this to worry about: "When you commit a blunder in teaching, somebody will grab you by the queue and shoot you like a live target." They said, "It is dangerous to be a teacher."

From their living ideas we came to realize profoundly that the remolding of intellectuals was a formidable and protracted task. The process of ideological remolding was, from beginning to end, associated with violent struggles, the focus of which was the question of "for whom we teach."

In accordance with Chairman Mao's teaching, "The question of 'for whom' is fundamental: it is a question of principle," and around the question of "for whom we teach," we vigorously launched a mass movement for the living study and application of Mao Zedong thought and unfolded revolutionary mass criticism in a deep-going and sustained manner. Refuting Liu Shaoqi's "theory of studying in order to be an official" and bearing in mind the living ideas of the teachers, we speeded up the transformation of their world outlook and, taking the road of integration with the workers, peasants and soldiers, further established the concept of teaching for the revolution. Our concrete methods were:

First, "five togethernesses" with the poor and lower-middle

peasants. As ordinary commune members the teachers joined
production brigades and settled down. They invited the poor
and lower-middle peasants to make "two recollections": to
recollect their past bitterness and think of their present sweetness; to recollect past miseries and think of exercising power.
They gave help in three ways: help in changing one's stand;
help in remolding one's ideology; and help in tempering one
through labor.

From the persons of poor and lower-middle peasants the
teachers saw their own weaknesses and found the gap between
them and the peasants. They learned about a clear-cut class
stand, deep class feelings, a lofty ideological domain and the
revolutionary custom of study of combining theory with practice.
They understood whom they should love, whom they should hate,
whom they should follow and whom they should serve.

Second, remolding old ideas in the course of labor. Separation from labor and contempt for the worker and the peasant
were the most fundamental problems concerning the teachers
trained in old schools. To remold their old ideas necessitated
putting the teachers through a course of arduous tempering during the three great revolutionary movements.

With this in view, we organized the broad masses of teachers
to go to the "May 7" school for cadres or to the countryside
and to take part in collective productive labor. For the first
time they lived in dwellings erected by themselves and ate grain
grown by themselves. Only thus could they really understand
the great truth that the world was created by labor. They realized deeply that "every grain of rice was soaked with the
blood and sweat of the laboring people and it was really shame-
ful for them to look down upon the workers and peasants in the
past." Many of them said that perspiration from labor had
cleansed their soul and that only by participating in labor regularly could they build an ideological Great Wall to oppose and
guard against revisionism.

Third, learning from workers, peasants, soldiers and students. We put the teachers and the students of the "new medical class" in the same group to practice "five togethernesses."

The fine qualities of workers, peasants, soldiers and students were at all times a source of education for the teachers. At the "native medical college" operated by themselves, students of the "new medical class" immediately sent their own towels to the poor and lower-middle peasants who were short of this article. On hearing that these peasants had finished the medicinal herbs they needed, the students quietly left to gather some during their rest period at noon.

In order to defend Chairman Mao's medical and health line, the students tested herbal medicine, practiced acupuncture needling on themselves and attended to patients in their homes. Deliveries of medicine were made to them in any weather. In order to persuade an old, apprehensive, poor peasant to go to a hospital for an operation, the students made five calls at his home to carry out ideological work. This moved the old man who said, "I've lived through three dynasties. I've seen the sick go to the doctor for treatment, but I've never seen the doctor call on the sick."

These incidents profoundly educated the teachers who felt that of all the gaps which left them behind the biggest was their lack of thought to serve the workers, peasants and soldiers.

Fourth, teaching the soul in the course of serving the poor and lower-middle peasants. The process of serving the poor and lower-middle peasants was a process of being reeducated by these peasants. It often happened that one visit or one delivery of medicine to the patient's home, or one action taken to treat or guard against disease turned out to be a criticism rally or a vivid lesson of education in class struggle and in the struggle between the two lines. In the past, quite a number of poor and lower-middle peasants, with the little money they had saved with difficulty, went to see a doctor in Guangzhou. Either they could not see the doctor or they were given the judgment that they had contracted an "incurable disease."

From the complaints lodged by the poor and lower-middle peasants against Liu Shaoqi's revisionist medical and health line the teachers could see their own past. Once, an elderly woman successively brought two children to see a doctor. One

was only slightly ill, but the other was a case of pneumonia,
having a high fever and in a serious condition.

A teacher asked her: "Why didn't you bring the seriously ill
child here first?" The woman said: "The first child was my
neighbor's and was placed under my care. This — the second
one — is mine." The teacher said with deep emotion: "Before
the great image of the poor and lower-middle peasants we are
forever primary school pupils and shall never be able to graduate."

Practice proves that the fundamental way to transform the
world outlook of teachers and solve the question of "for whom
we teach" is for the teachers to go among the workers, peasants and soldiers and to receive reeducation from them. In the
past year or more, the spiritual appearance of the broad
masses of teachers has shown a profound change. "To contribute the energy of their whole lives to the educational cause of
the proletariat" has become a common oath of the revolutionary
teachers.

Learn Warfare through Warfare; Foster New-type Teachers Expert in One Line and Capable in Many Other Ways

Because of their protracted "three separations," the original
ranks of teachers not only need to be reeducated politically and
ideologically but also have to study their special lines of knowledge anew.

In the past, many teachers concerned themselves mainly with
theory and had hardly any practice. "Specialists" in the study
of poisoning did not even know how to carry out experiments in
poisoning. Teachers giving basic lessons understood nothing
about treating the sick. Physicians had no knowledge of sur-
gery. Teachers of pediatrics could not treat the sickness of
adults. A person knew only how to talk about one kind of worm
or one kind of disease; even a single disease required two persons to lecture on it.

In the course of integration with the workers, peasants and
soldiers, the teachers deeply realized the pernicious influence

brought to them by the counterrevolutionary revisionist educational line and health line of the arch renegade Liu Shaoqi. They also felt the urgent need for a restudy of their professional knowledge.

In accordance with Chairman Mao's teaching, "In a certain sense the wisest and the most capable are the fighters with the best practical experience," we led the teachers to grasp tightly the remolding of their world outlook and, at the same time, to learn medical knowledge from the workers, peasants and soldiers. This enabled them to combine theory closely with practice and, step by step, to become new-type teachers of all-round development, combining traditional medicine with Western treatment, specializing in one line and being capable in many other ways. We used the following methods:

First, learning from the workers, peasants and soldiers. In the course of their protracted struggles with disease the broad masses of workers, peasants and soldiers have accumulated a wealth of experience in the prevention and treatment of disease. During the past few years, in particular, they used Chairman Mao's great philosophical thoughts as the weapon to repudiate the bourgeois "philosophy of servility to things foreign" and "doctrine of going at a snail's pace." They vigorously unearthed the medical legacies of the motherland, overcame many difficulties in medical science and wrought miracles hitherto unknown in the history of medicine.

We regularly invited PLA soldiers, barefoot doctors and veteran herbal peasants to impart their medical knowledge and help the teachers and students to run study classes. In the first six months of last year alone, 81 terms of classes to study new methods of medical treatment and 118 terms of classes to study traditional herbal medicine were operated. At present, the teachers have generally learned how to identify and apply nearly 100 kinds of herbs and how to cure patients with new methods of acupuncture.

Second, learning in the course of work. In accordance with Chairman Mao's instruction, "Learn warfare through warfare," we organized the teachers and students to learn skills to serve the people while giving medical treatment to the poor and

lower-middle peasants. For example, in a planned manner we
arranged for the preclinical and nonsurgical teachers to join
surgical or ophthalmological teams so that they would after a
period of training be able to grasp initially the whole process
of checking the patient's conditions, making preoperation
preparations, performing the operation and administering post-
operation care.

In the past, a teacher formerly of the anatomical teaching and
research group knew only how to cut dead bodies but could not
operate on a live person. Now, he is able to carry out medium
and minor operations of a general nature and to remove ophthalmological cataracts. Moreover, he can lead students to go
deep into remote villages and treat the sick, poor and lower-
middle peasants. This has enabled many people to see the red
sun with joy.

Third, teaching one another and learning from one another.
In accordance with Chairman Mao's teaching, "Officers teach
soldiers, soldiers teach officers and soldiers teach one another," we teamed up in a planned manner teachers of traditional and Western medicine, of preclinical and clinical courses
and of this and that subject and organized them into mutual-aid
teams. We also let the teachers form "pairs of red" with the
students or with the barefoot doctors so that they would teach
one another, learn from one another, and overcome one's weaknesses with the strong points of another. In this way they would
gradually rid themselves of the onesidedness of their specialized knowledge and develop themselves into experts in one line
and versatile teachers in many others.

A physician of the "new medical class" organized a mutual-
aid team with a traditional herbalist. They learned as they
taught. After a year's practice, this physician had learned
initially how to treat patients with methods which integrated traditional medicine with Western treatment. In addition, he was
able to lecture his students on methods of "dialectical medical
treatment" which represented an integration of traditional medicine with Western treatment. This was welcomed by the students.

After more than a year's restudy in their profession, the teachers of our college have basically become new-type teachers who can do as well as talk and practice traditional as well as Western medicine. They are experts in their specialized fields and are capable of doing many other things. On this momentous change a preclinical teacher has said with great emotion: "I was a 'cripple' during more than a decade's teaching in an old school. Participation in the educational revolution for not quite a year has turned me into a 'versatile worker.'"

**Seriously Carry Out the Party's
Policy Toward Intellectuals, Tightly
Grasp the Remolding of
Teachers' World Outlook***

Party Branch of Baijiazhuang
Worker-Peasant-Soldier School,
Beijing Municipality

In the past two years and more, obeying the great leader Chairman Mao's great teaching, "The problem of educational reform is mainly a problem of teachers," we have seriously carried out the Party's policy toward intellectuals, tightly grasped the remolding of the teachers' world outlook and gained preliminary results in this concern. A group of activists who are determined to carry out the proletarian revolution of education through to the end have emerged from among the teachers, giving an impetus to the deep-going development of the revolution in education.

Earnestly Carry Out the Party's Policy Toward Intellectuals

In early 1969, after the worker-PLA Mao Zedong thought propaganda team was stationed in our school, a leading group in the form of "three-in-one combination" comprising workers, armymen and representatives of cadres, teachers and students of the school was set up very quickly. In September of the same year, a Party branch was formed. At the time, we felt obvi-

---

*Guangming ribao [Guangming Daily], October 13, 1971. Translated in SCMP, No. 5005 (November 2, 1971), pp. 64-69.

ously that a force of teachers of the proletariat must be organized in order to implement Chairman Mao's proletarian line
of education and consolidate the leadership of the working class
over the schools. We made investigations and analysis of the
current situation of the teachers of the whole school and discovered two things, namely, most of them came from other than
working class families and most of them were not content with
educational work.

In view of this state of affairs, some leading members had
two erroneous views: Some of them held that the revolution in
education wouldn't work if reliance was placed solely on these
teachers and it was necessary to make a "big reshuffle"; the
others were of the opinion that the tasks of teaching were so
heavy that it was impossible to spare time for remolding these
teachers and it would be all right just to "bring them together
and use them."

These two erroneous views showed that some of our comrades
did not understand the Party's policy toward intellectuals and
underestimated the progress the teachers had made during the
Great Proletarian Cultural Revolution. For this reason, the
Party branch held that it was necessary first to imprint the
Party's policy toward intellectuals in the minds of the leading
members before this policy could be carried out among the
teachers. Obeying Chairman Mao's great teaching, "The question of the intellectuals is above all one of ideology" and "The
overwhelming majority of the intellectuals in our country want
to make progress and remold themselves, and they are quite
capable of remolding themselves," we made a historical, all-
round and concrete analysis of the current situation of the
teachers, examined and banished the two erroneous ideas of "a
big reshuffle" and "bringing them together and using them," and
understood the Party's policy toward intellectuals by raising
it to the high plane of the implementation of Chairman Mao's
revolutionary line, thereby raising our consciousness.

We attached primary importance to firm grasping of the
teachers' living study and application of Mao Zedong thought.
With reference to the problems among the teachers, we carried

out "everyday reading," held study classes, fought against self-interest and repudiated revisionism, thereby raising the teachers' consciousness of the class struggle and the struggle between the two lines. We paid particular attention to helping the teachers establish the idea of "being faithful to the Party's educational cause" by standing on the high plane of training successors to the revolutionary cause of the proletariat, thereby rousing the teachers' enthusiasm for participating in educational revolution.

We should correctly handle the ideological setbacks the teachers show in the course of progress. Chairman Mao teaches: "A thorough change in world outlook takes a very long time, and we should work patiently and not be impetuous." In the past two years, from the three setbacks the teachers of our school suffered in the course of ideological remolding, we discovered that each time the teachers slackened their ideological remolding and were plagued by more problems than usual was precisely the moment when the leadership confined its attention to their progress and slackened its efforts to educate and remold them. For this reason, whenever the teachers showed ideological setbacks, we always refrained from being impetuous and exerting pressure on the teachers but made efforts to combat arrogance and do away with complacency at the higher level and to enlighten and educate the teachers at the basic level.

For example, in July and August last year, some teachers thought that their remolding was "near completion" and they sometimes became arrogant and opinionated, particularly when they were commended by the leadership for the good results they produced in teaching lessons in the school-run factory and putting Mao Zedong thought in command of the cultural lessons. The Party branch promptly launched a rectification movement and roused the masses to air their views to the leadership. After that, obeying Chairman Mao's teaching, "we must be good at directing the petty bourgeois ideology in our ranks to the track of the proletarian revolution," we organized the teachers to visit and learn from Qinghua University and to find their own shortcomings by comparing their achievements with those of the advanced units. Subsequently, the teachers imposed higher demands on themselves, made strenuous efforts to study and apply Chairman Mao's works in a living way, took an active part in the revolution of education and worked more vigorously.

In the course of carrying out the Party's policy toward intellectuals, we paid attention to working meticulously on people of three kinds: First, those who had comparatively complex political history; second, those who had made mistakes which were relatively serious but were not of the nature of a contradiction between the enemy and ourselves; third, the so-called "advanced elements" in teaching rated under the revisionist line of education.

Accordingly, we made concrete analysis of the different conditions and carried out the Party's policy on each of them. With regard to the teachers who did not have a good family background, we helped them to draw a line politically and ideologically between themselves and their exploiting class families, to eliminate the influence of their families on their own thinking and to stand on the side of the proletariat.

In handling the comrades who had made serious mistakes, we helped them look at themselves through the viewpoint of "one dividing into two," so that they saw the seriousness of their mistakes and the fact that they could go on advancing only so long as they would receive education and correct their mistakes. We did more educational work on them, urged them to change for the better, and focused our attention on their actual deeds.

With regard to the so-called "advanced elements" in teaching in the past, we helped them study Chairman Mao's concepts of the revolution in education, transform their world outlook, criticize and repudiate arch renegade Liu Shaoqi's revisionist line of education and eliminate its pernicious influence on themselves. We gave them free rein in work and allowed them to remold and temper themselves in the course of practice, so as to fully rouse their enthusiasm in participating in educational revolution.

Organize Teachers to Receive Reeducation from Workers, Peasants and Soldiers

Obeying Chairman Mao's teaching, "The majority or the vast

majority of the students trained in the old schools and colleges
can integrate themselves with the workers, peasants and soldiers, and some have made inventions or innovations; they
must, however, be reeducated by the workers, peasants and
soldiers under the guidance of the correct line and thoroughly
change their old way of thinking," we adopt three methods for
organizing the teachers to go through tempering in labor during
the practice of the Three Great Revolutionary Struggles:

First, the teachers are organized in groups to receive reeducation and devote a few months' time to eating, living, laboring and studying together with the workers and the poor and
lower-middle peasants in factories and rural villages. In this
way, they find it easy to maintain ties with the masses and to
learn better from the workers and poor and lower-middle peasants. This method produces remarkable results.

Second, the teachers are organized to labor for a short period of ten to fifteen days. This involves only a short period
of time and not many teachers have to be taken off their job at
one time. It is easy to carry out this method in the current
situation when teachers are short.

Third, the teachers are organized to do labor during spare
time or on holidays. This method is good in a way that teaching
and learning is not affected and a greater number of teachers
can take part in labor. We have sent two groups of teachers,
totalling 30, to the factory and the countryside to go through
tempering in labor for a comparatively long period of time.
More than 20 teachers have participated, by turns, in productive labor and scientific experiment in the factory run by the
school.

In the course of tempering in labor, the teachers' mental outlook has gone through a change. We came to realize that, while
the teachers were being tempered through labor, it was necessary to strengthen ideological and political work on them, to
promptly eliminate the pernicious influence on them and quicken
transformation of their world outlook with reference to their
living ideas.

In the preliminary, intermediate and final stages of tempering in labor, the erroneous ideas of "getting a veneer of gold through labor," "manual labor relieves mental work" and "remolding has come to its peak" were prevalent from time to time among the teachers. Taking into consideration the pernicious influence of the "theory of getting a veneer of gold through labor," we guided the teachers to seriously study Chairman Mao's teachings about the integration of intellectuals with the workers and peasants, made them reveal their past conduct of "three separations," and understand more clearly the necessity of remolding of their world outlook.

With reference to the "theory that manual labor relieves mental work," we organized the teachers to seriously study Chairman Mao's great teaching, "Politics is the commander and the soul," and led them to learn modestly from the workers and poor and lower-middle peasants. When the erroneous idea "remolding has come to its peak" showed itself, we educated the teachers in Chairman Mao's viewpoint of "one dividing into two" and his viewpoint of classes and class struggle, thereby making them understand that the protracted nature and complexity of the class struggle determined that the transformation of the intellectuals' world outlook involved arduous work and would meet with setbacks, and making them realize that they must see their progress as well as their shortcomings, so that they could go on advancing.

Strengthen Transformation of Teachers' World Outlook in the Practice of Teaching

The teachers may easily show their problems of world outlook in the course of teaching. Therefore, the leadership should grasp the problems in the teachers' innermost being and strengthen transformation of the teachers' world outlook.

In teaching a lesson, one of the teachers twisted the political content of this lesson, made a mess of this lesson which gave prominence to proletarian politics, and said something politically wrong. The Party branch promptly made an all-round analysis and study of his problem and was of the opinion that this was a serious problem but he did not release poison intentionally and this problem cropped up because he usually did not pay attention to study and did not give prominence to proletarian politics. Accordingly, it decided to grasp this matter and use it to educate this and other teachers.

First, it organized the teaching of a lesson in comparison. Another teacher taught the same lesson after exhaustive preparations. The students were deeply educated in the proletarian political content of this lesson and by the teachers' strong proletarian feeling. After that, the activity of a "brief commentary," entitled, "Why is it that the teaching of the same lesson by two different persons produces entirely different results?" Eventually, this teacher was helped in seriously studying Chairman Mao's teachings and went among the workers, peasants and soldiers to prepare lessons and learn the deeds of the heroes and models among them. He taught this lesson in another class. Because his thinking and feeling had changed, he taught this lesson with better results.

We learned deeply from this matter that the question of the intellectuals was above all one of ideology. It is normal that they show some old ideas during their practice of teaching, and this question can be solved only by the methods of discussion, criticism, and education through persuasion. They must be allowed to carry out practice boldly. In the course of practice, they should be given help patiently in raising the level of their thinking and correcting their mistakes.

We should make practical analysis of the teachers' problems revealed in the course of teaching. We must pay attention to making a few distinctions, distinguishing the mistakes they make verbally and in writing because of their low political and ideological levels and their failure to concentrate their energies from their adherence to the reactionary stand and deliberate attack on the Party; distinguishing their failure to explain a question by combining theory with practice from their adherence to the old road of "three separations"; distinguishing their failure to put proletarian politics in command of cultural lessons from their objection to the bringing of proletarian politics to the fore.

In this way, it is possible to point out exactly the teachers' problems cropping up in the course of teaching, to convince them completely, and to make them display better the revolutionary spirit of daring to think, speak out, act and overcome difficulties during the practice of transformation of education.

We paid particular attention to bringing the worker-teachers in full play in remolding the other teachers who had taken up their posts for some time. In November last year, twelve distinguished workers were invited to serve as teachers in our school. Under the leadership of the Party branch, the worker teachers stayed on the first line of teaching and helped the other teachers of the school in overcoming the ideas of "wait," "fear" and "hardship" and taking an active part in the revolution of education; with reference to the problems revealed in the sphere of teaching, they and the other teachers and the students carried out revolutionary mass criticism and eliminated the pernicious influence; they led the other teachers to seriously study and carry out Chairman Mao's concept of revolution in education during their practice of transforming education, so that the other teachers might continuously raise their political thinking and level of professional attainments.

Appendix / IV:b:i

Teaching Is the Overriding Central Task in Schools*

Editorial, *Renmin Jiaoyu*

Over the last three years and more, teachers and students at educational institutions of different levels across the country have received a certain amount of education through their participation in various social activities. All these achievements should be affirmed.

However, here we must point out emphatically that quite a few cadres fail to understand that "teaching is the overriding central task of a school" and set excessive demands on teachers and students for their participation in social activities. As a result, a situation of urgency and confusion has been created, posing a serious obstacle to the teaching effort. We can cite the following examples:

In regard to institutions of higher and secondary learning, a student by the name of He Xulan — a League member and a freshman in the Department of Finance, Sichuan Provincial Finance and Economics Institute — spends 27 hours a week on social activities; there are only 27 hours left for her to study. Aside from 21 hours spent attending lectures, she has only 6 hours to review all the lessons. Teachers and students of Bobai High School in Guangxi Province are often sent by the county authorities on such errands as arranging meeting places and writing slogans. From last October to this January 15,

---

*People's Education, 1953, No. 3, pp. 4-5. Translated in CED XII:4 (Winter 1979-80), pp. 60-67.

Power in the Schools 263

they were called on to do more than thirty errands of this type. Language teacher Li Shiding and mathematics teacher Xu Xing-hua of the No. 4 High School of Zunyi, Guizhou, were dispatched on an errand to help plant trees on the commemorative site of the Zunyi Conference and to go to the countryside to press for seedlings. Merely because of this, they lost 25 teaching days. More than 20 students of the county high school of Fengcheng in Jiangxi were taken from their studies to help stamp receipts for the collection of autumn grain taxes. Ji'an Municipality transferred students to do propaganda work for legislative reform over a period of more than 20 days. Students of the junior normal school in Qingpu County of Jiangsu formed a spare-time music team. Following its establishment, the team would be invited to play whenever an important meeting took place in the county. They also had to be on call at all times no matter whether they were having classes or doing homework, whether in the daytime or at night. The situation is even worse in the primary schools. Take, for example, Cili County in Hunan Province. From September 1952 when it was time for schools to open, the whole county assigned more than 600 primary school teachers to do the work of measuring the land and fixing production quotas and then switched them to help with the collection of autumn grain taxes. As a result, more than one-third of the county's primary schools had not even opened by November 8. Teachers of the Siwei General Primary School of Yiyang Municipality were assigned to do outdoor school work 265 days in one year. In the first 40 days after the No. 3 Higher Primary School of Jiexiu County in Shanxi Province started its fall semester, four of its teachers were taken to do work outside the school for 39 days. Cadres of Yangfeng Township in the No. 2 District of Hui'an in Fujian Province ordered primary school teachers to stop their classes and participate in the construction of a highway. The teachers tried to hire others to do the construction in their stead, but were turned down by the township cadres, who beat the gong and shouted: "Everybody has to go personally." In the townships of Zilou and Heshangqiao in Changge County, Henan Province, whenever a township cadre got married, a cadre's child held a wedding ceremony, or even a neighborhood family gave a wedding feast, the schools had to stop their classes and have their pupils beat waist drums, do the yangge dance, and line up to welcome and bid good-bye to the guests.

Because of this situation, teachers cannot spend all their energy on teaching; nor are the students able to concentrate on their studies. There is a grave problem of skipping school and suspending classes, greatly affecting the quality of teaching. For example, in the No. 1 High School of Xi'an Municipality there are actually over thirty job titles for the students. Students who hold jobs in the general Youth League branch or the student union usually fail in two or three courses. Of the 59 students in the 1953 senior high class only 8 passed all courses in the first semester. Because of their participation in social activities, students of three schools in Gansu — Lanzhou High School, the Industrial School, and Jianguo High School — have, on the average, been absent from class for 96 periods, and an average of 44 to 69 percent of the students failed to pass the examinations. There are even more cases like this in the elementary schools.

What is at the root of this phenomenon? The main factor is that certain cadres regard school work as dispensable and teachers as "mobile cadres"; they take teachers and students away from school at will and make them work on other jobs over long periods of time. Second, there is multiple leadership without a unified plan. Aside from many government offices and organizations that are directly related to educational work, such as the administrative educational departments at various levels, the Youth League, and the educational workers' union, many other government offices and organizations not directly related to educational work also go to the schools. Without going through the necessary procedures, they directly assign at will a "central task" for the school, thus creating a great hindrance to school work. Take, for example, Xi'an Municipality. In the few months after the second semester of 1952 started, more than twenty units went directly to the school to

assign work. In Xingwen County of Sichuan the No. 2 district
government arbitrarily ordered the teachers of one elementary
school to recruit 504 peasants into agricultural cooperatives.
The post office of Xisi District in Beijing went to primary
schools and assigned teachers there to distribute newspapers
and magazines. Other units, such as police stations, courts,
the taxation bureau, the people's bank, commodity fairs, and
even department stores or cinemas can all go directly to the
schools to assign errands and jobs. Some district and township
cadres said to the primary school teachers: "Just doing a good
job of teaching doesn't count. Only when you have done a good
job with the central task can you be counted as having made
achievements!"

Of course, aside from the tasks and jobs assigned by different government offices and organizations outside the school,
we should not neglect the urgency and chaos created within the
school. For example, the headmaster of the Zhanggezhuang
No. 8 Central Primary School in a Beijing suburb holds eight
jobs outside the school, and in thirty days he attended forty
meetings. A teacher of the Central Primary School of Dongxi
District holds nine jobs besides teaching. Teachers at the
No. 5 Municipal Girls High School each hold three other concurrent jobs on the average. A teacher at the girls high school
affiliated with the Beijing Teachers' University holds too many
posts at the same time and consequently has to work as long as
102 hours a week. Some schools lack a plan or are not well
organized for their work; the headmasters have not assumed
their responsibility and fail to lay a firm hold on the teaching
work. A certain school in Beijing, for example, spent hours
on deliberation and discussion about sending a teacher to attend
a lecture. Quite a few headmasters are busily occupied with
such matters as funds, budgets, final accounts, the construction
and repair of school buildings, the purchase of furniture, the
evaluation of stipends, ... devoting most of their energy to
things outside of teaching. Inevitably this will cause chaos
among teachers and students.

Judging from the instances mentioned above, many teachers

and students are bogged down in busywork and confusion because of an excessive work load outside teaching. This is the
main reason that a great many schools do not fulfill their
teaching goals.

A planned and large-scale construction has begun today in
our new China. As far as our state's entire work force is concerned, "the plan is the law." All our work should be carried
out according to the plan. It is incumbent on each one of us to
do a good job in our work and fulfill our task to ensure the
completion of the state's entire plan. If we do not fulfill our
own work tasks, or we impede others' effort to fulfill their
work tasks, we are wrong in either case, and the mistake may
amount to a violation of the law. Failure to fulfill the tasks in
any field of work will invariably affect or wreck the state's
entire construction plan.

Educational work is part of the nation's planned construction. Without its supporting role — failing to train, in time,
qualified working personnel in adequate numbers, especially
technical personnel — the construction goals in different fields
of the entire state, especially economic construction, will be
prevented from being fulfilled. Therefore the central task that
the state construction plan delegates to the schools is to fulfill
the educational plan, do a good job in teaching, and educate the
students well. If the schools fail to fulfill these tasks, they
will jeopardize the central task of the state's economic construction and even tasks in other areas.

In light of this we must repeatedly make clear that teaching
is the overriding central task in a school. The main responsibility of a teacher is to do a good job of teaching, and the main
task of a student is to learn all his courses well. To judge
whether a school has done a good job with its work, one should
mainly examine its progress in executing the teaching plan;
there is not, nor should there be, any other criterion. Government at all levels, especially county governements, ought to
attach importance to educational work in the schools, constantly
exercising supervision over the principals and teachers of
primary and secondary schools and earnestly urging them to do

a good job of teaching in accordance with the teaching plan
published by the educational department under the Central People's Government. They should not be allowed to skip or suspend classes at will.

In order to overcome the urgency and confusion in which
school teachers are engulfed, we hold that from now on only
administrative departments of education, the Youth League,
and educational worker's unions or federations are allowed to
make limited use of vacation and after-school hours to mobilize
the teachers and students to participate in necessary social
activities — on the conditions that they do not hinder teaching
work or affect the teachers' health, and that they coordinate
with the objective of teaching. Aside from those mentioned
above, no other government offices or organizations have the
right to directly mobilize teachers and students to take part
in work and activities outside school. Even when administrative departments of education, the Youth League, and the educational workers' unions or federations want to assign social
activities to the schools, there should be contact and consultation beforehand. They should have a unified plan and procedures and avoid each going its own way. In assigning teachers
and students to participate in social activities, the assignment
should not extend beyond the time limit prescribed in the directives issued by the Administrative Council of the Central
People's Government and the Ministry of Education. The time
for school teachers at all levels to spend on social activities,
we hold, must not exceed an average of twelve hours a month,
and during vacations must not exceed one-sixth of the entire
time taken. As for the time students put in on social activities,
we must conscientiously carry out the stipulations set out in
the "Decision on Improving the Health of Students in Schools
at Different Levels" issued by the Administrative Council of
the Central People's Government in July 1951. That is to say,
students of colleges, universities, and senior high schools must
spend no more than three hours a week, students of junior high
no more than two hours, and students of primary schools no
more than one and a half hours on such activities.

If there is indeed some special occasion which calls for increased participation on the part of teachers and students, a
request must be submitted to the higher leading organ for approval before it can be put into effect.

Administrative departments of education at all levels should
immediately select one or two high schools as well as primary
schools and delve deep into them to understand how things
stand with the teaching in these schools and the problems of
urgency and confusion. They should study work methods,
formulate work regulations, and popularize good experiences
in an effort to thoroughly overcome all abnormal phenomena in
the schools. Currently, in Beijing, responsible comrades of
the Beijing Municipal Government, the Municipal Cultural and
Educational Commission, and the Municipal Educational Bureau
have formed a committee to visit separately the key experi-
mental schools to collect information and formulate work regulations. It is a good method. Furthermore, the experience in
Beijing indicates that the administrative departments of education also need to strengthen the planning of their own work.
They should clearly define the responsibilities of the teachers,
carefully consider their division of labor and relieve them of
an excessive number of concurrent posts, enabling them to use
their energy mainly for teaching work. We have heavy responsibilities on our shoulders today, and the tasks we will
have tomorrow might be even more formidable. Precisely because of this, we need to work out a rational division of labor
so that everybody can actively set to work and do a good job.
Leading educational organs at all levels must thoroughly overcome bureaucratism, find out, in time, how teachers at lower
levels actually carry out their work, and help them resolve
their specific problems.

Administrative departments of education at all levels should
educate cadres at the lower levels, especially the district and
township cadres, to make them understand the important role
educational work plays in the entire construction of our country. They should be made aware that the education of children
of the worker and peasant masses and the training of able peo-

ple for construction not only bear on our nation's fundamental
and long-term interest but also affect construction work already underway. It is necessary to educate these cadres to
change their work style of "monopoly" and "taking everything
into one's own hands," and learn the method of doing one's
work step by step in a planned way. They should be made to
understand that even though some work can be of primary importance or of secondary importance, everyone has his own
duties to fulfill. Only on condition that the major task of a
school is not hampered can they ask teachers of the school
to help with some other kind of jobs. As for the viewpoint
of regarding teachers as "inferior to others," it is particularly mistaken and should be strictly corrected. If the teachers
have shortcomings, we can offer criticism and education; but
we must respect and give assistance to their work.

Administrative departments of education at all levels must pay
special attention to encouraging the broad masses of people to offer
criticisms and suggestions regarding educational work. They
must make use of all the newspapers and magazines that can be used
to publicize the correct ways of viewing and handling educational
work and lay bare misconduct hampering our educational endeavors. Stern criticism must be made of cadres who hinder school
work, and in isolated cases appropriate disciplinary measures
should be meted out to cadres who behave extremely badly.

At the same time, from now on principals and teachers of our
schools at different levels must strengthen the planning of their
work and clearly bear in mind the principle that "teaching is the
overriding central task in a school." They must conscientiously
accord importance to teaching work, and overcome the urgency
and confusion created by themselves. Only in this way can they
truly achieve the goal of improving the quality of teaching.

At a time when the construction of our great country has
gotten underway, the effort to rectify the urgency, confusion,
and chaos in schools and strengthen attention to and leadership
of educational work are prerequisites for serving economic
construction. We educational workers must all exert ourselves
in improving the quality of our teaching.

Thoroughly Overcome Sectarian Sentiments*

Wang Benqing, Shaoxing County
Educational Bureau

I am a cadre doing personnel work in the administrative department of education, and the people I meet and see are mostly intellectuals. For a variety of reasons, intellectuals are indeed more prone to problems. Since I lack an adequate understanding of these problems, I have developed serious sectarian sentiments. Having studied the documents of the Eighth National Congress of the Party, especially Chairman Mao's opening speech and Comrade Deng Xiaoping's report on the revision of the Party constitution, I have received a deep education. In his opening speech Chairman Mao pointed out: "There still exist among our comrades viewpoints and styles of work that run counter to Marxism-Leninism, namely, subjectivism in ideology, bureaucratism in work, and sectarianism in organization." His words sounded the alarm for us.

In reviewing our sectarian sentiments, we find they first manifest themselves in the promotion of those who form the backbone of the school leadership. We tend to give more attention and promotion to teachers who are Party and League members or are young, and less attention to old or non-Party teachers. Young teachers, we believe, have a clean slate politically and can be trained even if their cultural and vocational

---

*Xiaoxue jiaoyu tongxun [Primary School Education Bulletin], 1957, No. 1 (January 5, 1957), p. 14. Translated in CED XII:4 (Winter 1979-80), pp. 68-70.

knowledge is inadequate. Old teachers have a complex historical background and are of a bad class origin. It is not easy to
clarify their problems, and we are afraid that if something
went awry in promoting them we would be held responsible.
We tend to make a fuss if we come across teachers with certain historical and political problems. Instead of energetically
helping them straighten things out, we "stay at a respectful
distance" and treat them as backward elements. Consequently,
we fail to promote those old teachers who deserve promotion.

Second, sectarian sentiments find expression in our handling
of teachers who have erred or are afflicted with serious shortcomings. Rather than "implement a policy of uniting with,
educating, and transforming the intellectuals" as set forth in
the political report of the National Congress, lending them
enthusiastic assistance and correction in connection with their
mistakes and shortcomings, we leave them out in the cold and
[even] take disciplinary action against them. Even those who
could be corrected through education, we simply deal with by
taking disciplinary action instead of using education. We fail
to adopt an attitude, toward those who have been punished, of
"learning from past mistakes to avoid future ones, and curing
the sickness to save the patient," as set forth in the report on
the revision of the Party constitution; rather, we think that
they are completely at fault and they are incorrigible. As for
those who have corrected their mistakes and are entitled to
have their penalty rescinded, we fail to do so because we suspect that they are "showing phony enthusiasm" and "pretending
to be honest"; we are fearful that they might "relapse" should
their penalty be canceled. In our county there are quite a few
teachers who were penalized around 1951 on charges of corruption or sexual misconduct and are now still being penalized.
As they have made mistakes and been punished, these comrades believe the leadership will not regain confidence in them
and they will have no promising future. Consequently they are in
low spirits and slack at their work.

Sectarianism also manifests itself in the reforming of the
wage system and the administering of welfare funds. Teachers

who are backward in thinking, have an undesirable class status, or have made mistakes are usually discriminated against.

Because of our sectarian sentiments, the relationship between the leadership and the teachers is affected, preventing teachers from displaying their enthusiasm and causing great damage to our work. It is just as Chairman Mao pointed out in his opening speech, a practice like this is detrimental to unity both inside and outside the Party and impedes the progress of our comrades and the cause. Chairman Mao teaches us that "we must strengthen intra-Party ideological education so as to overcome energetically serious shortcomings that affect our ranks." Under the correct leadership of the Party and following Chairman Mao's instruction, I am determined from now on to earnestly study the documents of the Eighth National Congress of the Party as well as its policy on intellectuals, modestly solicit the opinions of the masses of teachers, improve my ideology and work style, thoroughly overcome my sectarian sentiments, and push personnel work one step forward in order to better mobilize the enthusiasm of the teachers so they can strive to do a good job in the people's educational cause and surpass the nation's First Five-Year Plan.

A Discussion with Primary School Teachers
on the Issue of Joining the Party*

Party Members Administration Office,
the Organization Department,
CCP Zhejiang Provincial Committee

Recently, as the undertakings of socialist transformation
and socialist construction in our country have been moving
triumphantly forward and the Party has issued the great call
to "march on science and culture," especially as a result of
strengthened leadership by the Party over the work on intellectuals, the broad masses of primary school teachers across
the province have been greatly encouraged and their political
enthusiasm is running high. Not only are they energetically
pursuing vocational studies in an effort to elevate their level
of teaching, but are also eager to press forward politically and
step up their ideological remolding. Quite a few teachers have
already submitted their applications to join the Party, or are
in the process of striving to become a glorious Communist
Party member in a few years' time. Such political enthusiasm
is very valuable, and such a desire to progress deserves to be
encouraged. However, on the issue of joining the Party, there
are not a few teachers who lack an understanding on such questions as what is the reason for joining the Party, what kind of
people can join the Party, what formalities are needed, how
one can strive to become a Party member, etc. A number of
teachers still entertain some misunderstandings and misgivings. In order to help everyone acquire a correct understand-

*Xiaoxue jiaoyu tongxun [Primary School Education Bulletin], 1956, No. 13
(August 20, 1956), pp. 2-3. Translated in CED XII:4 (Winter 1979-80), pp. 71-79.

ing on the issue of joining the Party, we would like to discuss
with the teachers these few questions.

1. What is the reason for joining the Communist Party? A
clarification of this question is important. To join the Party
one must first of all have a correct motive. In order to acquire
a correct motive for joining the Party, one must have a correct understanding of the cause of communism and the Communist Party. As we all know, communist society is the most
ideal and happy society of mankind; but is is an extremely
arduous and formidable undertaking to build such a society.
To achieve this ideal and accomplish the task, the leadership
of the Communist Party is essential. The Party is the vanguard of the working class. History has proved that it is only
under the leadership of the Communist Party that the working
class and laboring people can overthrow rule by the exploiting
class, conduct socialist construction, and eventually realize
communism. The more correct the Party's leadership and the
stronger the Party organization, the quicker and the more
assured will be the victory of the revolution and the realization
of the cause of Communism. Therefore as far as a revolutionary is concerned, his purpose for joining the Communist Party
should be the dedication of himself to the cause of communism
in an effort to expand and consolidate the Party organization
and strive for an early realization of the communist society.
There should be no other purpose beside this. Some teacher
comrades raise the question: "Why is it that the Party now
stresses recruitment among intellectuals?" The matter should
be viewed in this way: our Party has consistently paid attention
to recruiting intellectuals; however, the Party places special
emphasis on recruitment among intellectuals today because
an upsurge of cultural construction has occurred along with the
high tide of economic construction. This is a move to
strengthen the Party's leadership over scientific and cultural
undertakings so that they can quickly overcome their back-
wardness, meet the needs of socialist construction, and catch
up with advanced international levels. In addition, this is also
designed to meet the political aspirations of the broad masses

of intellectuals and further cement the ties between them and the Party, so that we can better bring into play the role of intellectuals in socialist construction. Some comrades, when thinking of joining the Party, do not proceed from such a lofty purpose. What is in their minds is that admission into the Party will secure for them the honorable title of "Communist Party member," distinguishing them from others and making them a cut above the masses. There are also some who simply believe that they can count on more help from the Party once they are admitted; they then could make more personal progress. It should be said that such motives for joining the Party are not sincere or sound enough. True, it is an honor to be admitted into the Party and one will receive better education from the Party if one can become a member. As a revolutionary, however, one definitely should not join the Party in order to achieve the honor of being a Party member; nor should one regard the Party as a political school. When these are the motives, one should not be entitled to become a Communist Party member. Here it is important to read carefully what Lenin said in the article "The Workers' State and the Party Members' Recruitment Week" in October 1919:

We are not going to give these common Party members any promise or benefit because they join the Party. On the contrary, Party members must now take on jobs more difficult and more dangerous than usual.... Only those who are in genuine support of communism, those who are sincere and loyal to the workers' state, those true laborers, those who really represent the masses under the oppression of capitalism, ... are people we actually need.... The new Party members we seek are not needed for the purpose of staging a grand show but for the serious work they are going to undertake.

2. What kind of people can be admitted into the Party? This question arouses relatively more doubts and misgivings among the teachers. Some comrades, for example, raise the question: can primary school teachers be allowed to join the Party? The answer for this is yes. Teachers of the primary school are mental laborers; they are a segment of the working class. So long as they are qualified for Party membership, there should

be no reason for the Party to deny their admittance. However,
there are also comrades who contend: the qualifications for a
Communist Party member are set too high; it is very difficult
to meet those demands. True, admittance into the Party is
conditional. As we said before, ours is a political party of the
Chinese working class; it is an advanced and organized contingent of China's working class and has as its final goal the
realization of the system of communism in China. The nature
of the Party and its historic mission determine that not everybody can be accepted into the Party. But the qualifications for
Party membership are not beyond reach. The Party constitution stipulates:

Anyone who accepts our Party's platform and the Party constitution joins a
Party organization and works in it, abides by the Party's decisions, and pays
membership dues may become a member of the Communist Party of China.

To put it more specifically, all those outstanding elements who
have cleared up their past records, resolutely struggle for socialism, and gone through the real test of struggle of socialist
revolution may become members of the Party. Therefore the
point is not whether the qualification requirements for Party
membership are set too high but whether one has the determination to struggle for the cause of communism. So long as one
has such determination, it is entirely possible to achieve the
required qualifications through arduous efforts in actual work,
striving to become a member of the Communist Party. Some
teachers, because of their exploiting class origins, political
problems in their histories, or complex social connections, are
doubtful whether they are eligible for candidacy to Party membership. Naturally, we should dispel the misgivings of these
comrades. It goes without saying that since ours is a political
party of the working class we have to pay full attention to the
class status of its members. However, the Party does not follow a theory stressing the unique importance of class origin.
Though the Party requires that every applicant make clear his
political history and social connections, it does not demand a
clean slate — either in terms of personal political history or

social connections. As a result of the limitation arising from
past social and historical conditions, it is no surprise that
some teachers come from families of the exploiting class or
have comparatively more complex social relationships. Provided that these comrades can intensify their ideological remolding, strive to elevate their political consciousness, and
liquidate the bad influence their exploiting class origins and
complex social connections have had on them; provided that
they can make a clean breast of all their problems to the Party
in good faith, and through examination by the Party prove that
they have indeed made clear their political history and social
connections, then all such problems would in no way affect
their admittance into the Party (if they meet the qualification
requirements for Party membership in other respects). Lacking an understanding in this regard, some comrades do not
know how to assess their class origins, political history, and
social connections from the perspective of historical material-
ism and therefore constantly feel remorseful about themselves.
They believe that everybody has a promising future except
themselves, and adopt a passive attitude toward the issue of
joining the Party instead of actively creating conditions for acceptance by the Party. This is no good. It is hoped that comrades entertaining such ideas can turn themselves around.

   3. What procedures does one have to go through in applying
for Party membership? This question is comparatively easy
to answer. To ensure the quality of Party members, the Party
constitution provides a certain procedure that must be fulfilled
before one can be admitted into the Party. Every applicant
must personally submit an application to the Party and find two
Party members who understand him well as his sponsors. Then
his application must be examined by a Party branch and discussed by the general membership of the Party branch, which
will make a decision on the case and report it to the next higher
Party committee. The Party committee involved will send people over to interview the applicant and in the end will formally
approve him as an alternate member of the Party. What needs
to be clarified is that the application should be made of one's

own accord, for it is only when the political consciousness of
a revolutionary has reached the lofty level of communism can
he consciously set such a demand. Therefore each applicant
must take the initiative to submit his application to the Party
and voluntarily look for sponsors. Since it is the Party that
launches the recruitment drive, some comrades believe that
the Party would approach them on the question of joining the
Party, and there would be no need for them to submit the application themselves. This shows that they do not understand
the principle of applying for Party membership of one's own
free will. This also indicates that these comrades do not have
a pressing desire to join the Party. Since they have not handed
in the application, how can the Party forcibly drag them in?

4. How can one strive to become a Communist Party member? Before we discuss this question, we have to first dispel
a doubt. Some teacher-comrades have this to say: it is not as
easy for us primary school teachers to get into the Party
as it is for workers and peasants. Certain Party branches
show little concern for our political aspirations. Even if we
strive hard, what use is it if the Party does not understand nor
take an interest in our application? There are some grounds
for people entertaining such doubts. It is true that previously
certain Party organizations did not have enough understanding
of nor show adequate concern for teachers' demands to join the
Party. However, it is not true that the Party altogether ignores
or knows nothing about the political aspirations of teachers.
Especially since the Party Central Committee convened a
meeting on the issue of the intelligentsia, Party organizations
at all levels have strengthened their leadership over intellectuals and their work. What has actually taken place is also
proof of this. Over the last six months or so, the whole province has accepted into the Communist Party more than 300 outstanding elements from the primary school teachers. Therefore there is no more need for that doubt to linger.

As to how one should strive to become a Communist Party
member, it is most important, we feel, not to demonstrate
one's aspirations merely in words; rather, one should make

solid endeavor in actual work. To put it more specifically, [prospective members] should strive to do the following:

First, they should do a good job of teaching. A Communist should be the most valiant and active fighter on any front. It is stipulated as a duty of Communist Party members that everyone of them must "be proficient in his vocational work and play a model role in any revolutionary endeavor." As far as those who are striving to become Communists are concerned, they are obligated to make the same efforts. Primary school teachers have on their shoulders the glorious task of disseminating culture and educating and training the new generation. This requires that all of us love our own work, energetically strive to gain professional proficiency, and do a good job of teaching. At present some primary school teachers are not content with their jobs; they see their work as having no future in it and think of getting out of the educational field — "changing their profession." This way of thinking is incorrect, and should be criticized and rectified. Every comrade who is striving to become a Communist Party member should not only do his own work well but must also unite with and help the comrades around him so that they can improve together. This is because any revolutionary endeavor is a collective undertaking. Only by bringing collective strength into play can we do the work well. In light of this, every comrade must strengthen the spirit of collectivism and foster the fine work style of maintaining close ties with the masses.

Second, they should strive to raise their class consciousness and effectively reform nonproletarian ideas. This is even more important for elementary school teachers who come from a petty bourgeois class origin. In "On the Party" Comrade Liu Shaoqi instructed us:

Before and after joining the Party, revolutionary elements of the petty bourgeoisie in particular must devote more effort to political studies and remold their ideology. They must discard their old class stance and shift their position to the side of the proletariat, overcoming such deviations as subjectivism, individualism and sectarianism.

He added with emphasis: "Without such remolding, they cannot expect to become good Party members." His words clearly explain the importance of ideological remolding. To step up the process of ideological remolding, one must conscientiously study Marxist-Leninist theories and the Party's policies and decisions, and daringly conduct criticism and self-criticism. At the same time, one must take part in necessary social activities and strengthen one's ties with the masses so as to combine theory with practice. Only in this way can one gradually elevate one's ideological level to that of a Communist.

Third, they should take the initiative to get close to Party organizations and try to gain guidance and assistance from the Party. As Party organizations are yet to be firmly established among primary school teachers, there are, for the time being, certain difficulties in strengthening leadership over teachers and providing them with concrete assistance. Therefore, we wish teachers to forge close ties with the Party branch and Party members on their own initiative and constantly report on their work and what is on their minds so that the Party can understand them and lend them prompt help. If they have some political problems in their history or some major social connections which they failed to report in the past, now is the time for them to take the initiative to make a clean breast of them to the Party. Do not fear that one will lose the Party's confidence if one confesses one's problems. The Party always welcomes those who can sincerely make a clean breast of their problems and sees their confession as an indication of their elevated political consciousness. In doing this, moreover, one can alleviate one's burden, proceed with one's work in a cheerful frame of mind, and make continuous political progress.

Finally, there is one more issue that needs to be specially clarified, that is, what attitude one should adopt before the Party approves one's admission. Whether or not one can correctly handle this problem poses a test for every applicant for Party membership. We ought to be able to withstand such a test. If the Party has not yet approved one's admission, the implication is that in certain areas one has not been able to

meet the qualification requirements or the Party has not yet
arrived at a complete understanding of one's background. In
such circumstances, one should continue with one's endeavor,
rather than take a passive or pessimistic attitude and losing
one's confidence in securing admission into the Party; still
less should one blame the Party organization and alienate oneself from the Party. Anyone who adopts such a [mistaken]
attitude shows that he cannot stand the test of the Party. Before one's application for Party membership is approved, one
should have the correct attitude of maintaining one's confidence and determination to continue one's efforts, and, in light
of what one is lacking, strive to create the conditions necessary for admission into the Party.

Refute the "Don't Be Afraid of Delegating Power to Your Aides" View*

Ju Hongqi

Our country is a state of proletarian dictatorship led by the Communist Party. All departments and all work should be placed under the absolute leadership of the Party, rely on the broad revolutionary masses, and follow the mass line. Kuang Yaming, a representative of the bourgeoisie, has completely ignored the directives of the Party and Chairman Mao, and leaned on bourgeois "specialists," "authorities," and "professors" for running the University [of Nanjing].

Three years ago Kuang Yaming came to Nanjing University. The moment he arrived here he became busy calling on bourgeois "authorities" and "professors," saying that their "role" must be given "proper play."

In order to give "proper play" to the "role" of these "specialists and professors," Kuang Yaming, through the academic committee, did his best to expand their influence and power. He laid down the rule that manuscripts for the academic journal must first be examined and approved by the "specialists" and "authorities," that scientific research plans must first be discussed and ratified by the "academic committee," and that even the promotion of teachers also had to be examined and approved by them. When some people within the Party ex-

*Renmin ribao [People's Daily], October 13, 1966. Translated in SCMP, No. 3808 (October 26, 1966), pp. 3-5.

pressed dissatisfaction with this rule, Kuang Yaming said to them: "You should not be afraid of delegating your power to your aides," "you have many other things to do."

"You should not be afraid to delegate your power to your aides" — what a theory! Does Kuang Yaming, a representative of the bourgeoisie, want our Party to hand over to the bourgeois "specialists" and "authorities" the leadership power it has won after several decades of hard struggle, bloodshed and sacrifices? Does he want to follow afresh the line of "having professors run the university," a line put forward by the bourgeois rightists and which went bankrupt long ago? Is this not a revisionist advocacy, simple and pure? At no time must the leadership of our Party be allowed to "vanish!" He who dares to stretch his demoniac claws and snatch the leadership power of our Party will be totally destroyed by us.

Chairman Mao has long ago directed: "Intellectuals must continue to transform themselves, gradually discard their bourgeois world outlook and establish the proletarian, communist world outlook." Moreover, he stressed that "the change in world outlook is a basic change." Yet, Kuang Yaming, a representative of the bourgeoisie, openly and boldly opposed this directive of Chairman Mao. He divided intellectuals into four types: Those who are capable of "changing," those who can "catch up," those who "lag behind," and those who are "counterrevolutionaries." He said that while it was of course good to have intellectuals who could change (their ideas) and catch up, those who fall behind were not bad and even the counterrevolutionaries might not be interfered with by the university so long as they did not act.

At a forum of teachers, Kuang Yaming said that he who really wanted to pursue "learning" and obtain that kind of "knowledge" possessed by those "specialists" and "authorities" should not be afraid of becoming a rightist. He added that one who became a rightist might have more time to read. Here Kuang Yaming completely unmasked himself, further revealing himself as an out-and-out counterrevolutionary representative of the bourgeoisie. He is one who sets out to turn young teachers and students into bourgeois "specialists" and "authorities."

Kuang Yaming also inveigled young people into showing the "spirit of Zhang Liang, an ancient statesman, in looking for teachers" and into "self-consciously" doing "service" for bourgeois "scholars" and "authorities," such as cleaning their toilet rooms, looking after their children, and buying food for them. Only by doing so could they learn "techniques." This was tantamount to asking the youths of China to be the slaves and cattle of bourgeois "specialists" and "authorities," to learn the "techniques" in order to do so, so that the "specialists" and "authorities" could have more energy to spread bourgeois ideas and to oppose the Party and the people.

In all sorts of ways Kuang Yaming tried to satisfy the demand of the bourgeois "specialists," "authorities" and "professors" for better material living conditions. He did his utmost to meet their demand for "tall," "big," and "foreign" things. In order to arouse their "activism," he raised the pay for manuscripts for the academic journal. These bourgeois "specialists" and "authorities" treated him as a "bosom friend," saying: "Things would have gotten even better had he come here five years earlier." In the eyes of the bourgeoisie, Kuang Yaming deserves to be their representative.

In the midst of this Great Cultural Revolution, we must follow the instructions of Chairman Mao and completely alter the situation where bourgeois intellectuals rule our university.

**Persevere in and Intensify
the Educational Revolution [Excerpts] ***

*Investigation Report on
Middle School No. 23 of Tianjin*

Guangming Ribao

After more than three years of the Great Proletarian Cultural Revolution, the broad masses of revolutionary teachers
and students of secondary schools have criticized renegade,
hidden traitor and scab Liu Shaoqi's counterrevolutionary revisionist line for education and abolished the old educational
system of "three-separations." Great improvements have been
made with regard to the system of schooling, curricula, textbooks and method of teaching-learning. Can the task of educational revolution be regarded as accomplished? Will everything
be all right merely by giving lessons in accordance with the
new textbooks and according to a prearranged schedule?

Under the leadership of the Party, the workers' propaganda
team stationed at Middle School No. 23 of Tianjin and the broad
masses of revolutionary teachers and students of the school

---

*Guangming Daily, March 20, 1970. Translated in SCMP, No. 4631 (April 8,
1970), pp. 60-71.

have made a clear and definite answer to the question with their
own practice: The struggle between the two classes, two roads
and two lines on the educational front has not yet come to an
end. The educational revolution must be carried on perseveringly and intensively.

To Revolutionize Education, Party Leadership Must be Strengthened

If educational revolution is to be carried on perseveringly and
intensively, it will be necessary first of all to strengthen Party
leadership. The great leader Chairman Mao teaches us: "Without Chinese Communist Party leadership, no revolution can
succeed." Party leadership is leadership by Chairman Mao,
leadership by the thought of Mao Zedong, and leadership by
Chairman Mao's proletarian revolutionary line. This is per-
fectly understood by comrades of Middle School No. 23.
Some intellectuals of this school whose world outlook had not
been properly reformed used to express themselves stubbornly
and advertise their views, saying, "After all, they will have to
rely on us intellectuals for teaching reform." When resumption
of classes to make revolution began in 1968, they carried out
certain so-called "reforms" of teaching in accordance with the
bourgeois world outlook and not in accordance with Chairman
Mao's educational line, guideline, and policy. Instead of bringing proletarian politics to the fore, they "brought politics and
professional work to the fore by turns." Instead of thoroughly
criticizing old educational ideas, they carried out bits of revisions here and there on the basis of old textbooks. Instead of
thoroughly implementing the method of teaching advocated by
Chairman Mao, they went round and round within the old circle.
The Red Guard little generals said aptly that this was "patchwork reformism."
It was Chairman Mao's brilliant ideas of educational revolution that guided the revolutionary teachers and students in criticizing the tendency toward reformism. In view of the afore-
mentioned situation, the workers' Mao Zedong thought propa-

ganda team stationed at the school organized the revolutionary
teachers and students to study Chairman Mao's wise teaching
on proletarian educational revolution and severely criticize
renegade, hidden traitor and scab Liu Shaoqi's counterrevolutionary revisionist line for education, enabling all to realize
that reform meant going backward and must be opposed, and
that they must follow the road of thorough revolution.

After the Party rectification and Party building in June last
year, a new Party branch was inaugurated which conducted in
the school education to strengthen devotion to the Party. The
workers' propaganda team held a Mao Zedong thought study
class on "How to Continue to Make Revolution under the New
Situation." Members of the workers' propaganda team indicated
unanimously that they would consciously accept leadership by
the Party under the new situation, propagate Mao Zedong
thought even better, and make new contributions toward the
carrying through of the proletarian educational revolution to
the end.

The Party branch ceaselessly conducts Party education among
Party members and the revolutionary teachers and students,
and helps all to study the new Party Constitution, so they may
strengthen their devotion to the Party and increase their consciousness of obedience to Party leadership. After the present
term began, it has organized the teachers and students to study
that part of Marxism-Leninism-Mao Zedong Thought concerning
the mutual relations among leaders, the political party, political
power, classes, and the masses, and criticize various Right or
ultra-"left" bourgeois reactionary thought trends. They all resolve to continue to make revolution under the leadership of the
Party and be good fighters of Chairman Mao.

Leadership by the working class is realized through the Communist Party. In turn, leadership by the Party is realized
through the Party organization's leading the broad revolutionary
masses to execute the line, guideline and policies laid down by
Chairman Mao. After the inauguration of the Party branch, it
regards the implementation of Chairman Mao's series of wise
directives on proletarian educational revolution as its central

task. It has set up for the whole school study classes on
"Chairman Mao's ideas of educational revolution, so Chairman
Mao's ideas of educational revolution may go deep into people's
hearts. The broad masses of revolutionary teachers and students have correctly handled the relations between political
movements and educational revolution, those between political
education and cultural education and those between education in
war preparedness and teaching work, effectively implemented
Chairman Mao's educational guidelines and "May 7 Directive,"
and ensured the progress of educational revolution in the direction indicated by Chairman Mao.

Recently the school launched a struggle against the attempt
by a small handful of class enemies to corrupt and poison young
people, and as a result it had heavy tasks at hand. Some people
suggested stopping classroom work. The Party branch organized all to study Chairman Mao's great teaching, "Resume
classes to make revolution," heightened their understanding,
organically combined various items of work, and insisted on
carrying on classes, thus enabling the political movement to
develop in a healthy manner and the educational revolution to
proceed in depth.

Facts have taught all that with those intellectuals whose world
outlook has not been properly reformed assuming leadership
over the educational revolution, they will at most carry out
patchwork changes and follow the road of reformism, and that
it is only by strengthening devotion to the Party and leadership
by the Party and effectively implementing Chairman Mao's directives on educational revolution that proletarian educational
revolution can go on resolutely and in depth.

To Revolutionize Education, It Is Necessary to
Develop Revolutionary Mass Criticism

With educational revolution penetrating deep into the realm
of teaching and learning, there is much to be done in the way
of teaching reform. Will it be all right to relax a little on revolutionary mass criticism? In view of the living idea cherished

by some people that "mass criticism should be put aside for the time being in order to allow time for solution of practical problems," the leadership of the school organized all to study Chairman Mao's great teaching, "Without destruction, there can be no construction," and in the light of reality solved the problem of understanding revolutionary mass criticism.

Toward the end of 1968, some people did not carry on revolutionary mass criticism because they wanted to "solve practical problems." They completely occupied themselves with textbook "reform," saying that "everything will be all right so long as classes can be held." The result was some superficial changes, such as the changing of "one apple plus another" into "one book plus another," etc. The old system of educational thought was not touched at all. The appearance was new, but the essence was old. Essential problems were not solved.

"Destruction is criticism and revolution." "Only by destroying old and rotten things can new and healthy things be built."

Under the new situation of resumption of classes to make revolution, the Party branch of the school consciously led the revolutionary teachers and students of the whole school to bring revolutionary mass criticism to all aspects of teaching and learning and develop intensive, concrete revolutionary mass criticism against the old method of teaching and old textbooks. For example, the negative number concept in the first lesson in mathematics was always taught with the thermometer as an illustration. A one-degree drop from zero was described as a rise of minus one degree. It was not related to the reality of the Three Great Revolutionary movements at all.

Through such detailed analysis, the old textbooks were criticized for their error of not bringing proletarian politics to the fore and being separated from the practice of the Three Great Revolutions. The direction of textbook reform was thus made clear, and a radical change took place in the teaching of mathematics. In treating the negative number concept, the new textbooks cited the following actual example:

Master worker Hua, an old worker of No. 3 Rug Manufactory of Tianjin, used to weave carpets for the capitalists in the old

society. He earned only 6 yuan a month, from which 20 fen
would be deducted for meals if he did not work for a day. When
he was only fourteen, Master worker Hua was ill and did not work
for 25 days in April. A total of 5 yuan was deducted from his wages
for meals. He also borrowed 4 yuan from the management of
the factory for medicine. As a result, Master worker Hua did
not receive any wages for that month, but instead owed the
capitalist 3 yuan, which was a negative amount.

This is a mathematics lesson that is full of class content!
Some students did the problem with tears in their eyes.

Practice enabled all to realize that without criticism there
would be no revolution, and that without revolutionary mass
criticism there would be only reformism. With their understanding heightened, flames of revolutionary mass criticism
began to burn fiercely. Wall posters of revolutionary mass
criticism were put up all over the school, and revolutionary
mass criticism meetings were held in quick succession. Using
their tongue and their pen, they criticized the reactionary, feudal educational thought of the Confucian school, Kairov's reactionary "Education," Liu Shaoqui's counterrevolutionary revisionist line for education, and various manifestations of the
bourgeois world outlook. The broad masses of revolutionary
teachers and students brought revolutionary mass criticism to
the depths of their souls against their own thoughts, intensifying
educational revolution by degrees.

To carry educational revolution through to the end, it is necessary to uphold revolutionary mass criticism firmly to the
end. In view of the achievements already made, however, some
people said, "Mass criticism is more or less accomplished —
there is now little left for criticism."

Is that true? At the end-of-term examination last term,
some teachers wanted to "stimulate the students with marks,
so they may study with greater earnestness the following term."
Some students also tried to cheat in order to score better grades.
In view of these living ideas, the Party branch of the school roused
the masses to carry out revolutionary mass criticism from the
setting of questions to the examination and making of examination

papers. This turned the course of examination into a course of revolutionary mass criticism and further increased the ideological understanding of the revolutionary teachers and students.

The incident reminded many comrades of this question: "Intellectual development first" and "marks in command" were already criticized and repudiated in the past, but why did they have to be criticized again in the recent examination? It shows that the class struggle in the ideological domain is protracted. Things that have been criticized and repudiated can appear again, not to mention others that have not been criticized at all or only superficially criticized. How can we say "There is little left for criticism"? Practice shows that revolutionary mass criticism must be carried out throughout the whole course of educational revolution.

To Revolutionize Education, It Is Necessary to Launch Mass Movements in a Big Way

When teaching reform was first carried out in No. 23 Middle School, the school relied on only a few teachers who tried to carry out reform behind closed doors. They compiled and wrote textbooks, but were unable to break away from the old confines and got nowhere. Later, they asked several "experts" for their advice in an attempt to find a way to reform teaching-learning, but the result was that they were unable to solve any problem. Teaching reform was carried out rather lackadaisically.

"The people, and the people alone, are the motive force that creates world history." The only way to put an ultimate end to the old educational system is by adopting the revolutionary means of the mass line, and not the revisionist-reformist means. The Party branch of the school decided to rouse the revolutionary teachers and students of the school to strike at the old educational system by relying on the worker-peasant-soldier masses and on social forces.

However, some teachers, being afraid of everything and held back by "waiting," were unable to make progress. Some thought that educational revolution was the business of the leadership and did not concern themselves. In view of this fact, the Party branch of the school organized the teachers for repeated study of Chairman Mao's brilliant thought on educational revolution, and led them to criticize the "theory that cultural work is dangerous" and to discuss the dangers of the view that "educational revolution has nothing to do with me," thus increasing their consciousness of continuing revolution.

Meanwhile, the Party branch also resolutely implemented the Party's policy toward intellectuals, trusted and relied on the overwhelming majority of the teachers, moved them to the first line of teaching reform, ceaselessly reformed them while boldly using them, and boldly used them on the basis of continuous reform, thus greatly rousing their enthusiasm. The broad masses of revolutionary teachers turned "fear" into "daring" and "waiting" into "pioneering," and actively joined in the practice of teaching reform. The school leadership also extensively roused the students to take part in the educational revolution. Student representatives joined the educational revolution organizations at the school, year, and class levels. They also joined forces with the workers and teachers in a three-in-one combination in preparing lessons and giving lectures.

In order to realize proletarian educational revolution, "participation by the worker masses is necessary." In accordance with Chairman Mao's teaching, the Party committee and revolutionary committee of the No. 3 Rug Manufactory, which had cooperative relations with the No. 23 Middle School, stationed a workers' Mao Zedong thought propaganda team, formed of outstanding representatives of the working class, in the school to assume leadership. In addition, they also took the following measures:

They organized the worker masses of the whole manufactory to study Chairman Mao's wise directives on proletarian educational revolution and regularly made known the situation and progress of the educational revolution in No. 23 Middle School, so the worker masses of the manufactory might take part in the practice of educational revolution.

To better occupy and reform the educational position with
Mao Zedong thought, they stationed a standing committee member of the revolutionary committee at the school to take part
in its management. In addition, the Party committee and revolutionary committee of the manufactory also regularly discussed
and studied problems of educational revolution.

To enable Mao Zedong thought to occupy the teacher's platform, they organized a lecturers group of more than 30 old
workers and selected 4 workers as full-time teachers.

To arm the students with Mao Zedong thought, so they could
directly acquire the outstanding qualities of the working class
and become cultured laborers with socialist consciousness, and
to provide a base for the study of industrial production, they
admitted different batches of students into the manufactory to
do labor.

To reform the world outlook of the teachers with Mao Zedong
thought, they approved the sending down of teachers to do labor
so as to reeducate them.

By means of "sending out and inviting in," the No. 23 Middle
School threw its doors wide open and relied on the broad masses
of workers, peasants and soldiers in carrying out educational
revolution. During the summer vacation last year, all teachers
of the seven academic groups of the school went out to conduct
social surveys. They went to factories, rural villages, armed
forces units, stores and wharves more than 300 times and
widely solicited the views of the workers, peasants and soldiers
on educational revolution.

In the past year they established connections with more than
70 units and united with the worker-peasant-soldier masses in
carrying out teaching reform. Take for example the question
of institution of science courses. Some of the teachers favored
the establishment of a composite "industrial foundation course"
in which students would be taught a few kinds of industrial work.
Would this be all right? The master workers pointed out that
basic knowledge of mathematics, physics and chemistry was an
important instrument by which to carry out the Three Great
Revolutions, that since our object in training students was to

make them "cultured laborers with socialist consciousness,"
they should be versatile hands and not just workers who knew
several kinds of industrial work, and that therefore courses in
mathematics, physics, and chemistry should be instituted separately. However, the master workers pointed out, the old system of teaching of mathematics, physics and chemistry was
full of the images of foreigners and ancients as well as definitions and laws, and it must be smashed, and teaching should be
under the command of Mao Zedong thought and oriented toward
the Three Great Revolutionary movements.

With the help of the worker masses, the teachers understood
better Chairman Mao's ideas of educational revolution. All the
teaching reforms so far effected were adopted after listening
to the views of the workers, peasants and soldiers. Every problem in the mathematics textbooks came from suggestions made
by factories, rural villages and the armed forces. The teachers
also regularly prepared lessons together with the workers,
peasants and soldiers. Sometimes they would bring their students to factories and rural villages to be given lessons by the
worker-peasant masses on the spot. Sometimes they invited
workers, peasants and soldiers to the school to teach. The
revolutionary teachers said with deep understanding, "Without
the help of the workers, peasants and soldiers, educational
revolution cannot go forward an inch."

To Revolutionize Education, It Is Necessary to
Reform the World Outlook of the Teachers

The great leader Chairman Mao teaches us: "The question
of educational reform is mainly a question of teachers."

At the beginning some teachers went to factories and rural
villages to work on teaching reform. However, they were there
primarily not to reform their own world outlook, but merely to
look for teaching material. As a result, they met with many
setbacks. For example, to find teaching material for negative
numbers in practical application, some mathematics teachers
went to more than ten factories, but could find nothing. They

then went to the goods yard of No. 6 Gate seven times, but still could not find what they wanted. Why?

With this problem in mind, they studied Chairman Mao's teaching, "Some people now go to factories and rural villages too, but some of them produce positive results while others do not. Therein lies the question of stand or question of attitude, or in other words a question of world outlook."

Chairman Mao's teaching lit up the minds and brightened the eyes of the teachers. For the eighth time they went to the goods yard of No. 6 Gate to labor and study together with the loading and unloading workers, placing in the primary position their reeducation by the working class and the reform of their world outlook. Their feelings underwent a change. The workers told them what they really thought of them, teaching them a profound lesson and enlightening them, and not only enabling them to settle the question of teaching material for negative numbers in practical application, but also showing them how to bring proletarian politics in the teaching of mathematics and combine it with productive labor.

They said with deep feeling: "If we go to factories and rural villages purely to collect teaching material instead of trying first of all to reform our own world outlook, we shall inevitably emphasize the mechanical relation of mathematical knowledge with production problems, and be unable to solve radically the problem of separation of teaching from the Three Great Revolutionary movements."

Even with new teaching material, teachers will not be able to teach from proletarian textbooks if their way of thinking is not changed and they continue to see things through the bourgeois world outlook. The following story is well known in No. 23 Middle School: When language teachers were preparing the lesson, "The Red Sun Shines Brightly on the Mountains of Anyuan," there was a struggle between the two world outlooks. In the text there was this song:

> A young man goes to work in the coal shed.
> As he grows old he carries a bamboo container on his back.

If you are sick they will kick you out,
And if you die you die like a dog.

What did "As he grows old he carries a bamboo container on
his back" mean? One of the teachers said, "As the miner
grows old, he can no longer carry a big basket of coal on his
back, and the capitalist naturally makes him carry it in a small
bamboo container." One of the master workers who took part
in the preparation of the lesson, however, said, "How can there
be such a kindhearted capitalist in the world? A capitalist
sucks the blood of his workers. As you grow old, he will kick
you out, and an old worker can only go begging for food with a
bamboo container!" The different interpretations of the same
phrase reflected an acute struggle between two world outlooks.

Comrades of No. 23 Middle School realize from practice that
the educational revolution is a big revolution of world outlook.
If they begin by reforming the world outlook of the teachers,
they will have grasped the most important thing. If on the other
hand they merely reform the textbooks and methods of teaching
and fail to grasp the soul, they will lose their bearings and may
head for reformism, preventing educational revolution from
continuing in depth.

The world outlook of the teachers will always make itself
clear in their teaching, and change of world outlook cannot be
effected overnight, but takes place only very gradually over a
long period of time. The No. 23 Middle School regularly holds
various Mao Zedong thought study classes and, in relation to the
situation and tasks, the living ideas, and problems of the practice of educational revolution, organizes the teachers to study
and apply in a living way Chairman Mao's relevant teachings,
ceaselessly struggle against self and repudiate revisionism,
find problems from the struggle between the lines, the gap (between themselves and the advanced) from thoughts and actions
and the cause from the world outlook, and energetically increase
their consciousness of the class struggle, the struggle between
the two lines, and the continuing revolution.

Take the following example: There was a problem in first-year mathematics which reckoned how much a poor peasant family in the old society had to pay in rent, repayment of debts, and taxes in terms of grain at the year-end, but did not reckon how much grain could be left for the poor peasant family. It was not an account of blood and tears of the poor peasant, but an account of exploitation by the landlord or rich man. Some of the students pointed out sharply: "Such a problem is designed to train us as accountants for landlords and rich men."

The Party branch of the school realized that this was a "revelation" of the teachers' world outlook. Grasping this problem, the Party branch held a study class. The teachers voluntarily examined their own class feelings, their stand and their own world outlook, and together with their students finally succeeded in finding out that there was only 36 catties of grain left for the whole poor peasant family after a year's hard work, while the landlord took away 1,764 catties. With these figures they exposed and condemned the wicked old society. The incident made the teachers realize that the first line of teaching was a vast battlefield and that it was in teaching such a lesson or problem that the teachers' world outlook was tested, tempered and reformed.

Going to the practice of the Three Great Revolutions and becoming one with the workers, peasants and soldiers is an important way of reforming the teachers' world outlook. In addition to sending down teachers by batches to do labor, No. 23 Middle School has also experimented with ways and means of preventing teachers in service from being separated from labor. The mathematics teachers have adopted a method of "teaching alternating with labor," by which each teacher does one week of labor and three weeks of teaching in a month. When doing labor, they carry out "four togetherness" with the worker masses (i.e., they study Chairman Mao's works together, struggle against self and repudiate revisionism together, labor together, and live together), and observe "three-fixed" (fixed workshops, fixed shifts and groups, and fixed time) and "three-combination" (combination of reeducation with teaching reform, combination of teaching with production, and combination of teaching-reform groups with production shifts and groups).

In this way the teachers' acceptance of reeducation by workers and peasants is promoted as well as relearning of teaching
in the midst of the Three Great Revolutionary movements. The
teacher and worker masses study production and teaching
problems together, so that the worker masses become the main
force for educational revolution without being divorced from
production while the teachers become laborers without being
divorced from teaching.

To Revolutionize Education, It Is Necessary to Rectify the Ideological and Political Orientation of Curricula

To revolutionize education, it is necessary to rectify the
ideological and political orientation of the curriculum. In this
respect there is also a struggle between two ways of thinking.

One way of thinking maintains the bourgeois ideological and
political orientation of the curriculum, puts politics and culture
in parallel positions, and advocates carrying out of political
education and cultural education. Or it separates politics from
culture, stops giving socialist cultural lessons, and denies that
culture should serve proletarian politics.

The other way of thinking brings proletarian politics to the
fore in the curriculum, maintaining that politics is the soul,
that politics must command everything but does not replace
everything, and that socialist cultural lessons should still be
given properly, to make it serve proletarian politics.

"All work in school is for the sake of changing the students'
thinking." The revolutionary teachers and students of No. 23
Middle School have refuted the compromise view that places
politics and culture in parallel positions as well as the formally
"Left" but essentially Rightist view that divorces politics from
culture, and firmly insisted on the proletarian ideological and
political orientation of the curriculum. They regard the training of cultured laborers with socialist consciousness as the
basic task of the school and making political education the cen-

ter of all other aspects of education.

Chairman Mao's works are their basic textbooks and living study and living application of Mao Zedong thought is their obligatory work. Political lessons are given in all classes, where Chairman Mao's works are studied every day and a summing up meeting is held to discuss and apply them every weekend. Revolutionary mass criticism is also conducted for the whole school for half a day each week. Old workers and poor and lower-middle peasants are regularly asked to give recollect-bitterness and think-of-sweetness reports. Class struggle is a principal subject and students are led to study and apply Mao Zedong thought in a living way in actual struggle, so as to increase their socialist consciousness.

In accordance with the great leader Chairman Mao's teaching that students should concern themselves principally with studies but should also learn other things, No. 23 Middle School has instituted under the command of Mao Zedong thought eight cultural courses, namely, language, mathematics, history, geography, physics, chemistry, abacus operation, and foreign language. In addition, there is also revolutionary literature and art and military physical culture. Textbooks used for these courses were all written and compiled from the practice of the Three Great Revolutions. They stress proletarian politics and unity of theory with practice, enabling students to receive education in Mao Zedong thought and at the same time learn socialist scientific and cultural knowledge.

The students learn industrial and agricultural work for one month each every year. They learn industrial work at No. 3 Rug Manufactory, the leadership of which has clearly and positively announced that they must not be used for labor power, but should regard political and ideological education as the primary object.

After the students arrive in the manufactory, they are first of all required to attend a study class for three days, during which time activists in the living study and living application of Mao Zedong thought of the manufactory will speak of the practical application of Mao Zedong thought, veteran workers

who suffered much and deeply hated the old society will make
recollect-bitterness reports, and responsible comrades of the
manufactory will speak of the struggle between the two classes,
the two roads and the two lines in the manufactory.

In the course of learning to do industrial work, each student
is led by a designated worker, who will give him ideological
and political education, technical education, and education in
production safety. The students labor for six hours and study
politics for two hours each day. They are educated in Mao Zedong thought through various channels.

In the past more than one year No. 23 Middle School has successfully resisted Rightist and formally "Left" but essentially
Rightist interference, firmly insisted, in accordance with Chairman Mao's instructions about educational revolution, on changing the "three-separation" method of teaching from one textbook
to another in the old school, combined classroom teaching with
on-the-spot teaching, combined teaching by teachers with teaching by the worker-peasant-soldier masses, combined theory
with practice, linked education to the Three Great Revolutionary
movements, and carried on educational revolution deep in the
domain of teaching. In the first year of the great nineteen-
seventies, they are resolved to hold still higher the great red
banner of the thought of Mao Zedong, further develop revolutionary mass criticism, and firmly persevere in the educational
revolution and carry it out in depth!

(Reproduction from Tianjin ribao)

**Effectively Strengthen Party
Committee Leadership Over the
Revolution in the Realm of Teaching***

CCP Committee of the Tianjin
Educational Bureau

Pushed forward by the movement of education in ideology
and political line and criticize-revisionism and rectification of
style, educational revolution in secondary and primary schools
in Tianjin is gradually penetrating into the realm of teaching.
In response to this new situation and continuing to take the two-
line struggle as the key link, the Party organizations on the
secondary and primary educational front of our city have
strengthened their leadership over the revolution in the realm
of teaching and further pushed forward the development of the
educational revolution in secondary and primary schools.

Put the Revolution in the Realm of Teaching on the Agenda of the Party Committee

Why must the Party committee grasp the revolution in the
realm of teaching and attach importance to its leadership over
teaching work? At first our understanding of the matter was
not quite clear. The general view of the Party organizations
of the educational agencies and schools of the city and the various wards was this: The task of the Party organizations was
to grasp political movement, and everything would be all right

---

*Renmin ribao [People's Daily] , August 3, 1972. Translated in SCMP, No.
5197 (August 17, 1972), pp. 146-152.

301

if they grasped the ideological and political work well; but
teaching reform was professional work and was the business
of the educational revolution groups and the teachers. Some
comrades also thought that "It is safe to grasp politics, but
dangerous to grasp teaching." They feared that they might repeat the mistake of "putting professionalism in command" and
"intellectual culture first," and so turned politics and teaching
into opposites. As a result, teaching work was for some time
not placed on the agenda of important business of the Party and
grasping of teaching was sometimes tight and sometimes slack,
so that many problems were not solved in time.

On two occasions we conducted open-door rectification and
widely urged the masses to make suggestions to us. The broad
masses of cadres and teachers sharply criticized us for not
having grasped teaching work and the revolution in the realm of
teaching. We conducted an investigation on the situation of educational revolution in secondary and primary schools. A mass
of facts enabled us to realize that, guided by Chairman Mao's
revolutionary line and relying on the broad masses of revolutionary teachers, students and employees, educational revolution in our city had made great achievements, but that as a result of serious interference and sabotage by swindlers of the
Liu Shaoqi type Chairman Mao's proletarian line for education
and guidelines were not implemented in their entirety, and in
particular, the quality of teaching could not meet the needs of
the Three Great Revolutionary movements.

In relation to the reality of educational revolution, we conscientiously studied Chairman Mao's instruction: "Our educational guideline should enable those who receive education to
develop morally, intellectually, and physically, and so become
cultured workers with socialist consciousness. Our socialist
revolution and construction urgently needs such workers. If
the Party committee does not grasp the revolution in the realm
of teaching and strive to improve the quality of teaching, the
growth of the successors to the cause of the proletarian revolution will be seriously impeded and education will not be able
to serve proletarian politics well.

Teaching activity is the largest activity in school, and the old ideas of the teachers and ideological problems of the students are often revealed through teaching practice. Therefore, ideological-political work in school must not only proceed around the Party's central tasks at various times, but also penetrate deep into the realm of teaching. If ideological-political work is not combined with teaching activity in school, it will depart from reality and will not be able to play its due role of commander and guarantor of teaching work. It is completely wrong to sever ideological-political leadership from teaching work and to oppose one to the other.

With understanding raised to a higher level, the Party organizations at all levels on the secondary and primary educational fronts of our city have put revolution in the realm of teaching on the agenda of important business. Analyses and studies are made at specified times and concrete measures for improving teaching work are formulated. The principal responsible comrades of the ward-level cultural-educational bureaus and many of the Party organizations of schools go deep into the basic level and the first line of teaching to take part in the preparation of lessons, listen to lessons, give lessons, take part in activities of teaching reform practice, foster models, sum up experience, and discover in time and help solve problems that crop up in teaching.

Give Line Education Deep in the Realm of Teaching

"The correctness or incorrectness of the ideological and political line decides everything." Having studied this instruction of Chairman Mao in relation to reality, we realize that to carry out revolution in the realm of teaching successfully and improve the quality of teaching, it is necessary to give line education deep in the realm of teaching.

The Party organizations of the educational agencies of the city and its wards have held study classes on many occasions for the No. 1 and No. 2 men of the Party branches of all schools, to give them line education together. They are organized to

study in earnest the Party's basic line for the historical phase
of socialism as well as its educational line, and to expose and
criticize in a concentrated manner the interference and sabotage by swindlers of the Liu Shaoqi type against Chairman
Mao's proletarian educational line.

The many facts brought to light by all show that the two-line
struggle on the educational front is exceedingly complex and
acute, that the revisionist educational line of "three separations"
is not yet criticized deeply and thoroughly enough, that the content, guideline, and method of teaching must continue to be reformed, and that it is absolutely impermissible to slacken our
fighting will. The damage done in the past few years to the educational front by the formally "Left" but essentially Right revisionist line of swindlers of the Liu Shaoqi type has been very
serious. Under the banner of "highlighting politics" they peddled bourgeois politics, freely indulged in formalism, and placed
politics and professional work in opposite positions, causing
many schools to slacken the teaching of cultural and scientific
knowledge and at the same time weakening ideological-political
work.

They vigorously advocated such reactionary fallacies as
"Learn what is urgently needed first" and "Learn in order to
produce immediate results," and freely indulged in pragmatism,
so as to undermine the dialectical relationship of unity between
theory and practice and between "Making study the principal
concern" and "also learning other things," causing many
schools to abandon political theory in their political course and
neglect systematic teaching of knowledge in their cultural
courses, and giving rise to an erroneous tendency to substitute
practical work for study and "also learning other things" for
"making study the principal concern."

They negated everything, freely indulged in nihilism, totally
rejected the outstanding cultural legacy of ancient times and
foreign countries, and abolished rational regulations and systems, so that serious anarchical phenomena appeared for some
time in educational administration and even in teaching work in
many schools.

In the course of giving line education, the necessity of conscientious reading and study and of grasping the weapon of revolutionary mass criticism is stressed. It is also stressed that leadership cadres must take the lead in making exposures, in making criticism, and in making themselves a target of criticism, so as to dispel with practical action the misgivings of some comrades, and so that they may speak without reserve and direct their spearhead at swindlers of the Liu Shaoqi type and their counterrevolutionary revisionist line. Meanwhile, these leading cadres must earnestly sum up their own experience and lessons learned in the two-line struggle, so as to really attain the object of increasing their consciousness of line struggle.

On the basis of heightened understanding, they have, in close relation to the reality of educational revolution, clearly drawn a line of demarcation between the two lines of education in respect of several principal questions: the demarcation line separating "Making study the principal concern" and improving the quality of teaching from "intellectual development first"; that separating study of teaching for the revolution and practicing of basic techniques from "putting professionalism in command" and "individualistic effort"; that separating resolute placing of proletarian politics in command from formalism; that separating resolute learning of other things from substitution of practical work for study; that separating the strengthening of teaching of essential basic knowledge from the divorce of theory from practice; that separating the promotion of the teacher's role and imposing of strict demands on the student from "the teacher is the center" and exercise of "control, restriction, and oppression of students"; that separating the essential classroom teaching from "the classroom is the center"; that separating "The ancients serve the modern" and "The foreign serve the Chinese" from revering of the ancient to the neglect of the modern and adoration of and fawning on foreigners; that separating attention to the age characteristics of young people and children from "the fostering of seedlings of revisionism"; etc.

After the conclusion of the study classes, the Party branches of all schools have been carrying out line education deep among the masses in close relation to the reality of their own teaching reform. Thanks to the importance attached to the work by the Party branches and the initiative of the leadership cadres, who insist on arming and mobilizing the masses with the Party's policies and carry out meticulous ideological and political work, most of the schools are conducting their revolutionary mass criticism in a lively and brisk manner.

The leadership cadres of some of the schools also go deep into the curriculum group and, together with the revolutionary teachers and students, conduct line education by grasping the special contradictions and principal problems of teaching of all courses of study, help the teachers deal correctly with some relationships and demarcations of the teaching of various courses, carry out repeated practice in distinguishing the two lines of education, continue to demarcate clearly the two lines in the practice of teaching reform, and ceaselessly sum up and popularize some experience in teaching reform.

As the cadres and teachers have raised their consciousness of line struggle and initially made clear the right and wrong in some questions of principle in teaching reform, paid attention to enabling students to gain moral, intellectual, and physical development, and combined "making study the principal concern" with "also learning other things," classroom teaching and book knowledge with social practice, and the teachers' enthusiasm of teaching for the sake of the revolution with that of students in learning for the sake of the revolution, the Party's educational guidelines are further implemented practically in many schools.

The broad masses of teachers have overcome their erroneous tendency of not daring to grasp the teaching of basic knowledge, not daring to study the work of teaching, and not daring to impose strict demands on the students. They earnestly reform the content and method of teaching, strengthen the teaching of basic knowledge and training in basic skills under the premise of resolutely putting proletarian politics in command, conscientiously prepare their lessons and deliver their lessons, correct the students' exercises, and carry out out-of-class tutoring, further improving the quality of teaching.

Rouse the Revolutionary Activism of the Teachers with the Party's Policy

Total understanding and execution of the Party's policy of uniting with, educating, and remolding intellectuals and full mobilization of the revolutionary activism of the broad masses of teachers is a highly important condition for properly conducting revolution in the realm of teaching and improving the quality of teaching.

"In order to remold, it is first necessary to unite." We organize members of the Party branches of the schools to study earnestly Chairman Mao's writings concerning the question of intellectuals, severely criticize the crime of swindlers of the Liu Shaoqi type in sabotaging the Party's policy toward intellectuals, and make a class, historical, and dialectical analysis of the condition of the secondary and primary school teachers of our city. We realize that an overwhelming majority of the broad masses of secondary and primary school teachers of our city, being fostered and educated by the Party and having experienced successive political movements, are good or relatively good and are willing to be and can be remolded. A number of activists who are determined to carry the proletarian educational revolution through to the end have already emerged from them.

In the great majority of secondary and primary schools in the city the two different categories of contradiction are correctly treated and the teachers are properly assigned work. All those involved in contradictions between the enemy and ourselves but are to be dealt with as if they were contradictions among the people are being correctly and strictly dealt with according to contradictions of the latter category, and they will continue to be examined, educated, and remolded while they were being employed. Most of the teachers are posted on the first line of teaching. A number of those who are good ideologically and politically and who have attained a certain degree of professional proficiency are doing leadership work as heads of class and study course groups or in leadership posts in the schools.

It is not enough for the leadership cadres alone to know how
to implement earnestly the Party's policy toward intellectuals
and correctly deal with teachers. The broad masses must also
be made to know that. Many schools are giving the students
policy education, urging the students to show respect for their
teachers' labor and accept the correct education given them by
their teachers. We have propagandized throughout the city the
advanced deeds of Comrade Xiang Wenhai, a good cadre and
member of the Party and a good teacher of the people, greatly
inspiring and educating the broad masses of teachers and changing the mistaken views of many people on the work of teachers.
Most of the veteran teachers are professionally expert in
certain fields and have a rich store of both positive and negative
experience. Full exploitation of their revolutionary activism
will be a great help to the successful prosecution of the revolution in the realm of teaching. Many comrades among them, because they came from exploiting class families or have made
this or that kind of mistake, are often excessively cautious in
their educational or teaching work, being unwilling to assume
responsibility boldly. The Party branches of many schools are
repeatedly propagandizing among them the Party's class line
and policy which "though recognizing the doctrine of family
background, does not regard it as the sole criterion but places
emphasis on an individual's political performance." These
Party branches help the teachers to unravel their ideological
tangles and increase their confidence, so they may advance
ceaselessly. Meanwhile, they encourage the teachers to carry
out practice of teaching reform boldly and support them in their
effort to improve teaching work.
In the course of their ideological remolding, the teachers
have suffered from certain relapses and revealed some old
ideas in their teaching practice. However, that is only normal.
In compliance with Chairman Mao's instruction, "Ideological
remolding is long-term, patient, meticulous work," we firmly
insist on sticking to the guideline of boldly employing those
teachers even when they are suffering from a relapse during
their ideological remolding, dealing with them according to the

formula of "unity — criticism — unity," and carrying out careful ideological educational work on them.

Lack of professional knowledge and a low level of teaching skill will necessarily bring many difficulties to the work of revolution in the realm of teaching and the improvement of the quality of teaching. We require teachers to emulate Comrade Norman Bethune in acquiring a "great sense of responsibility in their work" and "constantly perfecting their skill." We encourage them to study their profession actively for the sake of the revolution. Normal schools and teachers' training classes are established in the municipality, its various wards, and in some schools. Many schools have also organized lectures on special subjects, compiled reference materials for teachers, and launched teaching research activities of various forms. Care is taken to give free play to the professional expertise of the veteran teachers in certain fields. Veteran teachers are urged to lead new teachers and new teachers to spur the veteran teachers on, so they may learn from each other and improve themselves together. Party organizations of various levels adopt various means to encourage and commend those teachers who are loyal to the educational enterprise of the Party and who have made notable achievements in educational revolution. In the course of building the Party, the Party branches of all schools take care to enroll in the Party organization promptly those advanced elements of the proletariat who have emerged from the ranks of teachers.

**Firmly Adhere to the Philosophy of Struggle;
Carry Out Properly the Revolution in Education***

*Some Understanding on Bringing into
Play the Political Role of the Workers'
Propaganda Team in the School*

Workers' Propaganda Team of the
Maoming Municipal Middle School
No. 1, Guangdong Province

Under the centralized leadership of the Party, bringing into
play the political role of the workers' propaganda team in the
school is an extremely important question of continuing the in-
depth development of struggle-criticism-transformation in the
sphere of education, consolidating and developing the fruits of
victory of the Proletarian Cultural Revolution, and carrying
the revolution in education through to the end.

Since last year, we have studied over and over again the documents of the Tenth Congress of the Party and the series of
important directives of Chairman Mao and the CCP Central
Committee on criticizing Lin Biao and Confucius, vigorously
criticized the counterrevolutionary crime of Lin Biao in following the example of Confucius in "subduing one's self and returning to propriety" and his revisionist line, and from the plane of
class struggle and two-line struggle, summed up the practical
experience of the workers' propaganda team after mounting the
sphere of the superstructure, and further strengthened our de-

---

*Guangming ribao [Guangming Daily], May 9, 1974. Translated in SPRCP,
No. 56021 (May 24, 1974), pp. 192-199.

termination and confidence in occupying and transforming the ground of education.

Only by Firmly Adhering to the Philosophy of Struggle Can Our Political Role Be Brought into Play

In 1968, the great leader Chairman Mao issued the call, "In carrying out the proletarian revolution in education, it is essential to have working class leadership; it is essential for the masses of workers to take part." In the past five years, four workers' propaganda teams, with Party members and old workers as the main body, have in succession moved into the Maoming Municipal Middle School No. 1 "to take part in all the tasks of struggle-criticism-transformation there." Guided by Chairman Mao's proletarian revolutionary line, and under the leadership of the Party branch of the school, we have taken the basic line of the Party as the key link, brought education in class struggle and two-line struggle to the fore, and persevered in running the school with an open door. A profound change has taken place in the outlook of the school, and the situation of unremitting improvement in the quality of education is extremely gladdening. However, the struggle between the two classes and the two lines in the sphere of education has always been acute and complicated. Every step forward taken by the working class on the ground of education must proceed through a struggle.

After the workers' propaganda team came to stay in the school, the implementation of the Party policies for cadres and intellectuals, the operation of the school with the open door, and the reform of the old system and method of examination had all to undergo violent struggles. The practice of struggle tells us: The political role of the workers' propaganda team has to be manifested through struggle. If the struggle is slackened, the working class will have no political position in the school, and it will not be able to bring its political role into play.

The protracted and complex nature of class struggle in the historical period of socialism determines that the struggle-criticism-transformation in the school will be a protracted and arduous process. The influence of feudalism, capitalism and revisionism has been with us for a long time, the ground of education thick with intellectuals calls for socialist revolution. The leadership of the working class absolutely cannot be relaxed or weakened, and the political role of the workers' propaganda team must be brought fully into play.

In order to bring into play its political role in the school, the most important thing for the workers' propaganda team to do is to grasp the major issue, pay attention to the line, hold the fort well, struggle firmly against the revisionist line in education and various erroneous tendencies and guarantee the implementation of Chairman Mao's revolutionary line in education. In the face of the major question of right and wrong bearing on the line and the general situation, we should unfurl our banner and clearly make known our attitude on what we support or oppose. There could be no room for vagueness or for conciliation and compromise.

For a time, some people poured cold water on the method of running the school with an open door, and tried to cut down the small farms and close up the small factories. This put us on guard. Using the basic line of the Party and Chairman Mao's "May 7 Directive" for comparison, we carried out repeated discussion, and felt that we could not give way on the question of orientation and road of running the school. Under the leadership of the Party branch of the school, we seriously summed up the lessons and experiences learned and gained from the revolution in education, further ascertained the orientation of running the school with an open door, and persisted in keeping the small factories and linking them up with plants and production brigades.

In the practice of struggle, we realized that the antagonism between the two lines in education, in the final analysis, reflects the struggle between the two lines. Only by grasping the essence of the revisionist line and deeply criticizing and vigorously struggling against it could the correct orientation be firmly adhered to. Since the development of the movement to

criticize Lin Biao and Confucius, we have, under the leadership
of the Party branch of the school, firmly grasped this question
at the core of restoration and counterrestoration, and mobilized
the teachers and students of the whole school to criticize
vigorously the principle of "subduing one's self and returning
to propriety" in association with the manifestation of the backlash of the revisionist line in the sphere of education, thus raising the consciousness of the teachers and students in clinging
to the struggle against restoration.

Transform Conscientiously the Sphere of Teaching

Since the workers' propaganda team must grasp the major
issue, pay attention to the line and bring its political role into
play, does it mean that it can pay no or less attention to the
matter of teaching? From the practice of struggle, we have
noticed that the sphere of teaching has been very deeply affected
by feudalism, capitalism and revisionism, and that in each trial
of strength between the proletariat and the bourgeoisie on the
battlefront of education, a strong counteraction has always been
whipped up in this field. In particular, although the practice of
"three departures" in teaching has been criticized many times,
yet at the slightest opportunity, scum will rise to the surface
and impede the deepening of the development of the revolution
in education. Unless this sphere of teaching is conscientiously
transformed, the ground of education occupied by the working
class can never be consolidated and thoroughly reformed, and
it will also be impossible to pay proper attention to the line and
orientation of the school. Because of this, in the past few years,
we of the workers' propaganda team have all along persisted in
going deep into the forefront of teaching to persevere in placing
proletarian politics in command and vigorously grasping the
reform of teaching.

Should teaching serve proletarian politics? The answer of
the teachers to this question is in the affirmative. However,
in the practice of teaching they cannot always "take this course."
Some teachers have long been accustomed to taking the old road

of "three departures," and are unfamiliar with the new road of
"three-in-one" combination. For a long time, the teachers of
liberal arts have not taken a step out of the school.

We criticized together with the teachers the various evils
caused by "three departures" to the teaching of liberal arts.
This enabled the teachers to realize that: Knowledge comes
from practice in the Three Great Revolutionary movements and
the teaching of liberal arts could and should be carried out in
the Three Great Revolutionary movements. Everybody decided
to give it a try. When teaching "It is said that there is merit in
exploitation. Where is the merit?" language teacher Miao Qifa
organized the students to go to three production brigades to conduct social investigations. He used living examples of class
struggle and two-line struggle to give lectures and guided the
students to write investigation reports and mass criticism articles. By doing so, the students were given a more lively and
profound course of education in actual class struggle and two-
line struggle than what they could have learned in the small
classroom. After that, other teachers of political science and
language also stepped out of the school in great numbers and
closely linked up teaching in the small classroom of the school
with the big classroom in society. From then on, the form of
teaching has been diversified, and it has developed from the
teaching of a single course with an open door into the teaching of
several comprehensive courses with an open door, and from "making a hurried examination" into staying at a selected spot in a
factory or a production brigade for eight or ten days. The
teaching of academic subjects is combined with learning industrial work, learning farming and learning military affairs and
the criticism of the bourgeoisie to form gradually a kind of
system.

For the sake of seizing the initiative on the ground of transforming teaching, our workers' propaganda team carried forward the revolutionary spirit of the working class that is good
at practice and courageous in innovation and conducted some experiments together with the leading members and teachers of
the school. In the past, after the students spent 14 periods in

the study of the subject of senior middle school mathematics "solid of revolution" in the small classroom, they could only move in circles around lines and angles and memorize some formulas by rote. When tests were held, many people failed to make the grade, and even those who obtained "full mark" also did not know what was meant by "processing surplus," much less how to apply the knowledge acquired in production. By changing the method and bringing the students to the small factory operated by the school for their lesson, we studied as we worked, and the students took only five or six periods to complete their study of the fundamental knowledge bearing on the solid of revolution and were able to apply this knowledge in turning the waste iron sheets into brand new ash trays, biscuit tins and steel mesh trays. Some students also changed the production technique to enable a piece of old iron sheet which formerly could only be cut into five and a half pieces of material to be cut into seven and a half pieces. By doing so, they not only improved the quality of teaching and shortened the time required for the courses, but also lightened the load of the students.

In the past few years, our workers' propaganda team adhered to the system of collective attendance, analyzed and studied the problems found in teaching and made suggestions for reform. We also invited factories to send over 15 old workers with rich practical experience to help the school build a worker-peasant-soldier teaching corps, which played an important role in teaching reform.

Exercise a Firm Hold on Transforming the World Outlook of the Teachers

Whether or not the teaching force can be properly transformed is an important yardstick for measuring whether or not the workers can occupy firmly the ground of education. Our workers' propaganda team has all along paid attention to firmly grasping this link.

One salient feature among the teachers of the Maoming Mu-

nicipal Middle School No. 1 is that 95 percent of the teachers
are university and college graduates turned out after the liberation, and the majority of them are also from working class
families. They warmly love the Party, love Chairman Mao and
love socialism and are active in this work. However, the mentality of "born red" is rather serious among them, and they invariably are unable to face squarely the shortcomings and weaknesses in their world outlook and have sufficient knowledge of
the long-term nature of class struggle and two-line struggle.

A teacher of the physics unit is down-to-earth and hard-
working, but his world outlook is basically still that of the bourgeoisie. For the sake of helping him strengthen his consciousness in transforming the world outlook, we have arranged for
him to go to a structural metal plant to practice "three togethernesses" with the workers, and later, assigned him to look
after a small plant operated by the school together with the
workers and master craftsmen. Once, the small factory operated by the school required a unit of small plate-rolling machine. This teacher copied the blueprint of a plate-rolling machine from a large plant and was about to build a similar unit.
The workers and craftsmen suggested that the "double-gear
rolling machine" be changed into a "gearless rolling machine."
When the teacher heard this, he secretly grumbled: "I have
read quite a number of books, but I have yet to see a 'gearless
plate-rolling machine.'" However, the result showed that the
refitting not only was practical, but also saved labor, time and
capital, and the machine was also more convenient to operate.
From this incident, the teacher discovered his fault of not respecting the views of the masses of workers and peasants and
always believing himself to be wise and clever, and that promoted a transformation in his thinking.

The transformation of the world outlook is a long and even
painful process of disciplining. For the sake of helping the
teachers exercise a firm hold on the transformation of their
world outlook, we have, in accordance with the basic line of the
Party, carried out properly the work of uniting, educating and
transforming the teachers. When their revolutionary enthusi-

asm cannot be fully mobilized, we neither just sit back to wait, nor become rash or impatient with them. We firmly believe that the majority of them desire revolution, and patiently bring their revolutionary enthusiasm into play. When relapses appear in their thinking on the road of advance and they display arrogance toward the masses of workers and peasants, we do not appease or humor them nor do we let them have things their own way, but firmly grasp ideological education and help them use "one dividing into two" in dealing with them and pay attention ideologically to the protractedness of ideological transformation and keep on strengthening their consciousness in transformation.

Fight Well This Battle for Winning Over Young People with the Bourgeoisie

"All works in schools are carried out for the sake of transforming the thoughts of the students." The practice of struggle in the past few years has made us deeply understand that a violent struggle is going on between the proletariat and the bourgeoisie for winning over the young people. The focus of the struggle is collectively manifested on the fundamental question of what road are the young people guided to take and for which class are they trained as successors. In the past few years, we waged all the time a fierce struggle against various bourgeois influences around this question. Under the unified leadership of the Party branch of the school, we worked in cooperation with the teachers of various forms to organize the students to study seriously works by Marx and Lenin as well as Chairman Mao's writings, criticize the bourgeoisie, take part in actual class struggle and two-line struggle, and conduct activities in learning from such proletarian heroes as Lei Feng and Chin Xunhua. We helped the students break away from the fetters of various bourgeois prejudices and traditional concepts and actively take the road of integration with the workers and peasants.

Students reaching the senior middle school level invariably develop a special fondness of talking about their future and their

ideals. Given proper guidance, this can turn out to be the starting point of their advance on the road of the revolution. Any
relaxation in guidance would provide the bourgeois ideology with
an opportunity to gain a foothold. In class (No. 5) of senior
middle II, there was a student who happened to be the son of a
worker. Because of the corrosion of bourgeois ideology, he regarded eating well and dressing well as his "ideal" in life.
After an old master craftsman of the workers' propaganda team
discovered this, he visited his home many times, and asked his
parents to give him a course of class education by contrasting
the sufferings of the past with today's happiness. After repeated
meticulous ideological education work, this student was transformed. Upon his graduation, he actively applied for permission
to go to the mountains and the countryside. He settled down in
the rural area and took the road of integration with the workers
and peasants.

In order to enable the students to truly embrace the revolutionary ideal of taking the road of integrating themselves with
the workers and peasants all their life, apart from conducting
education in the basic line of the Party and the revolutionary
ideals and future, it is also necessary to conscientiously cultivate their profound feelings for the workers and peasants. When
organizing the students to go to the countryside and factory,
special attention should be paid to guiding them toward maintaining broad contacts with and receiving reeducation from the
masses of workers and peasants, so that they may understand
that the workers and peasants are the masters creating the
world, and hence, consciously break with various bourgeois
prejudices and traditional concepts that slight the masses of
workers and peasants, and gradually shift their stand ideologically and sentimentally to the side of the workers and poor and
lower-middle peasants.

With the correct guidance of Chairman Mao's revolutionary
line, and especially having been tempered in the Great Proletarian Cultural Revolution, the mainstream of this generation
of young people of ours is full of vigor and actively striving to
make headway. Revolutionary young fighters daring to struggle
against the old traditions and concepts have kept on appearing.

Our workers' propaganda team is on the one hand modestly
learning from these young fighters, and on the other hand,
firmly supporting their revolutionary action and opportunely
grasping the advanced models for educating and leading the
other students. For example, in the struggle to criticize Lin
Biao and Confucius, we have gradually raised the awareness of
class struggle and two-line struggle of the students. At the
beginning of this term, 21 revolutionary young fighters including
Chen Zhihong of class (No. 9) of senior middle II sent a joint
petition to the Party branch of the school asking for permission
to go to the mountains and countryside to take the road of integration with the workers and peasants. Under the unified leadership of the Party branch, we went separately to various
classes, and together with the teachers, mobilized the students
to learn from these 21 young fighters including Chen Zhihong.
Within a few days, more than 460 students of the graduating
class of the senior middle school expressed to the Party organization their determination to go to the countryside upon their
graduation.

Keep On Raising Political Awareness in the Struggle

From the very first day of its arrival at the educational battlefront, the workers' propaganda team has been faced with this
severe test of struggle: The bourgeoisie stubbornly tries to
occupy permanently the ground of education, but the workers
resolutely want to transform it. We have to fight in an environment we are not familiar with, but the bourgeoisie are offering
stubborn resistance in a hereditary domain which they have occupied for generations. The struggle is protracted and complex
and at times even very violent. This is not all, for the various
erroneous ideas and tendencies in society will also be reflected
in the ranks of our working class. Consequently, the workers'
propaganda team must shoulder a dual task in struggle: it has
to fight not only against the remnant pernicious influence of
feudalism, capitalism and revisionism, but also against various
nonproletarian ideological filth within our own ranks. Faced
with this situation, we on the one hand pay attention to going

deep into reality, learning struggle through struggle, striving
to master the law and characteristics of class struggle in the
sphere of education. On the other hand, we pay attention to unremittingly transforming the subjective world in the struggle,
raising our political awareness and eliminating all kinds of nonproletarian ideological filth.

In the past few years, we of the workers' propaganda team all
the time kept a close watch over our own study and improvement. On the basis of private study, the members of the team
adhered to the system of collective study. All sat together to
study seriously works by Marx and Lenin and Chairman Mao's
writings, practice criticism and self-criticism, and according
to the spirit of the basic line of the Party, sum up the lessons
and experiences learned and gained at each stage of struggle
with emphasis laid on solving problems in the following fields:
(1) Use the great historic mission of the working class and the
basic line of the Party to admonish ourselves, unremittingly
strengthen our determination and confidence in carrying the
revolution in education through to the end, and firmly embrace
the militant thinking of "staying permanently in the school."
(2) Understand correctly the centralized leadership of the
Party, correctly orient the positions of the workers' propaganda
team and the Party branch of the school, strengthen the practice
of making reports and asking for instructions from the Party
committee at a higher level, and under the centralized leadership of the Party, carry out the various work of the propaganda
team. (3) Handle properly the relations between bringing the
political role of the workers' propaganda team into play and
participating in various concrete tasks, pay attention to avoiding
getting entangled in the daily routine of the school, and be good
at discovering problems of orientation and the line from various
links of the daily routine of the school. This will enable the
workers' propaganda team to truly bring its political role into
play in various fields of school work, and under the unified
leadership of the Party branch of the school, unite and lead the
broad masses of teachers and students in unremittingly scoring
fresh victories in the revolution in education.

**People's Daily Calls for Reliance
on Professors in Running Colleges***

New China News Agency

(Beijing, March 29 [Xinhua]) Reliance on the knowledge of professors and other experts in running schools of higher learning is stressed in a commentary today in the People's Daily.

The leadership of the Communist Party over schools must on no account be weakened or done away with, the commentary states, but neither should the Party committees "monopolize everything."

Party committees must not take on tasks that ought to be done by professors and other educators.

On the contrary, the commentary advises, Party committees in schools should have full confidence in them and assign them the kind of work that will enable them to give a full play to their initiative.

At the same time, the commentary continues, the Party committees should help educators make progress politically, while providing them with the necessary conditions for their work and life.

The importance of having more experts on the Party committees is stressed in the commentary. Once promoted to such positions, professors and other educators should be given authority commensurate with their titles.

---

*NCNA (English), Beijing, March 29, 1980.

Meanwhile, if Party officials do not have specialized knowledge, they must try to learn it. The commentary states: "We cannot ask every senior member of the Party committee in a given school to be able to teach or do research like professors and other experts. Nevertheless, it is justified to demand that they know education."

Accompanying the commentary is a news story reporting how the Party committee of Nankai University in Tianjin has given full power to professors and experts. President of the University is Professor Yang Shixian, one of China's leading experts in chemistry.

Appendix / V:i

You Cannot Treat Primary School
Teachers That Way*

Shen Yang

On primary school teachers' shoulders lies the responsibility for bringing up and educating the children. They have a
heavy work load and they deserve to have our esteem. Nevertheless, among the cadres are those who, instead of holding the
teachers in respect, insult them, discriminate against them,
and show no concern for their hardship and needs. In order to
effect a change in the situation, I would like to present to you
the following examples.

Willfully Insulting Primary School Teachers

Certain district and township cadres, as well as cadres in
charge of culture and education at the county and district
levels, deliberately humiliate primary school teachers. A primary school teacher of District 4 of Lixian County in Hebei
Province reported to the district Party committee that village
cadres often played poker games in the school far into the
night. The cadres summoned the teacher to the village hall and
warned him "not to lose his senses." As a punishment for
teachers who were late for a meeting, cadres of Xingyi Township in Xichong County of Sichuan Province arbitrarily had
them stand at attention to listen to a report. A pupil of a pri-

---

*Gongren ribao [Worker's Daily] (Beijing), July 14, 1956. Translated in
CED XII:4 (Winter 1979-80), pp. 109-112.

mary school in the county seat of Yidu County in Shandong
Province failed to respond to a question put to him by the
county's culture and education section-head.   The section-
head singled the teacher out on the spot and yelled at him:
"The pupils you teach have no manners" (implying that the
pupil did not even show respect for a section-head like
himself).   "Tomorrow I'll check on your teaching."   The
next day he actually went to check on the school's work
and deliberately threatened the teachers, saying that he
would have the school closed because of its slipshod teaching.   One assistant administrator of cultural and educational
work in Cangqi County of Sichuan, without authorization
from above, deprived more than ten primary school teachers of their right to vote in 1953, and the decision has not
yet been rescinded.

They Are Used as Handymen

Certain district and township cadres also use primary
school teachers as handymen.   The central primary school
of Zuyingcun in Anqiu County of Shandong has only four
teachers.   As the school has no handymen, the teachers
have to prepare their own meals.   However, when some
county and district cadres came to the village on business,
they also had to have their meals at the school.   On one
occasion there were as many as fourteen cadres eating at
the school, and the teachers had to use their own work
hours to prepare food for them.   The cadres would even
lose their tempers if they were not treated to their satisfaction.   Yang Fuqing, a cadre of Sanguan District in Nanbu
County of Sichuan, went to work in Sanguan Township.   At mid-
night he woke up all the teachers who had taken medicine for
hookworm and had been on fast during the day, and had them
take notices on the protection of draft cattle to the villages and
do a house-to-house check on measures taken to protect the
cattle.   The four teachers went to eight villages and did not get
back until almost daybreak.

Difficulties in Daily Life

Primary school teachers have difficulties in their everyday lives. A large number of primary schools in Gansu Province do not have cafeterias and the teachers have no place for their meals. Besides, administrative departments of culture and education in certain counties and districts willfully make irrational decisions, which cause difficulties in the teachers' lives. For example, some peasants in Yuexi County of Anhui joined the agricultural producers' cooperatives. Once they failed to do a good job with their sideline productions; as a result, they fell behind in the payment of their children's tuition and miscellaneous school expenses. The county authorities then decided to deduct part of the salaries paid to the teachers to offset what the pupils owed the school and to have the deficit cleared by July. In Shangfang Primary School of Hetu District there are four teachers. Their salaries add up to 106 yuan in total, but the different payments the pupils owed to the school amounted to over 120 yuan. As a result of the deduction, the teachers received no money in June and went without food on a couple of occasions. They do not yet know how they'll get through July.

Their Political Aspirations Ignored

Certain cadres discriminate against primary school teachers because they hold that teachers are of a complex class status. In Wenxian County of Henan the Educational Workers' Union shares the same office with the Youth League and the Women's Federation. Comrades of the Youth League and the Women's federation even go so far as to forbid comrades of the Educational Workers' Union to receive primary school teachers in the office. The County Federation of Unions also goes to the extreme of not allowing primary school teachers who come to work at the Educational Workers' Union to eat at the mess hall. They tell the teachers to buy their food outside in the streets.

Precisely because of the alleged complex class status of
primary school teachers, the authorities are apathetic toward
their political aspirations.

Comrade editor: there are not a few examples similar to the
above. In some places people have this to say: "Those who
work on trains, in kitchens, in post offices, and in schools" are
the "four lowest of the low." In one place the supply and marketing cooperative calls the lowest priced cigarettes with the
trademark "Gold Coin," the "Teacher Brand" cigarettes.
And in one place the primary school teachers said, "All those
who wear a cadre uniform are our superiors." All of these
are manifestations of discrimination against primary school
teachers. In order to allow them to do a good job and bring
their initiative into play, I appeal to you on their behalf.

Difficulties and Worries of Women
Teachers in Primary Schools*

Abstract of a Speech Delivered Jointly
by Committee Members Shan Lingyi and Deputies
Wang Chuanfeng and Zhang Wenyu at the Third
Session of the First People's Political
Consultative Conference of Qingdao Municipality

We three are women teachers engaged in educational work
at the primary level. Here we would like to "air our views"†
about current problems involving the primary school.

Women teachers account for more than 70 to 80 percent of
the total faculty in primary schools. However, the Party and
the leadership in charge of primary school education fail to
take this special condition into consideration when conducting
their work. We believe that in order to improve the quality of
education in primary schools, we must make up our minds to
resolve the contradiction between the work of women teachers
and their problems at home. At the present time, more than
90 percent of women teachers are mothers. In the daytime
they teach millions of innocent, lively, yet naughty children.
They not only teach them in the classroom and in the office
after class, but sometimes follow the children to their homes
for more teaching. Whenever they have a little time at their
disposal, they use it to correct the pupils' homework. When
returning home in the evenings, their minds are loaded with
a series of problems involving their pupils, and on their shoulders are bags loaded with the pupils' exercise books. But once
they get home, they face the problem of feeding and clothing

---

*Qingdao ribao [Qingdao Daily], May 11, 1957. Translated in CED XII:4
(Winter 1979-80), pp. 113-115.

†The authors actually use two words which were part of the official Hundred
Flowers slogan. — G.W.

their own children and doing the mending and washing. Limited
by their incomes, few of them can afford to hire help. As a result, they have to take care of the pile of chores at home by
themselves; at the same time they must finish the work they
take home — preparing lessons and correcting pupils homework. In this way they do their housework perfunctorily and
rush through the work needed for their teaching jobs. Consequently they cannot take good care of their own children. One
falls ill today and another gets sick tomorrow. Today this
teacher asks for a leave of absence and tomorrow another
takes sick leave. The school is compelled to find substitutes
to look after the pupils in the absentees' classes. In this way
the health of teachers is deteriorating, and the school records
of the pupils are on the downgrade.

Party organizations at higher levels show little concern for
primary school teachers politically. This is especially so with
women teachers. They fail to educate and help women teachers
in light of their political aspirations. Since Liberation all
women teachers have sought progress in politics and in their
work, and not a few of them have submitted applications for
Party membership. However, Party committees have not paid
attention to their work in this regard. (There was some improvement after the movement to suppress counterrevolutionaries.) Lacking the education and help of the Party, women
teachers lose their steam for making progress as time goes
by. Quite a few cadres and teachers have the feeling that the
political atmosphere in schools is thinning out.

In light of the situation mentioned above, we would like to
offer the following suggestions for reference:

1. Allow a little more latitude in regard to the personnel
program in schools which have more women teachers so that
appropriate preferential treatment can be given to them.

2. Where conditions allow, try to improve welfare work for
teachers, with special emphasis on child care. Cancel the
"special treatment" of requiring women teachers to pay for
child-care expenses.

3. The Women's Federation should not forget their sisters

in the primary schools and should help them resolve their problems.

4. Party committees should constantly pay attention to ele-vating the women teachers politically and educate and train them as people who have a political future.

**Raise the Status and Remuneration of the
People's Teachers to an Appropriate Level***

Deputy Chen Yuan's Speech at the Third Session
of the First National People's Congress

Allow me to say a few words on the question of education
in teacher-training colleges.

This year a new situation has developed in connection with
enrollments in high schools and universities; that is, the
planned enrollment quotas exceed the number of graduates sitting for the entrance examinations. Graduates of senior high
schools are fewer in number than the planned enrollment of
institutions of higher learning, and graduates of junior high
schools are fewer in number than the planned enrollment of
the senior high and vocational schools. That is to say, a situation of supply falling short of demand has developed between
the junior and the senior high schools and between senior high
schools and institutions of higher learning. All this serves to
illustrate that socialist construction in our country is forging
ahead at a tremendous pace, and there is an increasing demand
for specialized personnel at the higher and middle levels.
This also makes clear that secondary education in our country
falls far short of our needs. We have to develop many high
schools; otherwise we will greatly hamper our national effort
for economic construction.

---

*Guangming ribao [Guangming Daily], July 1, 1956. Translated in CED XII:4
(Winter 1979-80), pp. 116-122.

Shortage of Teachers Poses a Serious Problem
— During This Year and the Year After, High Schools
and Primary Schools Will Be Short 290,000 Teachers

The most crucial obstacle to our effort to increase the number of high schools lies in the shortage of teachers. It is just as Education Minister Zhang Qiruo pointed out in his address to the congress: "The shortage of high school and primary school teachers poses an increasingly serious problem," and "it is estimated that during 1956 and 1957 we will be short some 90,000 high school teachers and almost 200,000 primary school teachers." What staggering figures! As I see it, the various measures adopted by the government, such as expanding the enrollment for teacher-training colleges and universities, developing short-term teacher-training courses, and tapping potential manpower are all of great importance. I personally fully endorse and support them.

However, I think there is still another question which deserves attention from all sides, namely: How should we enhance the emphasis and respect of society for the work done by the people's teachers so as to more effectively ensure the source of students to be enrolled in teacher-training programs and also reinforce teachers' love and sense of responsibility for their own work?

Over the last few years, hundreds of thousands of young people, owing to their understanding of the importance in the cause of people's education and also in light of their own conditions, have enrolled themselves in teacher-training schools. Many of these young people have already shouldered the sacred responsibility of becoming a teacher and are persistently cultivating the younger generation for the fatherland, through their diligent efforts on the educational front. This is the primary aspect of the matter. On the other hand, however, a group of the young people look down upon teacher-training schools and hold that being a teacher is disgraceful. They assert that teachers have no future; they are underpaid and have no opportunity to engage in scientific research. A few days ago the

editor's note in <u>Jiaoshi bao</u> [Teachers' News] carried this remark: some young fellows "lay emphasis on science courses
to the neglect of liberal arts; they have particular contempt for
the job of a people's teacher." Since the problem is described
with the term "particular," it cannot but draw our attention.

Why Does a Group of the Young People Hold That Being a Teacher Is Inglorious and Has No Future?

Underlying this phenomenon, I believe, are the following major causes:

1. <u>Ideological influence left over from the old society</u>. As
the ruling class in the old society did not want the people to be
educated at all, they paid no attention to the cause of education
and naturally set no great store by teachers. In the old society
teachers were always looked down upon by others; they stood
on a low rung in the social ladder and earned so little that they
could hardly feed their families and themselves. In consequence
some people described a teaching job as a "temporary shelter,"
and one would quit it as soon as one landed another job. This
is a natural thing. The lengthy influence of the old society cannot be liquidated all at once. It still remains, to a considerable
extent, in the minds of some of the people, and constantly exerts a conscious or unconscious influence over young people,
preventing them from viewing the people's teachers' status in
our new society in the correct light.

2. <u>Our failure to conduct constant and adequate education and
propaganda</u>. Young people are inexperienced after all, and they
tend to hold biased views on certain issues. It is incumbent on
government offices, schools, and the Youth League to help them
acquire a correct understanding about the roles that different
endeavors play in national construction, and guide and aid
them in making a realistic choice of their future studies.
They should be made to understand that every speciality has
its own importance, rather than improperly stressing the importance of one specialty at the expense of another specialty. A

teacher's job, for example, is in fact a very important one. However, some students regard it as not so spectacular as industrial construction, and cannot perceive the significance that the teaching profession bears for construction. If one is engaged in the construction of a reservoir or a bridge, one is likely to witness in a few years' time how the construction project one has participated in plays a great role and benefits the people. A teacher's job, however, is one that "brings up people by lifetime efforts." It takes sixteen to seventeen years for one to complete the course from primary school to the time of graduation from a university. It would be even longer if we count from kindergarten. The fruits of this sort of labor are not immediately discernible. As a matter of fact, what a teacher does is cultivate people. The accomplishment of his work imbues every construction project that benefits the people and takes effect in the person of every working personnel who has graduated from the school. As for such a fundamental construction effort, we must constantly publicize it among the young people, shaping a new public opinion in society so that the young and others can have a correct understanding about it. If we merely rely on giving some improvised guidance when enrolling students each year, the effect is always minimal.

3. The direct impact that teachers make on their students. It is teachers to whom students are most frequently exposed, and it is also teachers who exert the greatest influence over students. This issue should be viewed from two sides. On the one hand, if what the students witness is the teachers' hectic work schedule, poor living conditions, and even the lack of respect due them, then they would find it difficult to choose teaching as their career when making a choice for their future studies. On the other hand, if the teachers themselves do not pursue their professional studies, do not pay attention to their ethical cultivation, and even fail to commit themselves to teaching as their specialty and are not content with what they are doing, they exert a bad influence on students through an imperceptible process and make the students feel that a teacher's job is meaningless.

Adopt Concrete and Effective Measures to Liquidate
the Influence Left Over from the Old Society

In light of the above state of affairs, we must adopt concrete
and effective measures to attach greater weight to the training
of teachers and to the work of the people's teachers, raising
their status and remuneration to an appropriate level. Here I
believe we may refer to what the great teacher Lenin said in
his Diary Excerpts:

It is necessary to raise the status of our national teachers to a level that
teachers in a bourgeois society could never expect to reach. This is a self-
evident truth. To achieve this, we must work systematically and press forward with indomitable will. Not only should we endeavor to raise their
spirits but also must equip them with opportunities for cultivation in every
field so they can truly live up to their noble title. Most important of all is to
improve their material living conditions.

From now on we must not only step up our efforts in conducting
regular ideological propaganda and education, but must also
pay attention to resolving such practical problems as teachers'
political treatment, their social status, living conditions, salary, remuneration, etc. By doing thus, we will not only be able
gradually to clear away the influence left over from the old society but can give the people's teachers great stimulus both
spiritually and materially as well. As a matter of fact, our
Party and government have always set great store by and
showed concern for the work of people's teachers. Nevertheless, in certain areas what has been done is inadequate, and
some localities have not fulfilled what is required of them.

Is It True That Good Schoolwork Is Not Necessary
When Applying for Enrollment to
Teacher-Training Colleges?

As regards ideological education, I am of the opinion that
leading comrades at all levels from the Center down to localities must issue more and specific calls and directives to en-

able the whole society to acquire a correct assessment of the function of people's teachers. Hasn't Kalinin, one of the chief leaders of the Soviet Communist Party and government, left us many instructive articles and reports concerning education and teachers? Could it be that our leading comrades at different levels fail to direct adequate attention to this issue? Apart from this, I think it is also incumbent on Zhongguo qingnian [China Youth], Zhongguo qingnian bao [China Youth News], Jiaoshi bao [Teacher's News], and many other newspapers and journals to do more work in this regard. At least they must never carry an article like the one appearing in Zhongguo qingnian bao on April 30 of this year. This article was written in response to a would-be senior high school graduate who intended to enroll himself in the physics department in a university and sought "advice." In "advising" the student the article had this to say: "If you do not have a very good foundation in chemistry and physics, it would not be a bad thing for you to enroll in a teacher-training college." Advice like this is no different from telling young people that a person with a good academic background should not apply for a teacher-training college; if one is good at physics, it would be a pity should one really do so. As a matter of fact, can a student of the physics department of a normal college be allowed to have a poor foundation in chemistry and physics? For another example, a student had passed the admission examination for a teacher-training college and wrote to inform his parents about it. In reply, the parents said: "If you are so good in your academic work, why should you choose to enroll for a teacher-training college?" The implication was that they really felt disappointed about it. Instances like this are many; they are not just isolated cases. Is it true that good academic work is not needed for study in a teacher-training program? Let me ask the question: if all those who have a good academic foundation are "advised" not to enroll in teacher-training colleges and the quality of graduates from teacher-training colleges cannot be guaranteed, then what will happen to the academic quality of the students they are going to teach? This is a question deserving attention from all quarters.

Be an Engineer of the Soul Worthy of the Name

The last point concerns the teachers themselves. As a segment of the ranks of new China's working class, we teachers
should clearly understand that the political status of a people's
teacher is essentially different from that in the old society.
Teachers should acquire more understanding about their duties
and the significance of their work, bearing in mind the glorious
responsibility teachers hold for the future of our fatherland.
Rather than laying excessive emphasis on such problems as
one's material well-being and remuneration, one should set
strict demands on oneself, elevate one's communist awareness,
and foster a work style of plain living and hard struggle so as
to become an example in promoting a new social atmosphere.
Teachers must continuously elevate their political and professional levels, actively pursue educational theory to acquire a
command of educational principles, and strengthen scientific
research to improve the quality of education in an effort to become architects of the human soul worthy of the name. They
must strive to train, for the nation, qualified personnel who are
developed in an all-round way and have both ability and political integrity, so that they can be worthy of the Party and government's profound concern and love, and can live up to the
people's great confidence and trust.

I have no wish to lopsidedly stress the importance of teacher-
training colleges. My purpose is to inquire how we can prepare
more and better reserve forces for the various specialties in
construction. At present, there is a shortage of students in the
high schools, and teacher-training programs fall behind our
needs. Each year the enrollment in teacher-training colleges
and universities makes up a high percentage of the total enrollment quota, but a number of young people have a "particular"
dislike for the job of teacher. This is a grave problem that we
must make great efforts to resolve. Because of this, I wanted
to present my views. Kindly give me your advice and support.

The Question of How to Assess
Correctly the Status of Teachers*

Jiaoshi Bao Commentator

During the rectification campaign, quite a few people put
forward various kinds of opinions regarding the status of teachers. Using the methods of criticism and self-criticism, pre-
senting the facts, and reasoning things out, certain localities
have already conducted debates on this issue. Judging by the
experience currently available, debates organized this way
have great significance for our effort to distinguish between
right and wrong, raise the socialist awareness of faculty and
staff, and clarify their confused ideas.

Compared with teachers' status in old China, the status of
teachers in New China has undergone a fundamental change.
To begin with politics, teachers have switched from serving the
reactionary ruling class in the past to serving the people. It
is a creditable achievement. As we all know, aside from des-
potic gentry, landlords, and power-holders of the Guomindang
who also held teaching jobs, the old society prior to Liberation
did not confer any social status on the overwhelming majority
of teachers, especially those who taught in primary schools.
They were totally devoid of any social and political status except that of slavery under the oppression of imperialism and
the Guomindang and of forced submission in order to retain
their jobs. In new China, however, teachers have stood up

*Teachers' News (Beijing), January 24, 1958. Translated in CED XII:4 (Win-
ter 1979-80), pp. 123-132.

along with the people of the whole nation and become masters
of the country. Held in respect by the Party, the people's government, and the broad masses, they bear the titles of "the
people's teachers" and "engineers of the soul." A considerable
number of teachers have been elected representatives to people's congresses and political consultative conferences at all
levels from the Center down to the localities. In the category
of primary school teachers alone, Tao Shufan and three others
have been elected deputies to the National People's Congress.
Let us raise the question: did such a thing ever happen in the
old society?

The Chinese Communist Party has always set great store by
the intelligentsia. As early as 1939, the CCP Central Committee adopted a resolution on "Recruiting Large Numbers of Intellectuals" drafted by Chairman Mao. It is pointed out in the
resolution: "Without the participation of intellectuals, it is
impossible for the revolution to achieve victory." Except for
an extremely small number of reactionary elements who persist in their stance and perpetrate counterrevolutionary activities, since Liberation our country has paid attention to rallying
all intellectuals, helping them with thought reform, and bringing
into play their ability so as to put them in the service of the
cause of socialist construction. In order to build our country
into a strong socialist nation equipped with modern industry,
agriculture, science and culture, in 1955 the Party Central
Committee convened a conference especially for the purpose
of addressing the question of intellectuals and formulated a
series of general and specific policies in this regard. Did such
a thing ever happen in old China or in any capitalist country?

Second, in terms of job security, our teachers can always
be assured of their jobs so long as they are up to working for
the cause of socialist education. This is something no one
could dream of in the old society. Moreover, in order to help
improve teachers' political and professional levels, the Party
and the government have provided teachers with courses on
political and vocational studies. Such concern for teachers has
never been witnessed either in the period of Guomindang re-

actionary rule or in any dynasty in the past. On top of that, to facilitate teaching work, the people's government has newly built, expanded, and developed many schools at the primary and secondary levels. Various kinds of reference books, news-papers, and magazines needed by teachers have been published, and books, instruments, and equipment have been added and purchased. Let us [again] raise the question: did anything like this ever happen in the old society?

Furthermore, teachers' livelihood has been gradually im-proved in terms of wages and benefits. In the period of the First Five-Year Plan alone, the average earnings of primary school teachers in the whole country increased from 25 yuan a month in 1952 to some 40 yuan a month in 1956, an increase of almost 60 percent. Wang Zhongyu, a teacher of Niuzhuang District in Haicheng County of Liaoning Province, made a cal-culation by contrasting the present with the past. The figures he gave are representative. Converted into grain, the highest wages a teacher in the district earned during the period of the puppet Manchukuo regime were one hectoliter and two de-caliters a month. Middle-range wages were seven decaliters, and the lowest wages four decaliters. During the rule of the Guomindang, the highest wages were eight decaliters, the me-dium wages seven and a half decaliters, and no wages were paid to the lowest income bracket. They gave this bracket the fine-sounding name of allowing the pupils to pay "rice in re-spect for the teachers," and as a result, the teachers could not earn what they deserved. In contrast, the highest wages a teacher can earn today are three hectoliters and one decaliter, the medium wages two hectoliters and five decaliters, and the lowest one hectoliter and seven decaliters. The situation may vary in different localities across the nation, but compared with 1949, teachers' livelihoods have greatly improved, a fact that nobody can deny. Furthermore, a good many welfare mea-sures have been put into effect in schools since Liberation. For example, free medical service has been provided for teachers and a welfare fund has been set up. The state has also laid down different regulations to govern such matters as resignation, retirement, maternity leave for women teachers, pensions for the disabled and for the family of the deceased, etc. Could these things have occurred in the old society?

The above brief account of the situation bears ample evidence for the fact that teachers in new China occupy an important status in terms of either politics, job security, or material well-being. By no means can it be said that "they have no social status"; "what they have now is inferior to the past"; or "they are inferior to others," and so forth. In fact, their previous status bore no comparison to the one they have now. Precisely because of this, all those poor teachers who were hired, enslaved, and trampled on in the old society or those veteran and young teachers who resolutely take the stand of the people and are politically motivated are very satisfied with and treasure the status they have in new China. In addition, from the difference of teachers' status in the old and new societies, they are deeply impressed by the superiority of the socialist system. They are convinced that it is only under the leadership of the Communist Party and the working class that the intellectuals truly have a future and truly have social status. To talk about a teacher's status when they deviate from the socialist road or the Party's leadership is nothing more than telling a lie or experiencing a horrible nightmare.

This being the case, why should there still be people clamoring that "teachers are inferior to others" or "the present is inferior to the past"?

Currently those who shout that "the present is inferior to the past" or "teachers are inferior to others" mainly fall into two categories. One category comprises landlords, rich peasants, and power-holders during the Guomindang's reactionary rule. They resist thought reform, persist in their reactionary stance, and harbor discontent with the country under the people's rule. People like Ge Peiqi, instructor at the Chinese People's University and formerly a Guomindang major-general, Yang Tianbai, language teacher of Linying No. 1 Middle School and formerly a rascal in the Linying County Party Branch of the bogus Guomindang, and Dai Shihou, director of Dabao Primary

School and a rich peasant, all take an exploiting class point of view in assessing problems and intend to restore their reactionary class interests of oppressing and exploiting the people. Naturally they feel that "the present is inferior to the past." As a matter of fact, when they cry out that "teachers are low in status," they are merely putting up a false front. What lies behind it is their hatred for socialism and the Communist Party. They feel hatred and revenge toward the people for overthrowing their "paradise" and seek to reverse the verdict passed by the socialist revolution. These people make the loudest noise and are the most vehement. They are the mainstay among those who cry out that "teachers are low in status." The second category is comprised of people who are politically and ideologically unhealthy. Some of them are affected by relatively strong bourgeois individualism. With their personal desires ungratified, they are full of grievances. Some of them entertain a lingering love for the old society and retain their old ways of thinking; they either lack enthusiasm for socialist revolution or adopt a vacillating attitude toward it. In sum, whether in terms of their political stance or their ideology, they have not completely reformed themselves. People of this category tend to become the yes-men of the former group. They are either deceived by them or purposefully echo them of their own accord.

When the bourgeois rightists, namely, landlords, rich peasants, and those who were power-holders during the Guomindang reign, stick to their reactionary stance, call out for the "status" they had "in the past," is it possible for us to grant them that? Absolutely not. If we were to allow them to have such a "status," we not only would lose the status of the people's teacher we have now, as well as the fruits of victory we won through the New Democratic revolution and the socialist revolution, but we would also be in danger of losing the Party, the state, and our own lives! Between them and ourselves is a life-and-death struggle; we must resolutely fight it to the end. How things now stand is clear as day. The people's rule under the leadership of the Communist Party will "live forever,"

while the "status" to oppress the people enjoyed by the landlords, the rich peasants, and power-holders in the Guomindang's reign is gone, never to return. Right now the only re-
course for them is complete repentance, discarding their reactionary stance, pleading guilty, and starting anew. There is
no other way out.

As for those who are politically and ideologically unhealthy,
their future and "status" would be at risk should they fail to
reform themselves with effort but let themselves follow the
course of their current direction. Among them are some who
always like to compare themselves with others in terms of
status, remuneration, and enjoyment. They never compete
with others in work, hardship, or contribution. For example,
they do not emulate the cadres in tempering themselves through
revolution or in their loyalty to the revolution. They contrast
their working hours to those of the cadres, ignoring the fact
that they themselves have summer and winter vacations. Some
teachers who are not content with their teaching posts in the
countryside or mountain regions are fond of comparing themselves with people working in the cities in terms of wages
without considering the differences in expenditures and living
conditions. They dismiss from their minds the principle that
the more willing one is to shoulder a difficult job, the more
honor one has. Rather than comparing themselves with workers in terms of the arduousness of labor, some city teachers
yell that their "status is inferior to that of the workers" on the
one hand, while on the other hand, they look down upon workers
and peasants. They are obsessed with the idea that "all occupations are lowly; only the pursuit of learning excels." There
are also some who not only are fond of making comparisons
but have even gone to the point of "making a row" in order to
fight for position, remuneration, welfare, and fame. It is just
as Comrade Liu Shaoqi said:

When it comes to the questions of remuneration, enjoyment, and other personal
matters in life, [some] always seek to surpass others. They compete and
emulate those at the highest levels. They "seek comfort tirelessly," and brag

about it before others. However, when it comes to work, they want to compare themselves with those who are inferior. They try to evade jobs involving hardship and attempt to run away when danger is imminent. ... They want
to live in good houses and are fond of the limelight. They seek to enjoy the
honor of the Party. In sum, they intend to seize everything that is good and
bear no hand in anything involving "bad luck."

These comrades should be aware of the fact that bourgeois
individualism is the root of all evil. If anyone is infected
with such an ideology, they will degenerate politically, become lax in their work, and be depressed in their spirit.
If allowed to go on this way unchecked, they not only will
will cause damage to the cause of revolution but may also put
themselves on the road to destruction. Anyone in our revolutionary ranks, if they seek fame, gain, and status, can never
achieve their purpose. Only those who loyally serve the people,
who have lofty ideals, who are men of integrity, and who are the
first to bear hardships and the last to enjoy comforts can
render service to the people and make contributions to the
revolution. They will be held in esteem everywhere and can
truly have a future. Many of our teachers enthusiastically
serve the workers and peasants, identify themselves with the
masses, and do a good job in teaching the students and running
the school. Precisely because of this, they have the confidence
of the local people and are held in esteem by the Party and the
government. It is hoped, therefore, that those who are politically and ideologically unhealthy will criticize their own bourgeois ideas as reflected over the issue of "teacher's status,"
conscientiously remold themselves, pass the test of socialism,
and not go astray.

   In conducting their shameless activities to oppose the Party
and socialism, the bourgeois rightists often pose as persons
who speak up on behalf of the interests of the masses. Using
"teacher's status is low" as a magic potion, they deceive those
who are unaware of the truth or those who are politically and
ideologically unhealthy. In smashing the offensive launched by
the rightists, therefore, we must on the one hand thoroughly
expose their conspiracy through struggle, while on the other

hand we must improve in the course of struggle our ability to
tell right from wrong and liquidate the pernicious germs they
spread.

The rightists claim: "In saying that the social status of
teachers is inferior to others, I mean that there exists a common phenomenon of disrepecting teachers among cadres and in
society." Is what they say true or false? False. In saying
that it is "false," we mean that the rightists exaggerate facts
and confuse right and wrong with a vicious intention. This is
because, first, it is only in isolated cases that teachers are
disrepected. Besides, since the CCP Central Committee convened the conference on the question of intellectuals, Party
committees in different localities have conducted a series of
educational programs among cadres, and currently the phenomenon of showing no respect for teachers has, in the main, been
rectified. Second, the practice of disrespecting teachers violates the policy of the Party and the people's government.
Once wrongdoing like this comes to light, the Party will settle it promptly and may even take necessary disciplinary action
against those involved. The rightists try to generalize individual cases into a universal phenomenon and describe it as a
policy of the Communist Party and the people's government;
they stand facts on their heads and are really shameless! It
must be pointed out that the rightists make a fuss about this
issue in order to provoke some people to oppose the Party and
socialism. We must repudiate their views and not allow them
to spread poison. This is one side of the question. On the
other hand, speaking of the social origin of the question, there
are a number of people within the ranks of our teachers whose
political stance and moral quality hardly deserve esteem.
Quite a few teachers from landlord backgrounds, for example,
oppressed the peasants prior to Liberation and did not acquit
themselves well during the land reform movement. Some
teachers who are of a landlord or other exploiting class origin
failed to distinguish between the enemy and ourselves and held
a vacillating stand during such movements of socialist revolution as land reform, suppression of the counterrevolutionaries,

cooperativization, etc. There are still others who have a bad character, are morally degenerate, and violate the law and discipline. They make a very bad impression on the masses and pollute the noble title of a people's teacher. Let us ask the question: how can the people unconditionally hold such persons in esteem and place confidence in them? What other more correct demands can we make of persons like this than requiring them to honestly remedy their mistakes, earnestly reform themselves, and seek to gain others' confidence? "It is invariably the case that one first insults himself before others insult him." Side by side with the leadership's improvement of its work, let us aid these erring ones in earnestly reforming themselves.

Finally, we must make it clear that some teachers hold critical views about their wages and benefits not because of serious mistakes in their political stance and ideology, but merely as a result of their lack of understanding. True, we cannot say that teachers are already highly paid at present. But this is the consequence of the huge population, poor foundations, and backward economy of our country. Even under such circumstances, the state has already done its best to gradually improve teachers' living standards on the basis of developed production. In fact, wages of the broad masses of high school and primary school teachers in rural areas are not only higher than the income of peasants in general (not to mention their welfare benefits) but are also higher than the majority of district and township cadres. This is exactly an indication of the state's concern for teachers, and it is warmly approved by teachers in large numbers. Pursuant to Chairman Mao's directive of proceeding from our six hundred million people, we must in the future abide by such principles as "unified planning with due consideration for all concerned," "building up the country through thrift and hard work," and "being industrious and frugal in managing a household," and not widen the gap between the living standard of teachers and staff and that of the broad masses of peasants. Otherwise, it will handicap our effort to consolidate the worker-peasant alliance and alienate the teachers from the masses. This will do harm to the teachers themselves and therefore is a very important matter. It is hoped that when studying Chairman Mao's report "On the Correct Handling of Contradictions among the People," we will conduct repeated discussions and arrive at a clear understanding of this issue.

Teachers Are Needed for
the Revolutionary Cause*

Hong Jiaobing

The doctrine of "It is bad fortune to be a teacher" is a variant
of the doctrine of "going to school in order to be an official"
invented by renegade, hidden traitor and scab Liu Shaoqi. It is
a reflection of the violent struggle between the two classes, two
roads and two lines on the cultural-educational front.

The violent class struggle between the proletariat and the
bourgeoisie has never stopped. Moreover, the latter have constantly changed their strategy and tactics in the struggle. When
the working class first moved into the schools, a small handful
of class enemies impatiently rushed out crying that workers
"knew nothing about education" and "could not lead the schools,"
in a vain attempt to dislodge the working class from the educational positions. When the working class smashed their sinister
scheme, took firm hold of the leadership over the educational
front in its hands, and carried out reeducation of the intellectuals, the class enemies shifted from the Right to the extreme
"Left," attacking the working class by formally "Left" but actually Rightist means and loudly crying "It is useless to go to
school" and "It is bad fortune to be a teacher," in an effort to
distort the Party's policy of uniting with, educating and remolding the intellectuals, disintegrate the ranks of revolutionary

---

*Guangming ribao [Guangming Daily] , October 22, 1969. Translated in
SCMP, No. 4537 (October 22, 1969), pp. 6-9.

teachers, and sabotage the proletarian educational revolution.

The struggle between the bourgeoisie and the proletariat is in the last analysis a struggle for "power." Vice Chairman Lin teaches us: "Seizure of power depends on the pen and the gun." The doctrine of "It is bad fortune to be a teacher" is a new sinister scheme and a new trend of the class enemy to seize "the pen" from the proletariat under the new situation and finally to seize "the gun." We must be vigilant against it and criticize it.

Some people in the ranks of teachers have not yet reformed their bourgeois world outlook, and as a result they do not see clearly the essence of the reactionary bourgeois trend of thought that has recently appeared and are ideologically sympathetic with it. This is very dangerous.

Having received the full impact of the revolutionary storm during the Great Proletarian Cultural Revolution, these people have learned a negative lesson: They regret very much that they have chosen the teaching profession. They tell themselves that as teachers they "earn no credit but have to work hard and bear fatigue," and in spite of all this they are said to have committed mistakes. Accordingly they have formed this erroneous conclusion: "A man's sorrow comes from his eagerness to teach others." They are afraid to mix with their students, to go to the classroom and to be teachers. They are afraid of making mistakes again and of being criticized. They want to get out of the educational front and quit the ranks of teachers.

Chairman Mao teaches us, saying, "Man's social existence determines his thinking."

How should teachers be treated? Are teachers unlucky or is their responsibility very important and heavy? Different classes have always looked upon this question differently and people of different stands will answer it differently.

The proletariat has always attached great importance to the position and role of teachers. In the early years of the establishment of Soviet political power, Lenin directed that teachers be elevated to an unprecedentedly high position and very highly honored. Our great leader Chairman Mao teaches us: In order to build socialism, we "need a large number of people's educationalists and teachers." Chairman Mao also exhorts teachers to be "faithful to the Party's educational enterprise." The broad masses of workers, peasants and soldiers have entrusted the teachers with the important task of dissemination of Marxism, Leninism and the thought of Mao Zedong as well as teaching of mankind's most advanced cultural and scientific knowledge and the fostering of successors to the revolutionary cause of the proletariat. This is the greatest trust shown by the Party and the people to teachers, and revolutionary teachers should therefore realize the importance of their responsibility and the difficulty and gigantic proportions of their task.

Chairman Mao teaches us, saying, "Our forces are completely dedicated to the liberation of the people and work thoroughly for the interests of the people." He also says: "Everything we do is done in the service of the people."

Teachers serve the people and are needed for the revolutionary cause. It is most glorious to serve the people and the revolutionary cause. It is most glorious to fight in order to create a proletarian educational system. Only those who foster spiritual aristocrats for the bourgeoisie and fight against the proletariat for successors are really "unlucky."

Those who are poisoned by the doctrine of "It is bad fortune to be a teacher" should correctly assess themselves, correctly treat the masses and mass movements, ceaselessly raise their consciousness of the struggle between the two lines, strengthen their will to continue to make revolution on the cultural-educational front and make thorough revolution, voluntarily accept reeducation from workers, peasants and soldiers, thoroughly change their old ideas, and be intellectuals welcomed by the workers, peasants and soldiers.

Chairman Mao teaches us, saying, "Change 'fear' into 'daring,' 'I' into 'public interest,' and 'trust in oneself' into 'trust in the masses.'"

Being afraid of mixing with students, going to the classroom and serving as teachers is a question of world outlook. It is having "fear" in the lead and being bedeviled by "self-interest." Some people, influenced in the past by renegade, hidden traitor

and scab Liu Shaoqi's doctrine of "going to school in order to
become an official," doctrine of "the docile tool," and doctrine
that "the masses are backward," have pursued the idea of "ex-
celling in studies to become an official," upheld "the dignity of
the teacher," and restrained students with the rules and taboos
of the revisionist line of education. These include "respect for
the teacher and the way," "attitude toward the teacher is question of attitude toward knowledge," etc., which were intended
to make students behave meekly toward their teacher and obey
his every word.

Now the sunlight and rain of Mao Zedong thought nurtures the
revolutionary spirit of students and the torrent of the Great
Proletarian Cultural Revolution has breached the dikes of the
revisionist line of education. The old system of education is
swept into the garbage heap of history and the phenomenon of
domination of schools by bourgeois intellectuals is no more.
Today young students analyze and observe everything with the
microscope and telescope of the sharpest invincible thought of
Mao Zedong, and analyze the work of their teachers. This
shows that, after being tempered in the great proletarian cultural revolution, they have become even more promising and
ambitious.

Should a revolutionary teacher not cheer such a revolutionary
change? Why should he be afraid of it? To mix with these
vigorous young students, to make criticism and study together
with them, and "show concern for each other, love and protect
each other, and help each other" is exactly a favorable condition
for bringing about the teachers' ideological revolutionization
and carry out proletarian educational revolution successfully.

Chairman Mao teaches us, saying, "What is work? Work is
struggle. Where there are difficulties and problems, there we
are needed to handle them. We go to work and struggle in order
to solve the difficulties. The greater the difficulty, the greater
the reason for our going there. It is a good comrade who does
that."

Two attitudes may be taken in handling difficulties. One is to
meet them face to face and solve them; the other is to retreat

and avoid struggle. It is a question of whether one wants to continue to make revolution or not. Because their revolutionary spirit is not thorough and because they always waver, intellectuals whose world outlook is not properly reformed will try to escape struggle under the new situation, to seek a refuge from windstorms and heavy seas or a tranquil "Shangri-La" and leave this "land of disputes." This is contrary to the current great struggle-criticism-transformation movement and therefore extremely dangerous.

A revolutionary teacher must face the realities and know the situation. On the educational front the poisonous influence of the bourgeoisie and revisionists is really very extensive, but this also shows the necessity of persevering in struggle on this particular front. Instead of shunning struggle, we must firmly and resolutely stand on the forefront of struggle on this particular front, study hard and master Mao Zedong thought, rely closely on the broad masses of workers, peasants and soldiers, unite with the broad masses of revolutionary intellectuals, ceaselessly launch attacks on the bourgeoisie, and ceaselessly remove and discard the filth of the exploiting classes from the depths of our soul while carrying on struggle. In this way, no matter how obdurate the traditional forces are on this front, we shall not be corrupted or defeated by them, but shall be able to beat them, destroy them and reform them.

"It is bad fortune to be a teacher" is a corrosive agent that breaks our revolutionary fighting will into pieces, a poisoned arrow with which the class enemy opposes the occupation of the educational positions by the working class, fights for leadership on the cultural-educational front, and sabotages educational revolution, and a reactionary social trend of thought. We must increase our vigilance and thoroughly criticize it. People are poisoned by this idea basically because they have "self-interest" in their heads, think about personal interests instead of the interests of the revolution, base everything on themselves instead of on the revolutionary cause, and fail to correctly deal with the Great Proletarian Cultural Revolution, the masses, and themselves. The poisonous influence of Liu Shaoqi's revisionist

line is not yet completely eliminated from their heads, so that
they fall prey to the class enemy's sinister plan to seize first
"the pen" and then "the gun." In fighting the battle on the educational front, we must fight point for point and for every inch
of ground. We will surely fight the battle on the educational
front successfully and fight it out to the end, so as to consolidate the dictatorship of the proletariat.

The great leader Chairman Mao teaches us, saying, "Reform
of the old educational system and reform of the old guidelines
and methods of teaching is a very important task of the current
Great Proletarian Cultural Revolution.

In accordance with our great leader Chairman Mao's teaching,
"The question of reform of teaching is principally a question of
teachers," many revolutionary teachers have already taken the
first step forward. They study and apply Mao Zedong thought
in a living way and voluntarily and actively go to the midst of
the workers, peasants and soldiers to receive reeducation from
them, and for this they are praised by the workers, peasants
and soldiers. They boldly carry out pilot schemes in educational revolution and have already achieved initial results.
This is a praiseworthy phenomenon. All revolutionary teachers
should do the same.

Holding high the great red banner of Mao Zedong thought and
under the leadership of the working class, we must unite with
all forces with which we can unite, study earnestly, strive to
reform ourselves, strengthen our confidence, and advance cou-
rageously. We swear to be activists in educational revolution
and "proletarian revolutionaries who carry the great proletarian cultural revolution through to the end," and dedicate all
our strength to the propagation and defense of Mao Zedong
thought, so that Chairman Mao's proletarian educational line
may firmly occupy the cultural-educational positions.

Zhang Tiesheng's Letter Has Given
Impetus to the Revolution in Education*

Changes in the Tandong Municipal No. 6
Middle School Brought about by
"A Thought-Provoking Test Paper"

Renmin Ribao

After the publication of "A Thought-Provoking Test Paper" in succession in the Liaoning ribao and in our paper, it led to a discussion among some people. Some approved of the revolutionary spirit of Zhang Tiesheng in going against the tide, while some said that Zhang Tiesheng's letter was wrong. These two kinds of views reflected the struggle between the two lines and the two kinds of world outlook on the educational front. The Party branch at the Tandong Municipal No. 6 Middle School laid hold of this question, started a debate, conducted education, criticized revisionism and the bourgeois world outlook, and raised the awareness of the teachers. What they have done is correct and good. This is an example in grasping the major issue, grasping the line and grasping political and ideological work.

Renmin ribao Editor

*   *   *

Under the guidance of the basic line of the Party, a vigorous revolutionary scene has appeared in the Tandong Municipal No. 6 Middle School. For the sake of training "workers with both socialist consciousness and culture" and for the sake of adapting themselves to the needs of the educated young people sent to the mountains and the countryside, the teachers are actively carrying out educational reforms. Broader and broader strides have been taken in running the school with open doors. One by one,

---

*Renmin ribao [People's Daily], January 7, 1974. Translated in SCMP, No. 5544 (November 1, 1974), pp. 149-153.

353

the workers, peasants and soldiers have mounted the rostrum
of the school, and group after group of teachers have gone to the
countryside and factories to receive reeducation. One by one,
"groups for learning other things" have sprung up like dandelions
in a spring lawn throughout the school. The comrades of the
No. 6 Middle School said enthusiastically: Zhang Tiesheng's
letter is like a fire which has brought more and more vitality
to the revolution in education!"

In July last year the Tandong No. 6 Middle School first heard
of the news that cultural tests had to be conducted for students
enrolling for university. When the teachers recalled how matriculation was conducted in the past, they also were unusually
busy. Some squeezed in time to help the educated young people
who returned to the city to prepare for matriculation to catch
up with their lessons. In accordance with the written requests
of the educated young people, some seminar groups prepared
and printed thick volumes of reference materials for matriculation. Some teachers also carried out "study mobilization" for
students taking the university entrance examination. Some
teachers said delightedly: "If things go on in this way, there is
some hope for teaching."

It was at this juncture that the letter of Zhang Tiesheng, "A
Thought-Provoking Test Paper," was published in the paper.
It immediately brought a strong response from the teachers.

Some of them said: "This letter from Zhang Tiesheng is like
a ladle of cold water. It has completely dampened the glowing
enthusiasm for teaching."

Some said: "If even the university does not attach importance
to marks, what is the object of teaching!"

Some also said: "With the university taking in such people
as Zhang Tiesheng, what guarantee is there for quality? Can
we still orbit a satellite into space?"

There were also those who argued back with conviction:
"That is not so! Zhang Tiesheng's letter, in opposing the placing of marks in command, is full of the spirit of going against
the tide!"

The teachers started to discuss the matter and argue with

each other. At the meeting of seminar heads convened by the
Party branch, neither side could convince the other.

The arguments of the teachers moved Comrade Huang Dengke,
deputy secretary of the Party branch of the school and a responsible member of the workers' propaganda team, to deep
thought. Why was it that only the minority supported Zhang
Tiesheng's letter while the majority of the teachers laid so
much emphasis on marks? He looked back upon the course of
struggle of the revolution in education. In the past few years,
although very impressive achievements had been scored, there
still lurked deep in the minds of the teachers the thought of
"intellectual education comes first." Formerly, he had thought
that after several revolutionary mass criticisms the teachers
would be able to distinguish between the lines and change their
sentiment. As things stood now, this kind of thoughtless optimism was not in keeping with the basic line of the Party. He
felt that if the proletariat wanted to exercise a firm grip on
leadership over the revolution in education, nothing short of
thoroughly criticizing the revisionist line and vigorously transforming the world outlook of the teachers would do. He went to
discuss things with Wang Caoqin, a member of the committee
of the Party branch and a vice chairman of the revolutionary
committee of the school.

Prior to the Great Proletarian Cultural Revolution, Wang
Caoqin was responsible for leadership work at the school.
These days, she had also been contemplating all things arising
around the question of the matriculation examination. Why were
some teachers so enthusiastic over the former examination
system? What was the cause of their antipathy toward Zhang
Tiesheng's opposition to the placing of marks in command?
She strongly realized that it was a basic fact that for 17 years
after the liberation the bourgeoisie had all along exercised dictatorship over the proletariat on the educational front, and that
the world outlook of the majority of the teachers was basically
bourgeois fundamentally was a condition that could not be over-
looked. When she heard the view of Huang Dengke, she said
delightedly: "We both think alike!" At the meeting of the Party

branch, they unanimously endorsed the controversy arising around the letter, "A Thought-Provoking Test Paper." They guided the teachers to make a thoroughgoing criticism of revisionism, to criticize the bourgeois world outlook and to shift their stand.

As the broad masses of teachers of the No. 6 Middle School were making a thoroughgoing criticism of Lin Biao and rectification of the style of work in association with reality, the happy tidings of the victorious closing of the Tenth Congress of the Party was transmitted to them. By studying the documents of the Tenth Congress, the Party branch raised its understanding in grasping the major issues and the teachers strengthened their consciousness in transforming their world outlook. Many teachers said: "We must remind ourselves every day of the basic line of the Party and grasp every day the transformation of the world outlook, for only in this way can we carry on the revolution!" Under the unified leadership and arrangements of the Party branch, the teachers formed themselves into teaching reform groups, and went to the factories and rural areas to receive reeducation and make mental preparations for ushering in a new upsurge of the revolution in education.

Within three short months, the No. 6 Middle School had already organized three teaching reform groups for sending to the countryside and factories. The Party branch also firmly adhered to the system of sending each teacher to the lower levels on two occasions in each term.

The great changes in the outlook of the countryside, the vigorous growth of the educated young people and the socialist activism of the poor and lower-middle peasants in learning from Dazhai in agriculture gave the teachers a profound course of education. When a teacher was with the Kangda production brigade under the Changshan commune in Dongkou xian, he lived in the house of production brigade leader Tan. Although he got up early and retired late, the production brigade leader who had a tight program of work and labor got up earlier and retired later than he. From production brigade leader Tan this old teacher thought of Zhang Tiesheng and was deeply ashamed.

He said: "Before coming down, I always tried to find fault with Zhang Tiesheng's letter and could not understand his spirit of going against the tide because I did not understand the poor and lower-middle peasants and did not stand on their side."

Zhang Fangxun was a teacher who formerly adhered to the proposal of accepting students on their marks. After he heard the stirring deeds of the educated young people of Kangda production brigade who worked hard alongside the poor and lower-middle peasants to enable grain production to show a very substantial increase, there was a big change in his way of thinking. He began to realize that the rich knowledge obtained by the educated young people in the Three Great Revolutionary movements far exceeded the scope of several pieces of test papers! The mind of Zhang Fangxun could not help from churning with emotions: Actually true knowledge comes from practice, but he has one-sidedly shown blind faith in "marks." Doesn't this mean that he has been bedeviled by his idealist world outlook? Zhang Tiesheng's letter is filled with the materialist spirit and speaks the words in the hearts of the broad masses of educated young people! He picked up once again the letter, "A Thought-Provoking Test Paper," and the more he read, the more warm-hearted he became. He deeply realized that only by accepting such people as Zhang Tiesheng into the university could the quality of the university be improved!

In the past teacher Wen Pangxing invariably thought that "students going to university have a great future, and it would be a great waste to send them to the countryside." He thought that those who excelled in scholarship should be sent to the university. During an investigation visit, an old production brigade leader told him: "The schools of the landlord and bourgeois classes advocate getting learned in order to be an official, but our school must advocate getting learned for the revolution and for industrial work and farming. If it advocates getting learned for the individual, no matter how learned a person is, he is also useless to us poor and lower-middle peasants." These words provoked Wen Panxing's thought. That evening, he studied word by word the basic line and the educational policy of the Party and dissected his own thinking. He thought: "The fundamental difference between the old and new schools lies in that we proletariat must train the students into workers with both socialist consciousness and culture, while the Liu Shaoqi, Lin Biao and company wildly opposed this idea. The revolution in education has been carried out for several years. Why is our thinking still in harmony with the revisionist line?" When he thought up to this point, he felt that the cold water poured by Zhang Tiesheng had sobered up his mind, and that the influence of the revisionist line in education of the past 17 years could in no way be underestimated.

In the course of making an in-depth study of the documents of the Tenth Congress and after reeducation by the poor and lower-middle peasants, the several groups of teachers that returned to the school from the countryside all shared the same feeling: In the past, they resented Zhang Tiesheng's letter because their world outlook was fundamentally bourgeois. Because of the deep pernicious influence of the revisionist line in the past 17 years, they did everything to find fault with Zhang Tiesheng's letter. In the vortex of "intellectual education first," how could they understand Zhang Tiesheng's spirit of going against the tide! At present, the teachers of the No. 6 Middle School basically support Zhang Tiesheng's letter. This transformation is a transformation in their world outlook.

The higher awareness of the two-line struggle on the part of the teachers has enabled the educational policy of Chairman Mao to be better implemented and given impetus to the in-depth development of the proletarian revolution in education. The stifling atmosphere of engrossing themselves in grasping "cultural quality" of the past several months has disappeared, and an unprecedented wave of enthusiasm for the proletarian revolution in education has appeared. The doors of the school have been thrown wide open. Old workers, old poor peasants, Red Army veterans, people's constables, and mothers of martyrs have been invited back to school to give lessons in class struggle and the two-line struggle to the teachers and students and to serve as tutors. Such courses as "surveying," "accounting" and "tractors" which serve directly the Three Great Revolutionary movements in the countryside have been restored. The teachers are striving to place proletarian politics in command of teaching.

The school has at all times put the firm and correct political orientation above all else and there have been profound changes in the spiritual features of the students. Yang Xingbin, a 4th-year student, formerly felt that since he eventually would be sent to the countryside, it didn't matter much whether or not he studied hard. He regularly played truant and his lessons lagged further and further behind. After ideological education, there was a change in him. He appeared on time for school every day, and gradually caught up with his lessons. He said: "The Party is training me to make me a good successor to the revolution. If I do not study well, I shall be unworthy of the revolutionary forerunners and shall not be able to make more contributions to the revolution in the countryside in the future." Fourth-year student Zhou Liping is the child of a revolutionary armyman. In the past, she thought that she could have future prospects only by going to university and had never thought of becoming a peasant. In the course of study, she has learned the truth: The key to the future prospects of a person lies not in what he is doing, but in whether or not he has the thought of serving the people.

> The Reporting Unit of the Tandong Municipal Revolutionary Committee and reporters of the Liaoning ribao
>
> (Reproduced from Liaoning ribao and abridged by Renmin ribao)

For Product Safety Concerns and Information please contact our EU
representative GPSR@taylorandfrancis.com
Taylor & Francis Verlag GmbH, Kaufingerstraße 24, 80331 München, Germany